WINES AND CHATEAUX
of the Loire

WINES
& CHATEAUX
OF THE
LOIRE

T. A. Layton

CASSELL · LONDON

CASSELL & COMPANY LTD
35 Red Lion Square, London WC1
Melbourne, Sydney, Toronto
Johannesburg, Cape Town, Auckland

First published 1967

Printed in Great Britain by
The Camelot Press Ltd, London and Southampton

F.167

To LANCE K. COCK
who has corrected more than
a million of the two million
words I have written—mainly
on wine—and to whom I am
truly grateful

I must acknowledge my indebtedness to Vivian Rowe and his publishers, Putnam & Co. Ltd., for permission to quote from his excellent book Châteaux of the Loire, *on which I admit to having leaned quite a bit for some of the material in Chapters 11, 12, 14, 16 and 18.*

T. A. L.

CONTENTS

ILLUSTRATIONS

★ *Author's photographs*

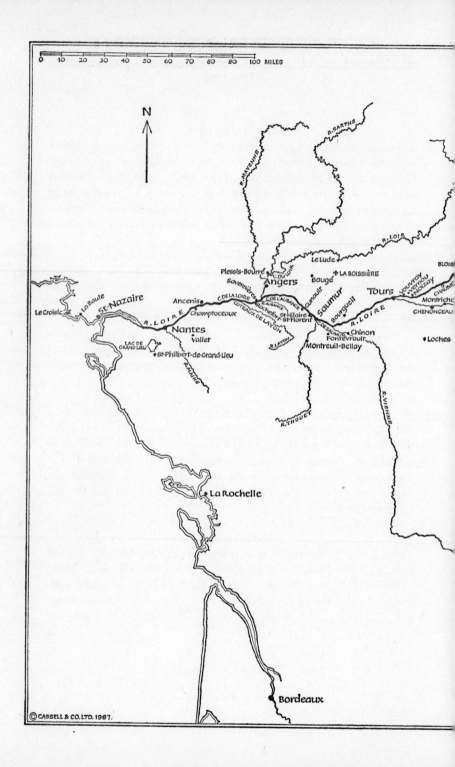

0 10 20 30 40 50 60 70 80 90 100 MILES

N

R.SARTHE

R.MAYENNE

R.LOIR

Le Lude

BLOIS

Plessis-Bourré
R.DU.LOIR
Savennières
Angers   Baugé + LA BOISSIÈRE

VOUVRAY
Vernou
Noizay
CHAUM

C.DE LA LOIRE
Ancenis   C.DE L'AUBANCE
Rochefort
Jaunault Saumur
Tours
Montrich

Le Croisic La Baule St-Nazaire
Champtoceaux CÔTEAUX DE LAYON
St-Hilaire St-Florent
Bourgueil
R.LOIRE
CHENONCEAU

R.LOIRE
Nantes
Vallet
CDESAUMUS Chinon
•Loches

LAC DE
GRAND LIEU
St-Philbert-de-Grand-Lieu
R.LAYON
Montreuil-Bellay Fontevrault

R.MAINE

R.THOUET

R.VIENNE

•La Rochelle

•Bordeaux

© CASSELL & CO.LTD. 1967

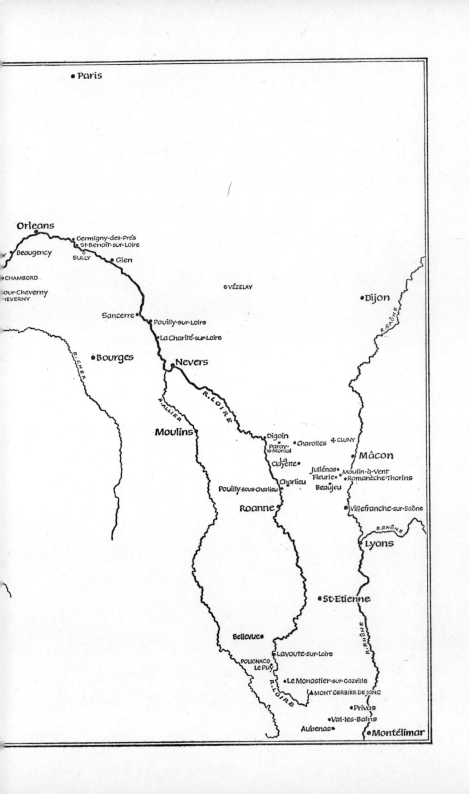

AROUND THE SOURCE OF THE LOIRE

MOST FRENCHMEN WILL BE SURPRISED when you tell them that, as the crow flies, it is only just ninety miles from the deep blue of the Mediterranean to the place where the Loire rises.

The actual spot is beside the five-thousand-foot peak called the Gerbier de Jonc, which is on the already immensely lofty plateau in the hilly, wild and impoverished department of the Ardèche.

Motoring up from the South of France, the nearest town on the Route Nationale from which to turn off into the by-ways is Montélimar; and it was from here that I set off to follow France's longest river the whole of the 625 miles to its mouth on the north Atlantic coast.

To celebrate the first day of my journey, I put up at the best hotel in the town, the Relais de l'Empereur ('Emperor's Posting-house'), described in the brochure as an historic hotel and as being owned by Francis and Roger Latry, late of the Savoy, London.

It was established in 1758 and Napoleon, we are told, stayed there no less than four times, his last visit being on the way to Elba in 1814 when, 'betrayed by his advisers and accompanied only by his ever-faithful Bertrand and Drouot', he was closely guarded by soldiers of the Austrian Empire and of the King of Prussia.

But whatever your feelings are concerning the diminutive Corsican, you will have had your fill of him after a night at the Relais; for letters, relics, photos and souvenirs all catch your eye from every living-room, hall and passageway, and, of course, your own bedroom, in the establishment.

To avoid a surfeit of Empire and Eagles, I wandered out into the town. Montélimar is the home of that sticky nut and sugar delicacy, nougat, and I found that the number of shops which sell it right inside the town is even more than those you see garishly placed on the main highway on the outskirts. None of it is now home-made but is produced by a small number of high-powered factories employing large staffs.

For dinner, I settled for the Hôtel des Princes, whose restaurant is situated in a vast Cistercian chapel, the only remaining portion of a group of buildings several centuries old.

The menu was large and varied, including the choice of two Tables d'Hôte (or should it be Table d'Hôtes?), one rather cheap and the other quite expensive. And as usual, my eyes being more greedy than my belly, I wanted particularly the Terrine Maison au Madère from the better menu and the rest of the choice from the cheaper. This greatly confused the waiter, who told me he would have to get authorization and, as the distances in this chapel-restaurant were so vast that I expected to be in for a long wait, I settled down to translate the history of the establishment which was printed on the back of the menu (and quite interesting it sounded).

The history of the construction of the hotel is lost in the mists of time; all that now remains is the Cistercian chapel, now transformed into a restaurant.

In 1136 Bernard de Clairvaux (St Bernard), after having founded the Abbey of Clairvaux, on this very spot created another small establishment for the purpose of observing the Cistercian rules.

The doyen of hotel-restaurants of the town from the fourteenth to the beginning of the eighteenth centuries, the establishment was called 'The Lodging of the Golden Griffin' for, in accordance with the practice in those times, there was a model of this fabulous animal in gilded wood over the entrance.

And when, in 1475, Louis XI started the system of postal relays, it was the Griffin that was selected as a stage point; which honour meant that over the next three centuries the establishment housed all the greatest personalities who came to or passed through Montélimar; of these one of the most important was the illustrious Marquise de Sévigné, who from there on 5 April 1673 wrote one of her inimitable and innumerable letters to her dear Madeleine.

But the most noteworthy guests to be received at the Griffin were the grandsons of King Louis XIV, the Dukes of Berry and Burgundy, on their return from Spain in the spring of 1701. And it was then that, among the presents that were offered by the Mayor of the town, nougat is mentioned for the first time.

It was also on account of this royal visit that the owner, Paul Audouard, set about modernizing the hotel and changed its name to the Hôtel des Princes, sending the old Griffin out by the back door.

I had just finished the translation when the waiter returned with the information that I could have the pâté and then go on to the duck with cherries, so on the strength of this I ordered, as well as my usual gin and double Dubonnet, a half bottle of Beaujolais.

The menu, though, continued to interest me; there were Oignons à la Grecque, Œufs en Mimosa, Tournedos Zingara and the usual (for this district) Quenelles de Brochet—pike—with a crayfish sauce. I decided that it would be a good one for my collection and that, the waiter being far from forthcoming, it would be necessary to 'win' it by my special technique. This necessitated the purchase of a newspaper from the seller who was just then conveniently making his tour and the pretended assiduous reading of the journal while slipping the menu discreetly between the folds. It is necessary to choose a moment when the eyes of all serving staff are averted, but as my man was continually in the kitchen I anticipated no difficulty here and, choosing what seemed an opportune moment, I quickly committed the minor theft and, nonchalantly picking up the newspaper, I asked for the bill.

He made it out and added his regulation tip and, because I felt that hoodwinking the poor fellow deserved a little extra largesse, I added a small sum over and above. Carefully he picked the money up from the plate and when, and only when, it was safely pocketed, he said:

'And may I have the menu back, please?'

*

From Montélimar to the Gerbier, the scenery becomes lovely whichever way you go; the slightly shorter route being by way of the most attractive little town of Privas with its excellently run Hotel Croix d'Or and the longer via the feudal town of Aubenas. I went round in a circle and so took in both towns.

Once, when asked what he meant by a medieval town, the historian Funck-Brentano replied, 'It is a castle which has known continued prosperity', and his description fits the town of Aubenas with its ten thousand inhabitants down to its last mellow stone. Situated just halfway between Avignon and Le Puy, Aubenas is in the centre of a region that, before France was divided into her modern departments (and we are now in the Ardèche), was known as the Vivarais. And because its situation has been that of a sentinel guarding the mountain passes, Aubenas has in its past seen more of wars than most places in this world.

Although this medieval town possesses a dozen and one old and interesting monuments, and although as an enthusiastic local guide says, 'One can spend hours savouring the poetry of the old stones', it is the castle, now the Town Hall, which is the main attraction. Those, however, who seek a *château fort* all in one style will be disappointed, for its charm lies in the way so very many building conceptions of so many centuries have been assembled to form a harmonious whole.

Inside, the most arresting exhibit is a statue of Olivier de Serres, which is the model for a monument planned to be erected in his honour—he was born in the Ardèche—and unveiled by Pasteur during a visit to Aubenas in 1882. De Serres was one of the great men of France; born in 1539, his studies in improved methods of agriculture were of sufficient merit for King Henri IV to commission a work entitled *The Agricultural Scene and the Management of Crops*. This earned him the title of the 'Father of Agriculture' and his name has become the French word for a greenhouse (it is not a *maison verte* but a *serre*).

Gastronomically speaking, Aubenas has a great reputation for its marrons glacés as well as its sweetmeat, chestnut purée, which stems from the fact that the Ardèche is by far the most important department in France for the cultivation of edible chestnuts.

Four miles from Aubenas just after Vals-les-Bains the road, now climbing up into the mountains, becomes truly spectacular; it twists as it climbs, but not to the extent of the curves becoming dangerous, and the road surface is excellent. Immediately before the summit, when the scenery is wild and bleak and the Loire can be seen to roll away into the distance, there is an official sign which, after one has motored for miles without seeing anything, really catches the eye— a clever piece of *tourisme* propaganda.

LIGNE DE PARTAGE DES EAUX
ATLANTIQUE—MEDITERRANEE

and underneath

←MEDITERRANEE   ATLANTIQUE→

It is quite emotive and also terribly precise; it is strange to think that after a rainstorm has fallen on those windswept hills some of the water finds its way down to the Mediterranean while the rest ends up flowing out into the sea at St Nazaire.

A few hundred yards from these signs there is a turning off the road and the ascent gets less steep; the road flattens out into a plateau and one arrives at the famous Gerbier de Jonc, so called because the little mountain does look like a corn stook (*gerbier*), though whether the Jonc is just a proper name or has anything to do with the fact that this word means a flowering rush is not clear.

Though it was well out of the season when I got there, there were signs that this vast, open, green, hilly plateau was a good tourist draw in the summer, for the first thing to greet the motorist is a huge sign outside a very modest farmhouse turned hotel.

ICI

SOURCE DE LA LOIRE
INDIQUEE SUR LE PLAN CADASTRAL
ET LA CARTE D'ETAT MAJOR

VISITEZ LA !—MEILLEUR ACCUEIL

A *cadastral* is 'a public register of the quantity, value and ownership of the land of a country'—a sort of Domesday book, in fact. As I got out of the car to obey the instruction, a man, very much the farmer I judged by his attire, came out of the doorway of a barn and, seeing my camera slung over my shoulder, struck up a 'Photograph me, please' attitude in the doorway of the building. I duly obliged and then said, 'Now, where is your source?'

'It's in here,' he replied, pointing to a spot inside the barn. I walked in and saw a little trickle of clear spring water bubbling up from the ground and then making its way down to the valley.

'Yes,' said the man, 'and remember that it is the real, true source of the Loire as shown on the Ordnance Survey map.'

I didn't quite follow what he was driving at but thanked him and got into the car to motor near to the Gerbier itself. After a few hundred yards the narrow little road suddenly spread out to seven or eight times its former width and, as I cast my eyes around, I saw two more buildings, one another modest farm dwelling and the other a small hotel-cum-café, each with signs saying that theirs was the true source of the Loire. The first farmer's comment was now abundantly clear.

The café establishment was well built and spacious, affording some idea of the large number of trippers who must come along in the summer. Alas though, it was quite deserted and the entrance was locked. There was, however, a small house attached to the café and, looking through the window, I saw a family just about to sit down to lunch. I tapped upon the frame and made a sign of puffing a cigarette, scribbling a postcard and having a drink. These being understood a man got up, walked through to the café and opened the entrance door.

'So you have come to take that photograph', he said.

'Actually I have come to get some postcards of the place and have a drink', I replied.

He seemed surprised. 'Don't you want to take a picture of the original source of the river we have behind the hotel?'

'I'm afraid I don't understand', I answered.

The man took a harder look at me and then made a clucking noise with his teeth in astonishment.

'I'm sorry,' he said, 'but an Englishman with the same make of car as yours has just left here. He said he was writing a book all about the Loire and would like to photograph my barn, where the spring is housed, which is the original and correct source of the Loire. He said he would walk up to the top of the Jonc and then come back and take photos. He bought quite a lot of things here,' he added hopefully.

'Well!' I said, 'I'm not walking up that mountain but I am also writing a book on the Loire and I'll have a few packets of cigarettes.'

*

After the Gerbier de Jonc the road winds slowly downwards and one of the tiny villages one reaches, still on the mountain, is Le Béage; a more ugly, untidy, depressing little hamlet I have yet to encounter. But the inner man was calling loudly, for at the last three villages I had passed through on leaving the Gerbier people had said that none of the restaurants there did meals, save in July.

The restaurant I had been directed to in Le Béage was up an alleyway and hard to find, but well worth the visit. It was, I presumed, the headquarters for the *pétanque* players of the region. This game, ideally suited to the rugged, sandy waste verges of Marseilles and the hot South of France, seems to me to be moving north and gaining respectability as it travels. It can best be described as a sort of poor man's aerial bowls. All you need for equipment is a stretch of flat ground some twenty yards long and as narrow as six feet, and a small wooden ball about the size of those used for golf; each player has his own pair of large, heavy brass or steel balls, a little larger than a cricket ball. The most popular way of playing is in teams of two or more a side and, as in bowls, one man throws the jack as far or as near as he likes. The game is to get all the brasses as near as possible to it.

Quite a number of cafés in the countryside have open-air alleyways for the game, but here there were no less than four almost entirely enclosed, and with the 'pitches' raked over and covered with what was clearly imported sand. At one of them, though it was a weekday afternoon, a lively game was in progress and in one team a hefty woman was, to my surprise, taking part.

Inside, the room was of ample proportions; to the left a bar and a great number of tables, and, to the right, many more of them which gave the vague impression that, in the season, meals might be served. I went up to the bar and ordered a cherry-base aperitif that I had become rather fond of. I also asked if there was anything on to eat.

The person who served me was a very young boy who did not look to me to be more than ten or eleven years old. He poured out my drink most professionally and then shook me by saying, 'I won't be a minute with the menu', implying a certainty I wanted it that was uncanny. He was as good as his word and as I had moved outside to watch the play, he followed me out and produced the menu. This also was a surprise, for it was actually printed on a large, heavy piece of wood the approximate size and shape of a shove-ha'penny board, but not quite as thick. Both sides were covered with a great deal of beautiful type and the whole was then glazed over.

'It's beautiful', I said.

'My great-uncle is a printer down the road', said the little boy nonchalantly. 'He used to be a chef all over the world.' At the top of the board there was a charming little drawing of an animated game of *pétanque* and under the word 'menu' was—freely translated—the following.

POLICY

Between 1900 and 1924 before motorized transport changed things, French regional cooking was definitive and dishes from one locality would not be found in any other; they were the culinary glory of France. Came the war and all this was changed.

Only a very few of these dishes are on each week but when they are they are authentic. Some are seasonal, some take days to make, so, to save embarrassment, will clients accept what is on or make do with one of my special omelettes.

ACHILLE GINESTET

Of the dishes that followed some struck me as being horribly filling, some as dull, and some superb, but to me, as a professional restaurateur, there was one thing—would that one could say this of all 'regional' cookbooks—that was as plain as a pikestaff: they all rang true.

And Monsieur Ginestet was the man for me, for his hors d'œuvre section was the fullest of all. Here is a selection: (I have left the actual name in French but translated the description underneath; the district is also given).

Hors d'Œuvre

Cerneaux au Vinaigre
   green walnuts seasoned and pickled in water and white vinegar—Orleans

Jésus de Morteau
   a very large sausage flavoured with aniseed—France Comté

Pâté de Foie aux Prunes
   pig's liver chopped with plums and fat bacon sprinkled with brandy and baked with onions

Crépinettes de Ménage
   pig's blood with chopped bacon rolled in a curl and then fried—Dauphiné. [Ugh! T.A.L.]

Croquettes Reinequet
   pancakes filled with chopped chicken, ham, mushrooms and dressed with a Béchamel sauce; served with a tomato sauce—Dauphiné

Cœurs de Chardons aux Alpes
   raw heads of Alpine thistle served with vinegar—Savoy

Poutargue
   a sort of desiccated caviar mixture of the roes of grey mullets grated and mixed with chopped hard-boiled eggs, onion and oil—Provence

La Fèche Sec
  marinated pig's liver sauté, pickled in vinegar and served cold with sliced
  radish and chopped parsley—Languedoc

Anchoïde Corse
  braised anchovies garnished with figs and garlic, served on slices of bread
  sprinkled with olive oil and chopped onions

Les Saucisses aux Huîtres
  sausage of pork forcemeat mixed with white wine and grilled, served hot
  with oysters—Bordelaise. [Sounds scrumptious! T.A.L.]

Le Pain dausse
  onion mashed in rough cider with coarse salt and served on slices of
  thickly buttered bread—Picardy

and so on.

On the other side of this splendid wooden menu were the main
dishes. Some were wildly cranky-sounding, for example, Le Sobron-
ado (a very thick soup of haricot beans, pork liver, chopped fat bacon,
diced ham, parsnips, celery, onion, cloves, nutmegs, chopped parsley,
figs and garlic served on slices of bread—Guyenne) and Le Chamango
aux haricots, or La Magnagna Basque (pickled pig's skin—'Chamango'
—boiled with leeks, cabbage, diced bacon, carrots, pimentos and
haricot beans and served with pickled pimentoes—Basque country).
Excluding those which were strange bedfellows, the four I liked best
were:

Morue à la Morlaisienne
  fillets of cod and lobster poached in cider covered with a Béchamel sauce
  and then baked between two pancakes—Brittany

Côtelettes chevreuil* à la Solognote
  venison cutlets browned in olive oil and butter, served on a long piece of
  thin brown bread and with mashed celery and sherry sauce—Orleans

Quenelles de veau à la Valentinoise
  quenelles of veal, poached with butter, cream, yolk of egg and nutmeg;
  garnished with thyme and served with a thick sauce of butter, flour,
  bouillon gravy, tomato juice and dry white wine—Dauphiné

Sardines grillées à la Niçoise
  fresh sardines [gorgeous fish! T.A.L.] dipped in whipped eggs, sprinkled
  with crumbs and grilled, served with black olives—Roussillon

  * But *venaison*, if male.

9

Then came the sweets:

Marrons à la Lyonnaise
   mashed chestnuts, mixed with vanilla, yolks of eggs, cream and baked in
   a mould—Lyonnais

La Flamusse aux Pommes
   minced apples mixed with milk, flour, eggs, sugar and semolina and baked
   —Nivernais

Le Clafoutis
   stoned black cherries covered with a custard mousse of eggs, flour, castor
   sugar and baked, served hot—Périgord

The child returned just as I had finished absorbing the menu—I
suspect he had been warned to give people sufficient time to take it all
in. The only hors d'œuvre which was on that week was the plum pâté,
which I jumped at, but the main course speciality was an elaborate
affair of tripe and pig's blood which gave me the shudders.

'What is the speciality omelette like?' I asked. 'You say that is
always on.'

'Morning, noon and night three hundred and sixty-four days of the
year', he replied.

'You mean three hundred and sixty-five,' I said.

'No, we are always shut on Christmas Day.'

The young man was too much for me.

'Well, what is the omelette like?'

'It is an omelette Lyonnaise which consists of poached chicken
livers, diced truffles, onion, fried croutons and cream mixed into the
omelette.'

'That's for me,' I said, 'and another aperitif', and I went on looking
at the game. The woman was clearly a dedicated player and was by
far the best performer. She was also drinking more eau de vie de marc
than the rest.

It seemed only a few seconds before my table was laid up and the
first course was served, which I ate in a trice, washed down by a large,
crisp, pleasant glass of unknown white wine. I was now ready for my
omelette and was vaguely wondering how long this would take when
the child came out and beckoned to the woman. She frowned but
stopped playing and disappeared indoors. A few seconds later the
omelette arrived. It was superb!

After eating it, and quite replete I lit a Gauloise and picked up the menu again to try to memorize its contents, for there was no question of 'winning' this one. At the bottom, my eye caught a list of several spirits and liqueurs and one in a slightly heavier type than the others. It was Foudraine liqueur, made of sloes, baked, poached and soaked in brandy and filtered.

This seemed a must, so I ordered one and at the same time asked for my bill. The child brought the drink but he took the bill out to the woman, who put it on a plate and came over to me. As I paid I complimented her almost fulsomely on the omelette, but could not help adding:

'I see you leave everything to the child except the final touch of the omelette.'

'No,' said the woman, 'he does that entirely.'

'But didn't he ask you in from your game to do it?' I persisted.

'No,' she said, 'he called me in to check his reckoning of the bill. But, as usual, it was quite correct.'

A twinge at the back of my skull told me there was something odd here, but I was too contented to let it bother me. But as I got to the door, I realized.

'But, Madame,' I said, 'it is of no consequence, but when you went inside to check the bill, I had not *then* decided to have your Foudraine and yet it is on the bill.'

The woman gave me a really pleasant open smile which was clearly meant to be a compliment.

'Practically everyone falls for the drink!' she said, 'so it is easier to put it on straight away.' Then she looked at me again as if to say 'I'm sure you are in our game', and continued, raising her glass to her lips, 'and if they don't have it, we say it is the house service charge.'

'You are refreshingly frank, madame,' I said. 'By the way, how old is that infant Carême? I put him at ten, but he must be older.'

'He was nine a couple of months ago,' said the woman.

*

The next place on my way to Notre Dame du Puy was Le Monastier. Ah! Le Monastier-sur-Gazeille!—dull, tiny town of only five thousand inhabitants, little did you know that just on ninety years ago fame was to descend on you. It was here that Robert Louis Stevenson bought his little ass which he christened Modestine and then set off on his famous

journey which only took thirteen days—from Sunday 22 September
to 4 October—and which was to become famous as his *Travels with a
Donkey in the Cévennes*. The work starts 'In a little place called Le
Monastier, in a pleasant highland valley fifteen miles from Le Puy,
I spent about a month of fine days.'*

The travels continue, 'Monastier is notable for the making of lace,
for drunkenness, for freedom of language, and for unparalleled
political dissension. There are adherents of each of the four French
parties—Legitimists, Orleanists, Imperialists and Republicans—in this
little mountain-town; and they all hate, loathe, decry and calumniate
each other.'

Stevenson only crossed my Loire-following path at Le Monastier,
for he was travelling south, so we must leave him here; but the way he
makes an utterly uneventful trudge with the slowest, stupidest,
laziest donkey in the world bristle with activity is a marvel.

R.L.S. was a chronic invalid all his life and especially so while he
was a boy. According to one life of him 'through the long northern
winters he could never cross the threshold without catching bron-
chitis or pneumonia', so it shows a deal of courage that he planned with
Modestine to sleep several nights out in the open.

To this end he had sewn up for himself a curious huge sleeping-bag
made out of 'green waterproof cart-cloth without and blue sheep's
fur within' and off he set.

All goes disastrously! Modestine crawls at snail's pace and Stevenson, convinced she is doing her best, does nothing save ponder on the
miserable time he will go through with the animal for a week or more.

Then he meets a peasant.

'*Your donkey,*' *says he,* '*is very old?*'
I told him I believed not.
Then, he supposed, we had come far.
I told him we had but newly left Monastier.

The peasant roars with laughter and 'plucking a switch out of a
thicket' he begins to hit Modestine 'about the sternworks, uttering a
cry'.

This causes the donkey to break into a 'good round pace' and
R.L.S. concludes that 'her former panting and shaking had been, I
regret to say, a piece of comedy'.

* There seems hardly any doubt but that R.L.S. meant this to be a variant of
Cervantes' opening to *Don Quixote*.

The references to wine in the work are few, which is not surprising since this was and is one of the least vinous parts of France. At the beginning of his journey, Stevenson takes along with him for 'his more immediate needs' a leg of cold mutton, a considerable quantity of black bread (mainly for Modestine) and a bottle of Beaujolais. Later, near the end of the journey, he cannot stand this any longer so he pours it away and replaces it with some 'generous scented Volnay', a description which fits it pretty well nearly a hundred years later.

There are two references to the Phylloxera, that little vine insect pest which ravaged the vine all over Europe in the last quarter of the nineteenth century. In the first place the author describes drinking not wine at dinner but 'a most economical juice of the grape—La Parisienne, they call it'. This was made by placing the grapes whole in a cask and filling it up with water. One by one the grapes burst and fermented and so what was drunk in the day was replaced at night by water; 'a feeble beverage but very pleasant to the taste'. Stevenson notes that, also because of the Phylloxera, he saw some men at work on a cider press. He was not quite sure what it was that they were doing, so he asked and they told him, adding 'just as in the North', as though the region was going to the devil.

The one thing at Le Monastier-sur-Gazeille that is not mentioned by Stevenson is a very fine and unusual old abbey-church which brings crowds of tourists to look at it.

LE PUY

THIS TOWN, WHICH IS PRACTICALLY ON THE LOIRE, has been called the most picturesque spot in the world, an architectural freak, and the best place in Europe from which to study the evolution of religion. It can, I think, sustain all these claims; the curious topographical features of the landscape; the bizarre but beautiful cathedral; the enormous bronze statue of the Virgin and Child built on a pinnacle; and the old Byzantine chapel built on yet another pinnacle—all add to the picture.

The city itself is situated in an immense basin or hollow and is surrounded by a whole conglomeration of sky-piercing, turreted pinnacles of volcanic rocks. According to the angle of the sun's rays the effect is either bizarre or grandiose.

On a spur of the largest pinnacle of them all is the Cathedral of Notre Dame du Puy. It was built there because of a pagan legend connected with the spot but those early evangelists were clever; when they sensed it would be useful to put an end to a heathen myth, they christianized it, and all was well. That is what happened here.

Towards the end of the third century A.D. St Georges, the first bishop of Velay, arrived in the province of Velay from Rome. The capital then was Ruessium, some ten miles from Le Puy.

During his episcopacy a devout woman who was ill of a fever had a vision. In it the Virgin Mary appeared to her and said, 'Go and place yourself on a black stone which you will find at the top of Mount Anis and I will cure you.'

The woman finds the stone, which was probably part of a dolmen or cromlech—a huge stone under which a man or beast could crawl— and after being cured she receives a further message telling her to build a sanctuary on the holy spot.

She goes to Bishop St Georges to persuade him to help her carry out the Virgin Mary's request and they set off on a hot July day. But when they get near the place it is, wondrous to relate, snowing and they cannot find the stone. But wonder follows wonder and a stag leaps out of a thicket and leaves hoofmarks in the snow which lead them to the stone. The bishop is greatly impressed, but as funds are low all he personally can do is to plant a hawthorn thicket around the spot to act as a marker.

Two centuries later another woman, this time a paralysed one, is cured by lying on the stone and again the Virgin Mary appears and tells the cured woman to call on the bishop and ask him to build a church there.

This time the bishop (who is called Vosy)* happens to be a rich man and with his money and his energetic drive a Christian church is raised on the site of the 'Fever Stone', as it by now has become called.

Around the church there grew up the small town of Anicium† which later, in the eleventh century when the cathedral became clearly outlined, was called Puy-Sainte-Marie.

Soon the 'Fever Stone' in the then new cathedral was joined by a small statue of the Virgin and then by another, and for some years pilgrims flocked to pay homage to both of them. Little is known of the first statue—it inexplicably disappeared after the thirteenth century anyhow—save that it was not black, and that it probably looked like the design on the pilgrims' medallions given to travellers to Santiago in the thirteenth century.

The second statue, the 'Black Virgin', was far more famous and its end well recorded and very tragic. It was brought to France from Palestine and given to the cathedral by King Louis IX (St Louis) in curious circumstances. Louis, one of the world's worst generals, got himself captured on his first Crusade and, while waiting for his ransom to come from France, did some sight-seeing, during which time he was shown a mysterious black statue representing a mother and child. The ransom paid, the Sultan in typical oriental fashion asked Louis to choose a parting gift and was greatly disturbed when the small statue was selected. Pride however won and St Louis sailed off with his gift, little realizing that it was in fact an image of Isis and her son Horus.

* He was helped by an architect called Scutaire whose name is carved on a fifth-century lintel, found recently during extensive repair work.

† It has been suggested, that Anis, then Anicium, derives from the Egyptian goddess Isis, whose cult was introduced into the Roman Empire and became popular mainly because of the splendour and mystery of its ceremonies.

The funny little statue must have made a tremendous impression on those who saw it for Faujas de St Fons studied it in such detail in 1778 that we know precisely how it looked; a cedarwood carving of the Madonna richly clothed in an embroidered gold dress; and if you did not look too carefully the small son's head appeared to be popping out of the fold of his mother's garment like a baby kangaroo. And there it remained for 539 years until 1794 when in the Place des Martourets the revolutionaries stripped the gold robe off the statue* and publicly burned it, while the poor priests came up one by one to take an oath of loyalty to the new government.

That great French art-historian, Emile Mâle, says of the cathedral, 'One of the most beautiful Christian monuments in the world; more than all others it sets the imagination working by its mystery, its strange half-Arab design, its confusing reminder of the Orient, its lovely cloister and its black and white arches which remind one of the great Mosque at Cordoba.'

For myself, in spite of the beauty of the cloister and the fascinating links with the Orient, the word 'ungainly' must be added to 'bizarre' and 'impressive', this latter word relating chiefly to the main entrance and the great flight of steps up to the cathedral itself.

The road leading to the main façade is called the Rue des Tables and there is a good painting of it showing how it appeared in 1911 in *Auvergne and its People* by Frances M. Gostling (Methuen, 1911). It shows a number of women seated on the steeply ascending steps outside their houses doing their tatting. High up in the distance can be seen the multi-brick coloured front of the cathedral. Ever upwards wends this very, very steep cobbled road until it changes into a stair-way of 132 steps which takes you to the summit. Until just a hundred years ago this approach must have been more curious still for the steps continued under the present porch through the nave and right up to the altar itself. Here the pilgrim found himself actually standing on the very Fever Stone which started it all.

'But the priests found it difficult to conduct divine service by reason of the swarming of sick folk', says Mrs Gostling in her travel book of the region. So the stair was altered and the rebuilding has been deplored by archaeologists ever since, for part of the building dates back to the

* Underneath the clothing it was remarked that the mother was seated on a kind of footstool, with her son on her knees, and, being Egyptian, they were bound with mummies' wrappings, both hands and feet.

tenth century while some less reliable enthusiasts have put it as early as the fifth.

After Rome by far the most important pilgrimage of the Middle Ages was to Santiago de Compostela in Galicia in the far north-west of Spain. It all started with the most wonderful Christian legend of all —the 'golden' one, in which St James the Greater's remains were pointed out by a star in a field in that part of Spain, now called Galicia. Quickly the fame of the spot grew and a church was built on the place where the saint's body was found—Santiago (St James) de Compostela (the field of the star). At least that was what it was thought to be for hundreds of years; more recently the suggestion is that Compostela is from two Latin words and means a burial place. And indeed there are several other Compostelas in Spain, which makes this interpretation likely.

As the shrine became more and more famous, travellers from all over Europe set forth on the pilgrimage, but because of the dangers of the brigand-infested route few people travelled alone. So it came about that there were four main rallying points in France which became more and more important. They were Paris in the north, Arles in the extreme south, and in the middle Vézelay and Le Puy. How truly exciting it must have been to have foregathered at 'The Peak', for that in Auvergne dialect is what Le Puy means, to lie on the 'Fever Stone', to embrace St Louis' Black Virgin and, most exhausting of all, to climb up to St Michael of the Needle.

The first pilgrimage started in A.D. 951 and was conducted by Bishop Godescalk, and what a crowd there must have been! For those who set out would be away from home for over a year! Thus at the rallying points mothers, daughters, wives and sweethearts also came to bid sad farewells. They met at the bottom of the Rue des Tables, ready to ascend the immense flight of steps on their knees and then to throw themselves on the Fever Stone. We have some idea of the density of the crowd when we recall that there is extant an old guide-book in which pilgrims are exhorted not under any circumstances to try to pick up anything they drop for fear of getting trampled underfoot.

I found present-day Le Puy a pleasant enough town; trying feverishly to attract those tourists who had been so singularly missing in the past; for until the earlier years of this century the place was very badly served by the railways; and three or four travel books of that time make quite a point of telling readers to be warned of places so very far off the beaten track. One book says that in 1911 there was only one hotel available.

Now, the hotel situation is quite good.

Actually Le Puy is still in a bit of a backwater, in comparison with the amount of tourism in France; and, infuriatingly, it seems just to miss out on every single sectional guide-book dealing with the country.

But the town *is* trying to get itself on the tourist map. I do not remember anywhere else, save perhaps Salamanca, where so many different official brochures were showered on me. *Holy City* and *City of Arts* is the main theme. One superb folder with a folding colour photograph of the whole town says that the place is *At the cross-roads of the Middle Ages* and then, just missing a good jingle, continues: *A place to halt—a place to stay—Puy en Velay offers you its valuable and artistic riches, numerous varieties of excursions—calm relaxing holidays.*

The next brochure draws attention to the gastronomic specialities of the region, all of which were to my mind quite bogus, save one. The exception is a big range of unusual aperitifs and liqueurs which are not to be seen elsewhere. One with a kick like a mule was a spirituous concoction of wild bilberries; it was not a cream, meaning very sweet, but an eau de vie, and very dry. But the real speciality of the town, advertised all over the place, is the very potent liqueur, or *digestif* as the French call it, called Ververine, which we call Vervein or Verbena.

A little aside at this point on the making of liqueurs because there are in the public mind certain misconceptions. In the first place there is no definition whatever, legal or official, as to what is a liqueur. Wine, beer and the various spirits are all beverages which have been described so accurately that if we order any one of them we know exactly what we will get. Not so liqueurs; for, apart from the fact that they are *generally* fairly sweet, they can range from a cheaply distilled spirit made from sugar beet, potatoes, or cereals flavoured with essences, to a very good brandy into which fresh apricots or cherries have been infused, to be gently matured in casks of oak (the perfect and only wood for maturing spirits) for many years. As for a 'liqueur' brandy, this is meaningless nonsense and the phrase as a sales gimmick went out of fashion among the better-class cognac shippers years ago.

There is one type of *digestif* which we in England class loosely as a liqueur but the French do not. These are spirits which are a distillation of the fruit itself . . . a fruit brandy, in fact. These are marketed as eau de vie de . . . whichever the (soft) fruit is, and the most popular is Quetsch. This is a small plum called also a mussel-plum. This drink is always water-white in colour.

The sweet liqueurs as we know them are *not* made this way but are basically the infusion of a flavouring agent into alcohol by two different methods: heat treatment or the cold method of maceration. The former is used for rather solid things full of essential oils, such as roots and peel. They are steeped in the alcohol for two days and then this alcohol is heated.

Fruit such as apricots, cherries, peaches, greengages, etc., after light mashing or crushing if the flavour of the stone is desired, is put into oak casks, brandy (for this is the basic spirit usually used) is poured on and it is left for many a twelvemonth.

When it is ready for bottling, in both instances the liqueur will be sweetened, usually by adding sugar syrup. The method used rather depends upon the laws of the producing country, though it is likely that saccharine as a sweetening agent will shortly be banned internationally.

*

That night I put up at the old-fashioned, rambling Hotel Bristol where I was obliged to park in their garage, which had such giant notices around the walls telling one not to lock one's car that I felt obliged to obey. As I was too tired to take everything up to my room, and as the garage doors did not look like being locked, I spent a highly nervous night.

But I had a good dinner first, for I did a lot of menu reading beforehand. Finally I settled for the restaurant of the Hôtel des Voyageurs but I can also recommend the Cygne or, less expensive, a Routiers restaurant called chez Michelet.

*

The next morning I went to look at one of the most massive monuments in the world, called Notre Dame de France, or by the locals the 'Virgin of Le Puy'. It stands on a crag, the Rocher de Corneille, behind the cathedral, is made entirely of bronze and is over fifty feet high. It was erected to perpetuate the memory of the proclamation of the Dogma of the Immaculate Conception and was blessed on 1 September 1860 in front of a crowd of a hundred and twenty thousand persons.

The Virgin is holding in her hand the Infant Jesus and, to get some idea of the statue's size, be it noted that the head of the child alone is a good deal taller than a man.

The erection of the statue was far from easy for it had to be put up in sections, that is, when sufficient metal had been found; and herein lies an extraordinary story—for much of the material comes from Russian guns captured at Sebastopol.

The French commander-in-chief, General Pelissier, had several times stayed at Le Puy and knew of the Rocher de Corneille and he wrote to the bishop, Morlhon, with the suggestion that, when the latter met Napoleon III, he should ask His Majesty for *the cannon that would be captured at Sebastopol.*

The Emperor received the Bishop of Le Puy on 5 September 1855 when the request was duly made. Upon which the Emperor said:

'The Russian artillery is made of cast iron.'

To which Bishop Morlhon replied:

'This metal would tempt one's cupidity if necessity arose.'

'But *when* the cannons have been taken, Monseigneur', replied the Emperor.

And on 8 September 1855 General Pelissier did capture Sebastopol, together with 125 bronze and 3,711 cast-iron cannon, which represented some 150 tons of metal for his statue.

*

But I retain the finest thing in Le Puy for the last, and all the other sights of Le Puy en Velay become mediocre compared with the astounding-looking St-Michel-d'Aiguilhe, or 'of the needle'.

We will come to the beauty of the little chapel at the top later, but the rock itself is such a dramatic little freak of nature that it is perhaps unique in the world. For, although it is over two hundred and fifty feet high, it is only five hundred feet in circumference at the very base and completely isolated from the flat surrounding land; a natural obelisk, a perfectly round tapering cone which geologists think could be the chimney of an extinct crater filled with volcanic rock and isolated by millions of years of erosion.

You need sturdy legs even now to ascend the two hundred and sixty-eight steps which take you to the top, but this is child's play compared with the ascent long ago; for there are still traces of the original steps which are almost perpendicular. No wonder that Bishop Truannus, who had the notion to build the chapel in A.D. 962, said, 'In other times even the most agile of men could hardly climb up.' One assumes that before he started building there was an even steeper pathway.

The chapel itself crowns the rock so perfectly that the ensemble has been rated by many to be the eighth wonder of the world, while others have said that the building itself now seems to have been built not by man but by time itself.

Two hundred years after Truannus started work, further extensive additions were made but it is interesting to note that, even in those remote times, there was an appreciation of older fine buildings for they took care to enshrine and build round the tenth-century architecture.

But the twelfth-century work was marvellous because they managed to add a five-tier belfry—an exact copy of the one at the cathedral. How they achieved this on the postage-stamp space available is a miracle.

In 1955 during the course of excavations the most charming little object was found: a crucifix on which is a Christ dressed in a colobrium, which is a short-sleeved tunic worn by the clergy of the early church or by kings at their coronation.

But let us leave Le Puy with a last thought of founder Truannus. He was the *doyen* of the cathedral chapter and he has left us something else besides his church, namely his Donation Charter.

Holy people of God both of the present and the future know ye that I, Truannus, wanted to erect a church on the lofty rock locally known as the Needle. I went before Bishop Godescalk who not only granted me a licence but also encouraged me greatly. Thus it was that my church was built, and I built an easy road up to the top and crowned the summit with a church which was good to look at in honour of Archangel Michael.

Now I leave the place to the canons of the cathedral but with this clause that all down the centuries they will every day pay three deniers for a mass for the saving of my soul and the soul of Bishop Godescalk.

And if anyone through avarice shall try to avoid the conditions of this charter and does not offer up prayers on the altar then they shall suffer the maledictions contained in the Old and New Testaments and thus chained by the cord of anathema shall go and rejoin for an eternity of torment the ministers of Hell.

This charter was finished on Thursday the fifteenth day of August in the eighth year of the reign of King Lotharius.

3

CHARLIEU
AND CLUNY

Leaving Le Puy to follow the Loire northwards, one comes to the pretty little village of Lavoute-sur-Loire. As there is no circumflex over the 'u', I take the word to be a corruption of *volute*, a volute or spiral, for this is what the river does here in a spectacular way. And high up above, perched on a crag and with a perpendicular drop to the torrents below, is the mighty, beautiful, first château of the Loire, Polignac, owned by those warring seigneurs of the same name since the Middle Ages and still to this day their summer residence. The river here flows fiercely and right up in the castle grounds the noise of the waters is like the shussing sound a strong wind makes in the pine trees.

My next village was Beaulieu, a hideous place quite belying its name and with an equally ugly castle made of semi-modern bricks which quite missed the effect the builders intended. The scenery here was as lovely as I had expected, for all my travel books of the early part of the century were unanimous on the subject.

A few miles on, and high up on the mountainside, I saw a sign: 'CHANTEGRAILLE 1·2 kms.' I went on and then thought—'It must be a picturesque spot—a sort of special singing grotto.' Should I go up? The ascent was terrifying.

I stopped a man panting up the hill on a bicycle and said, 'Excuse me, but is that place Chantegraille very beautiful?'

The man looked at me and scratched his head.

'It is a sort of natural spot', I continued, 'where one's echo comes singing back from across the mountains.'

This time the man gave me a very sharp stare and started, only I didn't realize this till later, to wag his head negatively.

'Thank you very much', I said. I turned the car round and when I got to the turning I saw a notice:

ROUTES DE FRANCE
OUVERT PAR 50 JEUNES VOLONTAIRES
DE JEUNESSE ET RECONSTRUCTION

Le Ministre d'Agriculture
Radio Luxembourg
La Tribune

The sign was beautifully and solidly made and superimposed above the writing were two wrought iron pick-axes.

'That's it!' I thought. 'The famous beauty spot inaccessible hitherto by car, and so the youth of France built a road up there.' And up I shot.

A wild exaggeration. I crawled! For though the youngsters had done a very professional job, the steepness of the gradient was horrific and I am sure it was farther than the sign said.

At the top was an ugly tumbledown farmhouse, outside which three children were playing. The scenery around, though, was terrific and the house was perched on the edge of a steep fissure in the hills, which rose again suddenly—the ideal spot for an echo.

I got out of the car into the drenching rain and, cupping my hands to my mouth, let out a 'hullo!' which would have made Roland's horn sound like a whisper.

Nothing happened. At least there was no echo. But the children stopped playing as if shot, and came running up, mystified and frightened.

'Where is the famous echo?' I asked.

They just gawped at me.

A thought dawned on me. 'Tell me,' I said, 'do you live here?'

'Yes', they said.

'With Mummy and Daddy?'

'Yes', they chorused.

'And they do farming?'

'Yes.'

'And you hardly see anyone else?'

'No.'

I went down a wiser man and found in my dictionary that night that a *graille* was a crow.

On to Malateverne, as ugly a village as the name sounded, through

Yssingeaux and quickly through St-Etienne, a hideous manufacturing town, to lunch at a Routier's just outside. When a Routier's food is bad, it is appalling; and here they sold me, as a supplement to a rotten meal, a portion of *fritures* which were tough, whole small fish fried in stale batter—it was like eating pieces of wire wrapped up in old leather.

Soon I got to Pouilly-sous-Charlieu.

Let us clear up the muddle about this name. Both *The Times Mid-Century Atlas* and the *Guide Michelin* list *four* Pouillys: Pouilly-en-Auxois, Pouilly-sur-Loire (which is dealt with later), Pouilly-sur-Saône and this one which is called plain Pouilly by *The Times* and not Pouilly-sous-Charlieu.

Neither of them makes mention of that Pouilly which is far better known to millions of wine-drinkers than all the other four put together. This is the miniscule hamlet (it is also the surrounding commune) of Pouilly, ten miles to the west of Mâcon, which has coupled its name with the village of Fuissé; from there comes much the best of the white wines of the Mâconnais, now called Pouilly-Fuissé.

Pouilly-below-Charlieu is about thirty minutes' car ride from Charlieu, a very fine little town indeed.

It was here that an incident occurred that made me decide that I had had enough of my half-grown beard, an uncomely sight and particularly so with my cheap Spanish peasant's all-blue shirt (oh! the linen it ruined when it was washed) and half-rim gold spectacles.

Charlieu is a tiny show-place town, which its inhabitants are rightly proud of, and its great pride is its Benedictine priory, which goes back to the ninth and tenth centuries. The place prospered exceedingly but despite this the inhabitants did not feel strong enough to remain independent after the break-up of Charlemagne's Empire. So in 932 they were obliged to call in aid from mighty Cluny near by, whose influence on certain parts of the building is noticeable.

It was just about closing time when I got to the priory and, terrified that the custodian might not let me in after so long a trip to see it, I slipped past him while he was selling postcards to some Danes.

Inside I found myself in a big courtyard with nobody to tell me where to go. I wanted especially to see 'the dungeon built of golden-coloured stones, supposed to have been made by Philippe-Auguste, a superb example of military architecture'. So I took a plunge down the only entrance which showed a descent.

Here I found myself in front of the most un-dungeon-like scene; two young men and two pretty teenage girls lovingly entwined and dancing to a languid tune being played on a gramophone. There was a long trestle table on one side of the improvised dance floor, upon which there were empty cups of tea and tumblers which clearly had recently held red wine, while on the other side of the room were two casks of wine with bowls under the leaking, ill-fitting taps. In the background there was a huge pile of vividly coloured children's swing-boats.

Seeing me, the couples stopped dancing, the girls untwined themselves from their partners and brushed back their long hair from their foreheads; the men went for more wine from the casks; none showed the slightest trace of nervousness. Not so me.

'I'm looking for the dungeon', I said.

'That's in the other corner', said one of the girls. 'There's not much to see', she added.

They were all very far from mod-rock attired; a very nice group.

'Would you care for a glass of wine?' said one of the young men, proffering a glass.

'Please,' I said, 'I am a London wine-merchant.'

'My father is a grower in the Beaujolais district.' So that was why the wine was so good! Never was ice so quickly broken.

'But what on earth are you doing here on a Sunday afternoon?' I said. 'And what are the boats for?'

'Waiting to get the go-ahead for the recording', said one. 'The boats are for the local fair and are stored here for the winter.'

Between drinks the story took shape.

Delighted with the setting and the acoustics of the priory's cloisters, a group of young people from the Mâcon had formed a society to make records of religious music, and the choir was at that moment having its final rehearsal upstairs, before going on the air live.

Looking around afresh, I saw a mass of recording equipment and at that moment a voice came over a loudspeaker.

'We will be ready to record in five minutes. Over.' One of the young men went over to a box, twiddled a few knobs and replied, 'O.K. Ready and out.'

At this moment one of the girls said to me, 'Would you like to watch the choir singing?'

Was it in good faith or did she know the upshot?

25

'It's a very pretty sight,' she said, clinching the matter, and I followed her pretty golden rat's-tail hair up the spiral stairway.

It was indeed an enchanting sight; some twenty attractive girls and perhaps half as many men; they burst into song as I got to the top of the stairs. We tiptoed along the side of the cloister so that I could see better and thus came into full view of the choir. Some of the girls took a somewhat surprised look at me and then buried their faces in their song sheets. A couple seemed to go purple in the face.

The singing continued only for a moment when a voice from the operators down below came over the air.

'Stop. We'll have to take it again. There's a funny noise come over.'

Downstairs later, after many more glasses of the cask-wine, I said, 'By the way, was that noise traced?'

'I think it was a couple of the choir trying not to laugh at your beard.'

*

There is a second priory at Charlieu. On the outskirts of the town is a Franciscan abbey with a beautiful cloister which the Cordeliers built in the thirteenth century. But the centuries have dealt harshly with this property and the final ignominy came in 1910, when an art dealer bought it and seems (piecing together four slightly different accounts one gets at the truth) to have actually dismantled the stones, ready to ship to America *pour entourer le tennis d'un de ses clients*. Whether it was real tennis or lawn tennis that was going to be enwalled is not clear. But the American client never got his cloister, because the state bought the stones back in 1913.

But Charlieu is full of lovely old buildings, including the much publicized and beautiful Maison des Anglais, though nobody knows why or how it became so called.

*

Phonetically, La Clayette is another Cirencester or Hunstanton, in that the inhabitants shorten it to La Claite. To the world at large it is known for its horse show, but to me, who put up there for some days, it was the only place I have ever been to where that old chestnut of *idées au-dessus de sa gare* made sense. For either the Station Hotel had truly had ideas of grandeur and moved, or La Clayette had been given the Beeching treatment. I never heard or saw a train, nor could I find a platform.

The Hotel de la Gare was excellent; quiet, renowned locally for good food, and with really cheap, good bedrooms; a useful asset if one is extending one's stay.

I used La Clayette as a jumping-off ground for mighty Cluny, and so, with no packing to do, got there too early the next morning. The custodian-guide was not yet ready to open and I was told to my fury that to be accompanied by him was compulsory.

'Are there a lot of valuable things then?' I said.

'Nothing whatever except the ancient ruins', he replied.

'Then what in the name of thunder is the idea of making people go round in silly herds?' I retorted.

'Those are the rules and one has to stick to them.'

Fuming with anger, I had to wait until the man was ready to take our party round. Three! A middle-aged Dutch woman, a young Frenchman and myself.

What a farce it was! The Dutch woman could not comprehend a single word of French, I sulked in a corner and tried to look as though I was not listening because I knew all about it, which left only the Frenchman to be addressed. Judging by one or two questions he put to the man, he probably knew far more than the guide.

This fellow was clearly used to addressing the huge summer audiences that gathered round him, for he boomed away like a fog-horn, keeping the Frenchman quite a distance away. Everything had been learned by rote and whenever the young man interrupted with a question, part of the speech had to start again.

But in spite of everything one could not help being fascinated. Cluny, 'light of the world', said Pope Urban II (who himself was a Clunisien) was second only to St Peter's, Rome. Built in 909 by William the Pious of Aquitaine, it enjoyed fantastic prestige until the fourteenth century and the great riches and ostentation of the monks of Cluny were a byword. 'They cannot journey five miles away from home but they must take with them sixty horses or more. A light surely does not need to be in a candelabra of gold or silver to give forth its brilliance,' said St Bernard in his bitter attack on their luxury.

But so much of it all is no more that it needs great imagination to conjure up the picture of its former almost incredible power and glory throughout the Christian world. It was systematically pillaged during the Revolution and on the grounds that its upkeep cost too much (it was completely abandoned from 1780 to 1798), the place was sold to a corn-chandler of Mâcon who, with state permission, started dismantling part of the buildings.

Personally, I thought that the most interesting place of all was the immense cereal storage room, dating from the thirteenth century and with its original roof still intact, because, said the guide, proffering the most interesting piece of advice of the tour, 'the chestnut, with which the enormous span of roof is made, is never attacked by wood-boring insects'.

Behind the abbey, in a magnificent setting, is a Haras National or Government Stud. It can only be visited in the afternoons out of season and it was with difficulty that I managed to persuade the concierge that my morning visit was of such importance that I must needs be invited in.

The young man into whose office I was eventually ushered was one of the best-dressed Frenchmen I have ever come across. He also had a cool, incisive brain which was now being used to control a mild irritation at being interrupted in his work and also to find out why a middle-aged English wine-merchant should be so interested in stallions.

Having heard in the town so much in praise of the establishment and being so near to success, I now wanted desperately to see the animals. I was on a pretty slippery saddle, until I remembered that I had recently been to Vienna and visited the stables of the famous Lipizzaner White Horses there. This did it! The atmosphere thawed considerably and we started our tour.

This particular Haras kept twenty-two breeding stallions for use in the departments of Allier, Loire, Nièvre, Rhône and Saône-et-Loire. They were an impressive sight, these massive percherons and cobs, and one could understand why a few farmers still preferred them to tractors.

I was surprised at the large number of English breeds used in France and I discovered that P.S.A., written so frequently alongside the name of the horse, stood for *Pur Sang Anglais*.

Although Cluny has the excellent Hôtel de Bourgogne in the Place de l'Abbaye with a splendid dining-room, I set off south again for I wanted to go to Mâcon to buy a book which was printed there. I was making good progress when I saw at a cross-roads a house on the outside of which was a huge sign: 'Cave de Dégustation'.

It was funny, I thought, that there should be a tasting cellar in this part of the world; then I realized that I was on the very edge of the Beaujolais district.

The author among the vines
on the Loire

The Loire, a few hundred
yards down from its source

The source of the Loire according to the Cadastral (the French equivalent of the Domesday Book) and the official map

The Gerbier de Jonc

The Basilica at Le Puy-en-Velay on a feast-day. At other times women used to sit working at tables on the steps leading up to the church

An awe-inspiring sign, to be seen about a mile from the source

Cluny Abbey: the famous
roof

The Ducal Palace at
Nevers. The
staircase, like the one
at Blois, was used,
in addition to its
normal function, as
a gallery from which
to watch spectacles

The place was in reality a sort of huge barn, empty and devoid of furniture on the customers' side. Behind the bar, however, was an array of bottles, together with exhortations to purchase, and a goodly collection of drinking glasses as well. It was all being looked after by a wide-awake, attractive woman of about twenty-five and I asked her if I could buy a drink.

'You would like to sample the wine first?' said the pretty woman.

'Not exactly', I said. 'I would like to buy a glass.'

The woman shook her head. 'Samples of our excellent wine are given away to those who want to buy bottles to take back to Paris.'

I hate getting free samples of anything; you are instantly placed under the obligation to be polite about the product when you might wish to castigate. And with wine how much more so! Most of my holidays have been spent digging out little growers and tasting the produce of their vineyards by the light of guttering candle-ends in damp, dark cellars and I like to be brutally frank about what I taste.

But by Jove! I was thirsty. What with going around Cluny with that dreary guide, then the trek around the stud which had left the smell of horse still in my nostrils, I was parched. So, in exchange for free drinks, I prepared to be polite.

'I'd like to try the wine', I said. 'Tell me, have you been open here long?'

'We started yesterday', said the woman, pouring out a glass. 'My father's property is tucked away at the back here and so far from the main road that no motorists ever pass. And we want to go direct to the public and not to have to sell our wine to the wholesalers in Mâcon, who just lump it all together into one great blend.'

This really sounded interesting. She offered me another glass of white wine which was even better than the first, dry but not thin, full but not flabby.

'So we suddenly remembered that we had this old property on the main road and my husband and father talked me into coming down here', she continued.

'May I try the red now?' I said.

My thirst was now assuaged and this was a greater compliment than can be imagined for, though I can quaff as much white wine before a meal as you are pleased to give me, the consumption of red on an empty stomach automatically gives me the most unpleasant pain, which lasts for about twenty minutes. Strong tea does the same, so I suppose it must be the tannin which is present in both but not in a white wine.

The red wine was good too; far better than anything I had had while in the district. Could I have stumbled on a not so 'little' wine that would be worth shipping to England, I wondered?

'Would your father consider exporting to England?' I said.

'Well, he has to Denmark and Sweden. I don't see why not.'

'I could go and call this afternoon,' I said, and explained that, though I had started by just looking in for a drink, I was in fact a London wine-merchant but had not expected, on this trip, to be buying wine.

'Why not go right now?' she said.

'Then I shan't get my lunch', I replied.

She frowned.

'The restaurant of the Croix Blanche next door to you', I said. 'It looks good from the number of cars outside, so I went in to order lunch and the man said I had better hurry or it would all be gone.'

'He's Italian and he is not given to conversation. But you will be able to get some of our wine there.'

'Where's your property?'

'Oh, it's called Château de Byonne. Just ask anyone.'

'And your father's name?'

'Thomas.'

'Thomas what?'

'John Thomas.'

At the restaurant I had one of the best meals for the price ever and I thus forgave the Italian owner, Georges Amalfitano, for being the tersest man ever. I also had the greatest difficulty in getting my half-bottles of white and red Byonne to come with the correct courses.

The dining-room was tiny and everyone seemed to have got into conversation with everyone else, mainly through the good offices of an enormous Boxer dog who was so beautifully kept and so well-behaved that it was impossible to resist feeding him when he came up and put his chin on your lap. Requesting food was obviously what he had been trained to do.

He belonged to a clearly well-to-do couple of dealers in antiques, who traded by touring the country for old pieces of furniture left abandoned in peasants' cottages. The dog must have been a valuable asset for getting into conversation with strangers.

When they heard I was a Londoner, the woman exclaimed:

'Why, we have been to London, haven't we, *chéri*?' and they recounted how they had been commissioned to erect some wrought iron in the café of some cinema in the very heart of the West End.

They had forgotten the name of the cinema and were dying for me to help them recollect; it being newly built, they were emphatic, and in the West End.

'The Empire', I said.

'No,' they replied.

'The Columbia, then?'

'No', again.

I tried harder and extended the 'West End' to Chelsea and Kensington. No go. It was intriguing. They described with meticulous care the café, where they seemed to have spent every single hour of the eight days they were in London.

'Our hotel was in the West End too', said the woman.

'Yes. Ealing', said the husband.

'Oh!' I replied.

More wine arrived for me. I was pressed harder. It all seemed so important at the time to find out where they had worked.

Then the wife said, 'You know, now I come to recollect, it may not have been a cinema they were building below.'

'That's it!' said the man. 'I remember now. It was a bowling alley. Ah! I've got it. Cricklewood, eh?'

'Oh yes,' I said, 'and in the very centre.'

*

The Château de Byonne was very hard to find, mainly because it looked so vastly different from the sketch of it on the front of the wine list that the girl had given me. For, although the château itself was dignified, superbly proportioned and very ancient, the surrounding outbuildings were an untidy mess and gave every appearance of having been used by an unsuccessful mixed farmer; chickens, ducks and geese were scuttling everywhere and weeds abounded. Eventually Monsieur Thomas appeared, a small dapper-looking man with the air of a French aristocrat. I could not understand it. This man went with the neat presentation of his wines down at the *dégustation* place and not with this messy muddle. But the answer was soon forthcoming.

'The place was let by my grandfather under an agricultural tenancy,'

31

he said, 'and I have only recently got it back. I thought I would get the vineyards back into production first.'

As we went round, I noticed that there were, indeed, signs that the vinicultural side of the establishment had been given a distinct boost.

Inside all was different; elegance reigned everywhere and I guessed the furniture to be valuable. A manservant brought glasses and bottles on a salver and we sat down to sample again.

Then: 'So you come from London, do you? I would like to see it again.' I waited for the much older man to reminisce.

'Yes, I was an assistant chef at the Queen's at Eastbourne and then I went up to London to work at the Ritz. That was from March 1909 to October 1914 when we came back for the war.'

'We?'

'Yes. My brother came with me; he went as a butcher in the Charcuterie at Benoit's.'

I sensed a story here and so said, 'Were you a chef elsewhere?'

'Oh no! It was the Phylloxera that started it all. It practically ruined my grandfather, so we boys had to leave school and take up temporary jobs.'

Gradually the story was told. Of a family with rich vineyards and therefore a comfortable income seeing them wither away before the dreaded vine louse, whose depredations none knew how to stop. Then, when the cure had been found, the ruinously expensive replanting which had to come before the boys' education.

I had heard of the misery and poverty caused by the Phylloxera ever since I had rinsed out the dirty casks in the *chais* in Bordeaux, but this was the very first time I had come up against anyone who had personally been hit by it. Nothing could have brought home the disaster more clearly.

The eastern side of the Rocky Mountains of North America is the original home of an insect of the Aphidae family called the *Phylloxera vastatrix*, from the Greek *phyllon* (leaf) and *xeros* (dry). Its life-cycle is so curious and so complex that one is rather hard put to it to find a beginning.

The first time that you know that your vineyards are in for trouble is when you see leaf galls on the underside of the leaves, for it is then that the aphids hatch out, a sure sign that parents of both sexes are at work down below. Two different sorts of aphid are hatched out. The more deadly one remains in the soil, takes up its abode there and gets to work on the roots of the vine; the other is content merely to suck the juice of the leaves and stays above ground.

The ones that stay in the soil seem to be able to reproduce themselves for many generations, after which they come to the surface as winged insects which lay their eggs on the stalks of the vine. Some of these eggs are male, others female. These mate on hatching, the gravid female lays further eggs and the whole cycle starts again.

But this is all rather simplified since, apart from there being several immature stages, there are four quite distinct forms of adult.

Until around the early eighteen-sixties the insect was unknown in Europe; but when it came—almost certainly brought over in some table grapes or young vines from the United States—it moved with dramatic speed, reaching as far north as Bordeaux in 1868. In the next five years the ravages were terrible.

In 1873 hopes were raised after Planchon, the great French entomologist, had ascertained that an acarid or mite, called *Tyroglyphus* (from two Greek words meaning cheese-carver, because cheese mites are in the group) *phylloxerae* was an enemy of *Phylloxera vastatrix*. But nothing came of this because, although the former was a true enemy in the Rockies, it failed to survive in Europe.

After this the depredations became terrible; it was costing the French £60 million a year and the hardship caused to the peasants (as an example see Stevenson's account of the wine in the Cévennes) was tragic.

Though Planchon had failed, the scientists did not give up and even bizarre remedies were resorted to. Rich men were to fantastic lengths to rid themselves of the insects and many tried flooding whole areas of their vines. But it was found that, even after they had been under water for over a month, only two out of every three aphids were killed and the soil was left so debilitated that very heavy manuring was needed.

The least harmful cure of all was by far the most expensive; it was also dangerous. This was to treat the ground with carbon disulphide, a highly inflammable chemical and somewhat toxic. None the less by 1895 about a quarter of a million acres of French vineyards had been thus treated. But the effect was transitory.

Then came the cure, dramatic and paradoxical, but to explain how it worked I must discourse a little on vines.

There are countless thousands of varieties over the face of the earth, from those that make lush table grapes down in Spanish Almeria to those that creep up huge trees in the jungle and produce pinhead-sized green berries that could never be made into wine. They are all of the order *Vitaceae*. Among these is the variety which makes *good* wine, *Vitis vinifera*, and is only found in Europe; there are fifteen hundred different types of this alone.

But also of the *Vitis* or *Vitaceae* family are further varieties of non-European grape-bearing vines which, however, do not make *good* wine. The result is a harsh, unpleasant brew with a typical 'foxy' flavour. Two of these vines are *Vitis riparia* (also called *vulpina*) and *Vitis rupestris*, whose natural home is in America.

Returning to the plant louse. Life was not as easy for it in the Rockies as it was when it invaded Europe, for the good reason that the roots of the mountain vines were so much tougher than the easily eaten European vines. So the solution came whence came the trouble. What was done (and still is done) was to graft *vinifera* on to the roots of resistant vines, mainly improved strains of *riparia* and *rupestris*. But it must be remembered that the American species are not one hundred per cent resistant and the struggle continues.

The cost of such grafting is very high and because of this, the French have been searching for half a century now for a hybrid which will make good wine and yet be resistant to the louse. The Government and also the makers of the really good classical wines do not think there is much future in these hybrids; on the other hand the 'hybridizers', as they are called in French wine circles, vociferously disagree. They are making such strides that even the powers that be are giving them increasing permission to plant hybrids in areas where great wine is not sought after. The two most successful 'hybridizers' have been Monsieur Couderc and Monsieur Seibel.

*

So much for Monsieur Thomas and his sad family history. However, he was making such good wine that I gave him an order for his white and red and then went on to Mâcon to call on Protat Frères for a book of some rarity.

A few months earlier I had gone to Santiago de Compostela solely because I had been told that the newly converted hotel, the Hostal de los Reyes Católicos, was for luxury, comfort, style and what the *Guide Michelin* calls atmosphere alone worth the visit. It was! A millionaire's hotel at well below millionaires' prices. A place of such vastness that you could wander round the corridors for days discovering new rooms and courtyards, and yet so superbly proportioned that the size was never oppressive.

The A.A. of course gives it top five-star rating and informs you that there are 157 rooms, all with P.B. (private bath or shower). Actually all the bathrooms are quite large. It gives you some idea of the ground size of the place when I say that all these rooms are situated on only the second and third floors above and around the four patios or courtyards of Mateo, Marcos, Lucas and Juan, as the four Apostles are known in Spain.

They give you a plan of the whole hotel in colour when you book in and I did a little measuring on it. The main dining-room, coloured in red, shows as a tiny corner beside one of the patios. It seems a very long, narrow room but its *width* is probably twice the length of the dining-room of a good hotel in any large town in Britain.

Anyway, on the way back from Santiago I suddenly realized that by a coincidence I had been following the old pilgrims' road to St James' tomb and the whole subject got quite a hold on me. I found that nearly every French and Spanish book on the subject referred to a remarkable twelfth-century *Guide for the Pilgrim*, written in Latin and translated into French by Mlle Jeanne Viellard, which I at last tracked down to a printer, Protat Frères of Mâcon.

The book is a delight. The author was probably one Aimery Picaud of Parthenay-le-Vieux, and certainly a Frenchman from either the Poitiers or Saintes district, a holy pilgrim full of devotion for St James the Greater. This work, now in the archives of the cathedral of Santiago, was written around 1139.

What a brave, wild journey it was, especially when one got into the north of Spain. Some people are villains, as we see in chapter seven.

THE NAMES OF COUNTRIES WHICH THE ROAD TO ST JAMES TRAVERSES AND THE CHARACTERISTICS OF THE INHABITANTS

If by chance you cross [the department of] the Landes in summer do take care to protect your face from the gigantic flies which breed there and are called wasps or ox-flies.

Having crossed this country you find yourself in Gascony which is rich in white bread and excellent red wine. The Gascons are verbose, mocking, debauched, drunken gluttons. They are shockingly clad in tatters and have no money. None the less they fight well and are remarkably kind in their hospitality towards the poor.

Around the fireside they are accustomed to eat without a table and all drink from the same goblet. They sleep upon their mattresses of rotten straw and it does not shame them to sleep all together, master and mistress with the servants.

Poor Gascons! Still, they are not as bad as the people from Navarre who 'on hearing them talk one would think that dogs were barking' and who indulged in the most immoral of practices with animals.

I have digressed disgracefully and even in the next chapter I am not as close to the Loire as I should be, but the wines made in the Beaujolais region deserve more attention than they usually get.

4

THE BEAUJOLAIS
DISTRICT

THE GROWERS IN THE BEAUJOLAIS AREA feel with reason
that, if only they can get the motorist off the great auto-highway from
Lyons to Paris, he (the motorist) will fall bacchically by the wayside
and so become converted to their wines thereafter. Consequently, one
gets showered with leaflets telling one to make the short detour,
especially coming up from the south, from Villefranche-sur-Saône
up to five miles south of Mâcon. This is called the Rapid Itinerary
and goes as follows:

Arnas—St-Etienne-des-Ouillières—Odenas—St-Lager (wine-tasting takes place here, and there is a beautiful panorama over southern
Burgundy)—Cercie—Villié-Morgon (wine-tasting cellar here, run
by the local wine Cave Co-opérative)—Chénas—Juliénas (wine-tasting
here in the cellar of the old church)—Saint Amour–Bellevue—
Chanes—Crèches-sur-Saône.

Then comes the bigger detour, called the Touristic Itinerary, with
many a place for a good wine-tasting, especially at the villages so well
known to the British drinking public, like Beaujeu, Romanèche-
Thorins and the ever famous Moulin-à-Vent.

The village of only two thousand inhabitants which has given its
name to the district, Beaujeu, is the ancient capital of the region. The
castle of the Seigneurs of Beaujeu was destroyed by Richelieu's orders
in 1611.

I do not usually recommend museums but the one in Beaujeu is,
for the wine fancier, worth a visit. Here you see a remarkable collection of old Beaujolais wine-making tools and, as well, implements
connected with two industries well-nigh defunct: wooden shoe- and
cask-making. There is also a room devoted to dolls dressed in authentic,
ancient costumes.

Wines have made the fortune of this little place, and all around, the hillsides are one carpet of vines. For the non-wine-loving visitor there is an eleventh-century church of St Nicholas consecrated in 1129 by Pope Innocent II which, on account of its romanesque tower and its curious construction of locally hewn black rock, attracts annually a vast number of sightseers quite disproportionate to its small size.

Perhaps though, the most remarkable thing about the village is a curious statue which, bizarre as it is, at least makes it vinously clear what its sculptor intended to evoke. There was in Lyons an actor of the Grand Guignol school named Gonafron who was inordinately fond of his Beaujolais 'Pots' (a specially shaped bottle unique to the district holding, most sensibly, three-quarters of a normal bottle). There he stands and sculpted around him are twenty-three casks; on each one is hewn the name of a Beaujolais district.

If you are in a lighthearted mood and want a good laugh, I think that the best place you can visit in the area is Juliénas. For a good sample glass of many typical wines among the most bogus of comic surroundings, there is nothing to equal it. The building is called the Cellar* of the Ancient Church, though how long it has been secularized I do not know. Whenever it happened, the monks must still be turning in their graves, for the vulgarity and near-obscenity of the hideous stained-glass windows and pictures is unforgettably shocking. The worst is an obese Bacchus astride a butt of wine, holding in his hand an enormous glass of red wine. Around him dance nymphs with the nakedest of breasts, who are being chased and caressed by a group of amorous fauns.

Some idea of the tone of the whole place can be gathered from the wording of the little folder with which each visitor is presented. The type used is Olde Worlde and the French is a sort of fake medieval, which in translating I have tried to copy:

> *Harke noble Seigneurs, gentle dames and sweet damsels; harke to Mister Francis Rabelais, spiritual patron of artists and writers who each year sing the praises of our verdant and gentle commune of Juliénas which verily lies betwixt Jullie and Pruzilly at the verily northernmost end of Beaujolais. Seek ye here for helthe, long life, inspirations and joviality.*
>
> *You who come from the north and you who come up from the south, welcome to our unforgettable Juliénas! Like a young damsel who laughs among her corset of vines, here she is stretching herself out lazily the length and breadth of a slow-flowing stream.*

* *Cellier* they call it, which is actually a wine store-room on the ground floor. If below ground it is a *cave*.

Here every vigneron's *house resembles a manor and here everyone dedicates himself to an ancient and amiable science; here everyone lives for wine and by wine.*

Here on the old Roman road which united Lutecia with Lugdunum did the first vines flourish and so did the first vintages.

As the document continues, the arch verbosity fades somewhat, and towards the end, we do get a little information.

More than three hundred growers and owners tend some six hundred hectares [around 1,500 acres], which produce annually an average of twenty thousand hectolitres [around two and a half million bottles] of wine. A wine which is purple in colour, light on the palate, yet withal fruity and full of ardour.

In order to produce that which you are about to drink, a wine which is robust, bouquetful, fresh on the mouth and to the lips, powerful yet elegant, much time, much knowledge and much care have been lavished on these hillsides or, in a word, much love.

Delicious in its youth, when it has all the aroma of youthful fruitiness, yet our Juliénas knows how to grow old gracefully like a Burgundy, which is not always the case with all Beaujolais wines.

The final paragraph is sheer corn.

Enter then, oh visitor, for whom we have been waiting, enter the cellars of the Old Church. Everything here is planned for you to meet, in his best form, His Highness Juliénas. For his Excellence a great mansion was needed and here, oh ye travellers, it is. We vignerons of Juliénas had a happy dream and that was that you should taste, and in comfort, the wines which are the very soul of the district which welcomes you. Taste then and, once you have done so, we are supremely confident as to what the result will be.

It is generally accepted that Juliénas makes the best Beaujolais, even if the commune of Moulin-à-Vent is the best known.

But, though the tasting room in the church at Juliénas is vulgar, and although the other *caves de dégustation* are a little gimmicky, I would not miss visiting as many as I come across, and buying sample glasses at them, for the world. Nor should you; for the atmosphere is charming, the quality of the wines offered is far better than you will get at the neighbouring café and those who serve are, invariably, enthusiastically talkative. You will be pressed to buy bottles of the region in excellently convenient HandiPak cartons, corkscrews, dripmats, and very sexy postcards whose motif is the same—that you will perform in the nuptial bed far better on vast quantities of Chénas (or whatever commune you happen to be in) than without it or with the wine of any *other* commune.

The outputs of the most important Beaujolais growths are as follows:

	VINEYARD ACREAGE	OUTPUT IN BOTTLES
Brouilly	2,000	3,200,000
Côte-de-Brouilly	500	800,000
Chiroubles	700	1,000,000
Fleurie	1,700	2,900,000
Chénas	530	800,000
Juliénas	1,500	2,100,000
Morgon	1,580	2,300,000
Moulin-à-Vent	1,700	3,000,000
St-Amour	560	800,000

Note that the number of bottles to the acre does not follow a mathematical pattern; that is because the amount of wine made to the acre varies.

The best vineyards of Moulin-à-Vent are Les Carquelains, Le Moulin-à-Vent and Les Champs de Cour.

Those of Fleurie are Les Viviers, Le Garrand, La Roilette and Le Point-du-Jour.

How do you like to drink your Juliénas, your Fleurie and so on? You have doubtless read page upon page of the delights of drinking it as they do in Lyons, slightly chilled and very young.

Be that as it may, there is another aspect of the subject which may have escaped you. In 1952 Alexis Lichine's book *Wines of France* (Cassell) was published and had an immediate success among the public for its readability, and among the experts for its knowledge. And although the author is the owner of one of the great chateaux of the Médoc and has done much to improve the quality, it is more for the Burgundy chapter that the wine trade in Britain remembers his book; and I agree.

Here is what he has to say about Beaujolais, Lyons, and drinking.

The wines of Beaujolais flow to Lyon as inevitably as the Rhône and Saône, and a parable on the wall of almost every café and restaurant throughout southern Burgundy reads thus: 'Three rivers bathe Lyon, the Rhône, the Saône, and the Beaujolais.' No doubt it's true. Lyonnais claim that one of the modern wonders of the world is the fact that the city lets some Beaujolais get away from them, to the rest of France and even overseas.

Lichine then tells us that Fleurie is the best of the communes to be served chilled; that the Morgon wines last longest of all in the area and that *very* young Beaujolais should be drunk from a carafe (i.e. directly from the cask) and slightly chilled; and that 'none of the wines show much improvement after five years'.

Then follows an intriguing paragraph:

These wines of southern Burgundy are different from the great Côte d'Or wines in another way: you swallow them, you don't sip them. The reason is simple. That's the way people seem to like to drink them. It is almost impossible to take swallows of the Chambertins, or Musignys, or even Cortons, and it is difficult to take large swallows of the lighter Beaunes. But when you get to southern Burgundy, all that changes. When drinking, one has a desire to take big draughts of the wine, in much the way one drinks beer or cider. One reason may be that cold drinks can be drunk faster than hot ones. But it is more than that. The wine itself is light and refreshing and makes you want to have a lot *in your mouth at once. And this is particularly noticeable when you are eating food. The Côte de Nuits produces sip wines, the Cotes of southern Burgundy produce swallow wines. By the time you get down to Provence, the wines are guzzle wines. It is not a question of temperament, but of geography.*

In the above paragraph I have taken the liberty of emphasizing those six memorable words, for this is a most original, observant and accurate comment.

As for guzzling Provence wines; you either hold your nose between your finger and thumb when you drink or leave them alone.

5

CHAROLLES
TO VEZELAY

TO THE NORTH OF THE BEAUJOLAIS DISTRICT and wending our way back again to the banks of the River Loire, we come to the little agricultural town of Charolles. Not all the nearly four thousand inhabitants are occupied in raising the beef cattle which have become so famous, for there is also a century-old ceramic industry which does a thriving trade. The Charollais cow is a relative newcomer in the bovine world and I noticed that the great Fream, in his mammoth work on agriculture printed in 1907, makes no mention of them; yet they are now the second largest breed in France, exceeded only by the ubiquitous Normandy.

If ever there was a contented cow, it is the Charollais breed. Pure creamy white all over, the animals stand in the lush pastures so immobile that at times you wonder if they are real.

To get back to the River Loire from Charolles, one motors along the valley of the Bourbince until one gets to the town of Paray-le-Monial. This little town hasn't changed much in the last half-century and after a stay there I found little to quarrel with what the artist F. A. Gethin had to say of the place at the turn of the century. He was killed in his forties in the 1914–1918 war, but before then he had been making quite a reputation for himself with his sketches of churches.

His most important book is devoted to churches in this district and the towns are described with charm:

Paray-le-Monial is a little town embedded in shady sleepiness and sur-rounded by meadow and is so drowsy that, even on the brightest day, it only seems to wink and rub its eyes and turn over again. It was very full of clothworkers in the seventeenth century, until Louis XIV bethought him of revoking the Edict of Nantes and making life intolerable for the active Huguenot population. A reminder of the prosperity of these people is to be seen in the fine Town Hall with its carved front, once the habitation of the Jaillet family. The chief industries—traffics, rather—nowadays are in the horses and big white oxen of the Charollais, renowned breeds both of them, and in retailing emblems of the Sacred Heart.

The Town Hall that he refers to is, indeed, a marvel. Jaillet was a very rich draper and he built the house in 1525, covering the intricate front with its funny little turrets and the low windows with medallions of famous personages and also, very prominently, with fan-shaped scallop shells. The latter are, indeed, so dominating that one wonders if he had been on a pilgrimage to Santiago de Compostela.

The town's present source of income comes from tourism, in the shape of pilgrimages to one of the most wishy-washy saints ever.

In the village of Verosivres-en-Charollais, Marguerite Marie Alacoque was born in 1647 to the Notary Royal of L'Hautcour. The substantial farmhouse, with its painted ceilings and the chamber of Marguerite now fitted out as an oratory, can be seen today. At the tender age of five, the little girl felt she was being sinful and she refused to play at soldiers, because she was afraid of offending God. When she went to stay with her godmother at the castle of Corcheval near her home, her greatest joy was to spend as many hours as she could on her knees in prayer before the Virgin. 'I had recourse to her', she said, 'in all my needs and she rescued me from great perils. I dare not address her divine Son.' A little later, however, vanity did take hold of her and at one time she even put on a fancy dress. But to no avail, and she soon realized that 'it was hard to kick against the potent pride of God's love'.

Then her mother wanted her to marry. The project was going along smoothly until Our Lord made it clear to her 'that He was the most beautiful, the richest and most powerful and most perfect and most accomplished of all lovers'.

In 1671, Marguerite entered the Convent of the Visitation at Paray, which she had chosen for its seclusion and rigour. Here she was put to watch an ass and its foal, for fear they should trespass on to the herb garden of the nunnery. Her novitiate over, she took her final vows and heard the Saviour say to her: 'Until now I have been thy betrothed; from this day onwards I will be thy spouse.' And thenceforth, she assures us, He commenced to treat her as such.

Marguerite Alacoque's claim to fame was that she was the one to popularize throughout France the worship of the Sacred Heart. The wound and heart of Jesus had been the theme of the holy fathers and saints from St Augustus' time to that of St Francis of Sales. It was the frequently expressed wish of St Francis that the Daughters of the Visitation should have their habitation in the pierced side and heart of the Saviour, though this was not specially preached at the Convent of the Visitation at Paray before Marguerite's time. On the Feast of St John the Evangelist (27 December) 1673, she believed she lay on the heart of Jesus and for the first time saw His heart, until then always kept secret.

In 1674 there was another vision and then a third in 1675, when she was told by Christ that the Friday after the Octave of Corpus Christi should be set apart by the Church for the worship of His Heart. From then on things moved apace; further visitations gave more detailed instructions as to how the adoration of the Sacred Heart should be propagated and a Jesuit father, expelled from England, took over the direction of the future saint and her mystic activities.

One thing the Saviour wanted, it was alleged, was that the Sacred Heart should reign in the palace of the King and that it should be 'painted on his standards and graven on his arms so as to render him victorious over his enemies'. Louis XIV unfortunately did not comply.

But the Papacy did accord a limited observance within the diocese and the first Mass took place in Dijon in 1679—the very year poor Marguerite Marie died, almost certainly from sores due to unbelievable, self-imposed privations.

During the eighteenth century the cult made somewhat slow progress; nevertheless, religious foundations and confraternities dedicated to it grew in number. But in the nineteenth century the position changed. In the first place her tomb was opened in 1830, when two miracles of healing occurred. Then, in 1864, she was beatified by Pope Pius IX and at Paray-le-Monial one hundred thousand people attended the festival which celebrated the event.

This, however, was completely overshadowed by the fantastic pilgrimage which took place in June 1872. A month was set apart for it but this was not long enough and the time was prolonged. This event took place just after the loss of Alsace to the Germans and among the procession was a contingent from that province with the inscription: 'Heart of Jesus, give us back our country'.

Pilgrims came from England, America and Poland—it was one of the greatest religious demonstrations of modern times.

The chapel erected to Marguerite Marie, on the spot where she saw her visions, is hideous and tawdry, while the shops outside selling cheap emblems are worse.

Such then is Paray, save that I have left for the end a description of the great Romanesque church with its elegant spires, which was started as far back as 1109 by St Hugh of Cluny. The simplicity of the lines is a marvel and the whole effect is made more beautiful by the fact that the church is built of the glorious golden-toned stone of the district.

Lunch-time was approaching and, also, one of the longest stretches of road imaginable. It was, too, the type of countryside where one felt nothing of interest would crop up and anything for a distraction would be welcome. In such a mood I came to a wayside, one-storied cottage which presented an extremely gay appearance, for all round the doors, nailed into the stone walls and affixed to the white railings, were disused wooden clogs painted in every conceivable colour and filled with nasturtiums, pansies and nemesia. A splendid photo, I thought, jumping out, but a woman came to the door with such a scowl on her face that I refrained and set the steering-wheel straight for Digoin—not to be confused with the mighty Dijon, home of mustard, cassis (blackcurrants) and a veritable city of all the arts.

Digoin is a dumpy little provincial town but with a curious minor claim to fame which the inhabitants, by dint of many a coloured photograph, have tried to turn into an attraction. Here is one of the only two barge-carrying water bridges in France.

From Digoin up to Nevers, the road hugs the banks of the Loire pretty closely and, at times, the river is touchingly lovely. What a fantastically busy river it must have been at the beginning of the nineteenth century, when the roads were so terrible and everything went by water transport.

The Loire in earlier times was like a small sea covered with white sails and was called the 'Road which Walks'; its praises have been sung by La Fontaine, Charles of Orleans, Madame de Sévigné, Balzac, Victor Hugo and countless others.

Here then is something of the river's history.

Although in the fourth century the Romans had used the river for navigation purposes, it was only around 1360 that there was formed a 'Worshipful Company of Merchants using the Loire'. It was situated in Orleans and operated from there. In return for keeping the channel of the river dredged, the members extracted what became known as the 'box charge', because the money due was placed in specially constructed boxes situated at various stages along the river banks.

The many sails must have been an impressive sight for the number of different types of boat was legion. Largest of all was the *Gabare*, or sailing barge, which was nearly eighty feet long and thirteen feet wide. Then there were the flat-bottomed barges without rigging; these were the most popular of all and are still in use today for the transport of cattle and hay. Another interesting boat was the *Sapine*. It gives some idea of the currents when I say that these boats, which were made of fir, would often be dismantled at the end of a journey (downstream they covered some twenty miles a day), the planks would be sold and the boatmen would make the journey back to their starting-point on foot.

The scene must have looked like a vast water convoy. First came the 'mother', a great *Gabare*, followed by the ever-decreasing sails of her 'daughters'. But the whole fleet was preceded by a wherry nicknamed 'the ferret', which took depth soundings and marked out the course with branches.

Dressed in blue, with great red sashes as belts and with large rings of gold in their ears, the *Chalandoux*, or bargees, were an extremely colourful race and so was their language, so much so that it has become almost legendary.

In Nevers lived the parakeet Vert-Vert, lovingly tended by the nuns, who were very proud of his perfect manners and speech. So popular was he that the nuns of Nantes heard of him and insisted on borrowing him, and off he went by barge to that capital. Horror! The bargees of the River Loire had taught Vert-Vert such foul language that to say the nuns of Nantes were shocked was like saying that Rome was no mean city.

Utterly scandalized, they sent Vert-Vert back to Nevers, where he came up before the Abbess, who condemned him to fasting, solitary confinement and, above all, a penitential vow of silence. The parakeet's vocabulary improved and all was forgiven. But then, 'stuffed with sweets and crammed with liqueurs', Vert-Vert died of indigestion.

Nevers is an extremely fine town, the capital of the Nivernais and a few miles from the confluence of the Loire and another important river, the Allier. You enter it by an enormous, square, fortified gateway with a splendid, vast, slate-covered roof, which is part of the old fortifications and dates back to the early part of the fourteenth century.

Inside is one of the largest churches imaginable for so small a town; its singularity stems from the fact that it contains every style of architecture from the tenth to the sixteenth century inclusive, and that the east side of the apse is Gothic while the west is Romanesque. This is seen elsewhere in Europe only in certain churches along the Rhine, especially of Worms (original home of Liebfraumilch) and at Mainz, ugly twin town to lovely Wiesbaden.

This Nevers basilica is called the Cathedral of St-Cyr and Ste-Julitte; a walk round shows an array of pinnacles, towers, bastions and so forth which give the building an air more of a Spanish fairy-tale castle than anything else. Inside, in addition to a weird eleventh-century crypt, there stands, most incongruously, a huge wooden grandfather clock inlaid in gold.

The ducal palace at Nevers is a marvel. Building was started in the first half of the fifteenth century by one of the dukes of Nevers, Jean Clamecy, because he was tired of the austerity of the old fortress residence alongside. The palace is now the Town Hall, and extremely proud the Nivernais must be to have such a place. It is perfectly symmetrical, of yellow ochre stone and roofed entirely in magnificent slate. At each extremity are two round towers, capped by rounded turrets, and in the centre a magnificent circular stairway of honour juts out, topped by a superb, octagonal slate spire. The building is on one side of a magnificently kept square, from where there is a gracious view of the countryside.

Vézelay was my next port of call and there were two minor incidents *en route*. I cannot say that the countryside was uninteresting, for the woods here and the curving hills are quite beautiful; but I wanted some relaxation from making notes on my trip; and bounding along I saw a scruffy little café called 'Au Clair de la Lune'. I know what I will do, I thought; raise a good laugh about 'Mon ami Pierrot'. They will think that very droll from a foreigner.

The café was incredibly crowded inside—a surprise, for there were no cars or bicycles out in the front. I ordered a glass of white wine which was one of the nastiest ever, and tried to catch the attention of people behind the bar and around it by just looking interesting and hoping that I would be dragged into the conversation.

No one took the slightest notice of me.

Perhaps, I thought, another glass will do the trick. I downed what I had without making too much of a grimace and ordered another, saying, 'Same again please.' (I had specifically ordered a small measure the first time so as to be able to have two.)

A new person behind the bar filled the tumbler up to the brim. This was too much! Normally, I would have nonchalantly wandered outside, pretending, with my back well turned to those who could see, to take a long swig and then emptying the glass on the forecourt.

But now I had a seat at the bar and was completely hemmed in from behind. Manfully I sat sipping this foul, though highly potent brew, hoping for a lull in the conversation.

If only there were something to take the taste out of my mouth!

'Have you any potato crisps?'

'Sorry, sold out', was the reply.

'Some nuts, then?'

'None left.'

'Have you anything at all?' I asked.

'There's cherries in brandy.'

On the counter there stood a huge, glass sweet-jar with a brown plastic top.

'All right', I said, 'give me a portion.'

The man behind the counter took a fair-sized soup ladle, unscrewed the top of the jar and reached downwards. When he came to the liquid, a very thin film of dust was seen to part. Down went the ladle to reveal a few moth-eaten cherries, which were eventually captured and with a great amount of liquid poured onto a soup-plate-like saucer. I was also handed a dessertspoon.

If the wine was execrable, what words are left to describe the ardent firewater which here went under the name of brandy? After a couple of spoonfuls I could take no more.

The idea of making a witty remark had now lost all appeal and I no longer cared whether I did or did not finish up the loathsome drink and the even worse 'appetiser' I had in front of me. On an impulse, I tipped the saucerful of cherry liquor into the wine, mushed up the cherries themselves and put them in too. I then gave a vigorous stir and took a deep swig.

I suppose readers have read a score of times that what makes a fine Cognac,* a good claret or Burgundy are those very ingredients which

* By the way, it is not just an old wives' tale, but I am one of hundreds whose heart definitely beats harder after a few brandies, whereas gin, vodka, etc., do not have this effect. Why?

the chemist is unable to analyse and which for that reason, I suppose, are called 'impurities'. They are minute traces of chemicals whose exact composition have eluded the test-tube expert. So, too, no scientific test will ever be able to explain how it was that, when my two obscenely horrible liquids were blended, the whole became a very passable aperitif.

At that moment too there was a lull in the chatter; my chance had arrived.

'If this is the "Clair de la Lune" ', I said to the proprietor, summoning up my best French, 'where is "mon ami Pierrot"?'

The proprietor looked across the counter towards a very fat man, who had clearly been drinking pretty steadily for quite a long time. I noticed that he was wearing a filthy, floppy, polka-dot bow tie and a different beret to all the others. At least that is how it looked but I suspect that it was the same make as all the others, but pulled about to look more artistic. He had a tiny cigarette between his lips, which he did not trouble to remove as he looked at me for a brief moment and said in a rather bored way:

'*C'est moi.*'

Then he turned back to his companions and the din of chatter started again, while I crept disappointedly away back to the road to Vézelay, by now a far from sober man.

Food and a siesta to sleep off my aperitif was now of prime importance and my luck was in, for less than half a mile along a straight, quite deserted road I saw a sign:

LE COTTAGE RESTAURANT

I did not expect for a moment that it would be open, but there was a long drive up to the house where I could sleep off my nasty alcohol away from a public road. To my surprise and delight there was a tiny restaurant attached to the bar and Madame offered to make me a herb and cheese omelette. She also insisted on standing me a drink, because she and her staff were preparing the food for an evening banquet—that was what she specialized in. They had just finished and would I care to go into the kitchen and take a look?

This I gladly and totteringly did. What a sight! Scores of lovely, boiled chickens, all covered with an aspic which (I tasted it) was the real thing and not one of your packet deals. Some of the birds were covered with pistachio nuts, with the initials of the two young marrieds for whom the party was being given, while others were decorated with slivers of black pickled walnuts (again I was invited to taste) which had been soaked for weeks in rum. I certainly had stumbled on a gastronomic hideaway.

My knowledge of culinary French is not bad and now I was able to use it in the most extravagant praise of what Madame had achieved, adding for good measure that I was a restaurateur in London. This called for another tumbler of wine and I now knew that I was getting up to my real limit of alcoholic intake before eating. I took a long swig from the glass (because when you have had a lot you need just a little more to make you speak cogently and efficiently) and told Madame in no uncertain terms that the omelette she had promised me really must be made quickly or else!

I wandered from the great kitchen and made my way slowly to where I thought the bar restaurant to be but instead took the wrong turning and found myself in a huge room with some fifty tables and matching chairs spaced around a dance floor, which had (most unusually) a dais right in the middle for the band—all clearly for Saturday night dances. But how could they get so many customers, so deep in the countryside?

I retraced my steps and there, waiting, was my omelette on a beautifully laid-up table complete with crusty bread, butter, radishes and olives, together with a further pitcher of wine. While I was eating, I set to wondering how such a house could ever have been called 'Le Cottage', for no building could have looked less like a cottage.* It was large and three-storied and square and could only be described as appalling Victorian French.

My bemused pondering was interrupted by Madame, who came to see how I was getting along. She was followed by her husband, who apologized for being so dishevelled (which was an understatement since he looked as though he had come from a bear pit) but said he had been laying up the tables in the village hall for that night's banquet. He further implied that it was a bad slip-up on his part not to have been there to welcome me, so would I join him in a *Fine*.

After that, he said, giving his wife a very amorous look, he would ask permission to leave me as they were going upstairs to *se reposer*,

---

* It is odd that the English word comes from the medieval French *cotage*, which is a Latinized form of *cotagium*, a sheep shelter; yet the Modern French word *cottage* comes not from the medieval French but direct from the English.

because they would be late that night. I replied that they need not worry on my account for I, in turn, was going to ask for the hospitality of their drive for a couple of hours, where I was going to sit in my car and have the sleep of a lifetime. I then told them of the events at the 'Clair de la Lune' and said that I was in grave danger of being pickled, foxed, three sheets in the wind, having one over the eight, seeing the wine when it was red, being half-seas over, tight as a drum—or, more concisely, inebriated.

Monsieur and Madame gave each other a very quick look and both came to the same decision.

'You poor thing! You certainly shall not sleep it off in your car. We have several spare bedrooms upstairs, which we let out in the season.'

And in no time at all I was stretched out on a fine bed, the counterpane turned down, the electric fire turned up and the curtains drawn. Two hours later, a knock at the door woke me and in came Madame in a charming house-coat, from out of which peeped a frilly nightie, and a cup of tea was put by my bedside.

Shortly after I was on my way—and I had forgotten to ask how the establishment got called the 'Cottage'.

*

Approaching Vézelay from the south-west you pass through superb undulating woody country. The village was, with Paris, Le Puy and Arles, the fourth great rallying-point for pilgrims going to Santiago.

There are two hotels and five hundred inhabitants, though walking up to the main street you would guess five thousand. The Hotel of the Post and Red Lion is a semi-sumptuous affair where you can have a *dodine** of jellied duck with truffles, snails from Mont Martre with Chablis and/or a fricassée of veal laced with old Burgundy, all washed down with Sauvignon de St-Bris and Irancy.

Actually, the correct name of the former place is St-Bris-le-Vineux (in the department of Yonne just south of Auxerre) and the growers there are not a little proud of the great quantities of white wine they ship to Germany to go towards the making of the best German Sekt,

* *Dodiner* is to rock a sifting machine; *faire dodo* is child's talk for 'go to bye byes' but, although I have seen *dodine* somewhere in a culinary connection, it is not in Escoffier, Francatelli, Dumas, Soyer or the *Larousse Gastronomique*.

as they call their champagne. And when indeed I expressed some surprise, the first man I spoke to was somewhat nettled.

'Whatever is so odd about that?' he asked. 'After all, our soil is of exactly the same composition as in the Champagne area.' The point he was making was that vines grown on chalky soil make wines with a slight tendency to sparkle naturally.

As for Irancy, this is a tiny hamlet a few miles from St-Bris set at the bottom of a vast natural amphitheatre, which I would have thought was the finest vineyard sun-trap in all France. But alas, as your car wanders tortuously downward, you see acre upon acre of erstwhile vineyards now returned to nature or planted with cherry trees. Though they make a certain amount of rosé wine, it is the red which has the controlled appellation rights—not a great wine at all.

But in spite of the galaxy of *Guide Michelin* recommended food and wine at this hotel in Vézelay I did not go there, since the girl at the cash-desk told me that the heating had been turned off for the winter. So I made instead for the Cheval Blanc, where I had a plateful of frogs' legs (they are really overrated things, aren't they?), a rather hard Camembert; and a soft bed.

Vézelay village is adorable; you march up the long narrow street (a little too full perhaps of souvenir shops) and then come to a big square where stand the remains of the monastic buildings.

That which is left is enough!

This great abbey's connection with England is so strong that I cannot resist the temptation to tell the history of the foundation at some length. For here came Thomas à Becket in 1164 when he was declared traitor and driven from England; here, in Holy Week of 1146, came Eleanor of Aquitaine, the future Queen of England when she married King Henry Plantagenet; and here came in 1190 Richard I the Lion-hearted, to set off on his fatal trail to the Holy Land.

If tradition is to be believed, the abbey church was not always placed so high but occupied a site near the road which leads to the charming village of St-Pierre-Perthuis, where there are some neglected graves in the shadow of a ruined church. The famous *Chanson de Geste* by Gérard of Roussillon, however, does not agree with this and having studied a curious account of how he and his wife, Berthe, after many vicissitudes (and some miracles) set to work to build themselves a church, we can be sure that Gérard did in the ninth century found the original abbey.

On his death he made it a condition of his grants that the abbey should be subject to no feudal lord or ecclesiastical superior, save the Pope himself.

Around A.D. 1000 it was discovered that the abbey which Gérard had founded contained in its shrine the true relics of St Mary Magdalene.

That was the cause of the beginning of the troubles. As soon as the miracles began to flow, so did a large number of pilgrims to the abbey. With them came votive offerings and in many cases the gifts of rich lands. The abbey became rich in the traffic of the saint's bones and a tidy population came to settle on the narrow ridge outside the abbey itself.

It was the old story; prosperity begets pride and pride begets a fall.

Soon Vézelay began to make enemies; the mighty Abbey of Cluny was one which had no liking for a rival. Its abbots acted as vice-regents, more or less, of the succeeding Popes and wanted, nay expected, to have the last word in matters of discipline and ecclesiastical preferment. Vézelay, however, maintained her claim to be exempt from all authority, save that of the Papacy itself, and was continually resisting Cluny's interference.

The counts of the House of Nevers (men of high rank and with considerable influence in the councils of France) were, however, the arch-enemy, nor can one entirely blame them for their ill-will. They viewed with envy and anger a rich body owning broad acres within their domain, who themselves exercised feudal rights to the full, yet refused in turn to render any feudal dues or observances.

And as the abbey grew and occupied with its vast building all the promontory of the spur, so the town increased and spread along its spine and down the slopes. At this period, the stream of communal liberty was flowing freely over Europe and many of the townsmen rebelled against the abbey's monopolies in such matters as the ownership of land, the grinding of corn and the pressing of the grapes.

So it was that these men listened avidly to the smooth talk of the counts of Nevers, when they promised them a fairer deal should they come under their protection.

Among the brethren at Vézelay was one who probably came from Poitou, since he went by the name of Hugh the Poitevin, and it is to him that we are indebted for a most detailed chronicle of the culminating struggle between the abbey and its opponents.

It is called the *Chronicum Vezeliacense sive Comitum Nivernensium Historia* and records with extreme candour the failures and deprivations of the body to which he belonged.

So frank, in fact, were his disclosures that someone at the abbey who succeeded him cut out whole portions of the manuscript; but a great deal of historical research in the last years of the nineteenth century has enabled us to get a true picture.

The author does not conceal his dislike for Cluny and he records with glee how the long struggle was won by Vézelay. He also lashes the townsfolk for their clownish insolence and he roundly denounces the town of Nevers and especially one Ida of Courthin, whom he calls 'a daughter of Jezebel of the seed of Amelek'.

His story opens in A.D. 1150 with the assault on a monk by a townsman who was found poaching in the abbey's preserves. At the time the establishment was run by Abbot Pons de Montboissier, to whom Hugh the Poitevin was first secretary and his real hero. Pons, who was feudal lord and ultimate judge, ordered the poacher's eyes to be put out. The townsmen, encouraged by the counts of Nevers, seized on the occasion to rise and demand reforms.

The Abbot refused their request. The townfolk, in turn, refused to pay dues or to respect the abbey's authority and formed themselves into a commune, electing councillors, or consuls, to govern them.

On a more practical scale they beleaguered the precincts, which resulted in a cessation of the great flow of pilgrims to the shrine of the Magdalene.

Fierce affrays ensued between the abbey retainers and the peasants and not even the presence of the bishops deterred them from violence. During this sad period the Count of Nevers played the most despicable of cunning roles, for he proffered protection to the Abbot if he would recognize him as feudal overlord, but at the same time fomented the rebellion as hard as he could.

Abbot Pons appealed to Cluny, to the Bishop of Autun, to the Duke of Burgundy and to the King. Louis VII behaved badly too; partly for reasons of state and partly through the influence of the powerful house of Nevers, he at first put off any positive action and merely initiated a series of discussions.

So for a long while the citzens ground their own corn, pressed their own wine, paid no dues and pillaged the property, while Abbot Pons' life was so endangered that he was compelled to take refuge elsewhere.

When, however, the blockade became so vigorous that the brethren had to eat meat on fast days, the state of affairs became a scandal to Christendom and Court. Finally the Pope took action by urging the King to do something positive.

Louis's anger was now considerably stirred and he summoned Abbot Pons, the Count of Nevers and the burghers of the newly formed Commune of Vézelay to appear before him at court.

Reluctantly they came; many of the commune were judged guilty of treason, perjury, sacrilege and homicide (worse than the Jackdaw of Rheims), while upon the Count of Nevers was imposed the unpleasant task of punishing the offenders and reinstating the Abbot in his rights.

The Count now realized that the King meant business and so when he had returned to his eponymous town, he sent warning to the citzens of Vézelay, with the result that, when he got there, he found a deserted place; the inhabitants had fled to the fastness of the Morvan.

As for Abbot Pons de Montboissier, he verily had his pound of flesh by seeing that the King's will be done upon the property. Furthermore, as and when they were caught, the offenders, says Hugh the Poitevin: 'were punished either by misery of prison or by loss of limbs . . . and so the Church obtained her due measure of Justice'.

The strife by no means ended here and for many years a bitter struggle went on until eventually the rights of the citizens were defined and consolidated in a charter. Still later the abbey, tired of incessant strife, which its claim to independence entailed, permitted Philippe le Bel to become its feudal lord and so found a peace of sorts.

Vézelay's period of supreme greatness, fame and power was during the whole of the eleventh century and the best part of the twelfth. But towards the close of this latter century and during the whole of the next, its decline set in. The *coup de grâce* came from Pope Boniface VIII at the end of the thirteenth century when he openly expressed doubts as to the veritable presence there of the body of St Mary Magdalene.

This terrible suspicion resulted in the saintly relic being unable to work any further miracles, and so of course the pilgrims ceased to come.

*

Now to the basilica itself.

The fact that there is a church here at all is due to the foresight of two remarkable Frenchmen, whose combined energies saved the building from literally crumbling in ruins.

Pillaged by the Huguenots in 1569 and again ravaged during the Revolution, the whole must have presented a sorry sight to Prosper Mérimée when he came across it in the nineteenth century in the course of his duties as Inspector of Historical Monuments. He drew attention to its greatness and its condition.

The rebuilding, however, was such a daunting task that none of the leading architects of the day would undertake it; but eventually a young man called Viollet-le-Duc took on the job with considerable success. He was under thirty at the time.

The glory of Vézelay lies in its narthex and in the sculptured capitals in this vast vestibule, and also in the nave proper of the church.

What is the function of a narthex? The word comes from the Greek and its prime meaning was a tall umbelliferous plant with a hollow stem. Then it came to be used to describe a small casket used for unguents. The usual architectural meaning now is a vestibule, or portico, stretching across the western end of early Christian churches.

But what exactly was it for? It may have been for catechumens, that is candidates being instructed in the Christian religion and awaiting baptism; or for 'penitents' who were not yet reconciled with God through the church; or was it a waiting place for women?

There is a fourth possibility which, though the most vague, is, I think, the most likely, and that is a sheltering place for pilgrims who may after a long journey have felt themselves too untidy and spiritually unready to enter the church proper.

If you should go to Vézelay try and remember to take a little spyglass with you, for the church is a lofty one and the little sculptures are right at the top of the capitals. There are a hundred and forty in all; perhaps a third are leaf carvings, while the rest are stories from the Bible admirably described in a wonderful little booklet on sale in all languages at the church shop in the square.

A few of the subjects in the narthex are as follows:

1. Men eating grapes
   In the Middle Ages Vézelay was a well-known wine producing region

2. Samson and the lion
   Samson, whose prodigious strength resided in his flowing hair, a symbol of consecration to God, overcomes the beast. (It is interesting to note that the sculptor would never have actually seen a lion but only knew what they looked like from drawings brought back from the East.)

3. The dragon and the woman of the Apocalypse
The Dragon (Satan) pours out fire against the woman (the Church), while the river quenches the animal's fire.

4. Isaac blessing Jacob ·
We see his hands covered with animal's hide, to imitate the hairy skin of his elder brother Esau, and Jacob receiving from the blind father the blessing due to the first born.

5. St Benedict tempted
Here a demon offers an attractive woman to the saintly founder of the Order to which the monks of Vézelay belonged. Benedict with God's help resists temptation and sits calmly there making the sign of the Cross. But to make matters doubly safe the saint throws himself on to a thorn bush.

6. Death of Cain
Hidden in the foliage, Cain the murderer is killed in his turn by an archer.

7. St Benedict brings a child back to life
You can tell the saint by his monk's label, the tonsure and the book in his hands, while he blesses the body of a child covered with a shroud and bound with wrapping at the foot of a palm tree. Watching is the father, a peasant with an especially sad look about him and leaning on one of his tools. Then round the side of the column we see the same peasant departing with his now alive son.

One of the most interesting sculptures in the nave is that of Lazarus and the rich man, and the death of Lazarus. This is a very popular theme, appearing several times on the capitals and, in fact, I have here described three carvings in one mention. Lazarus crouching at the rich man's door gives up his soul to God, to whom it is carried in a small glory* by two angels. The rich man on another is surrounded by prostitutes and dying in his bed as two serpents devour his riches, while demons tear out his soul with pincers.

Yes, for a quiet holiday I recommend to you Vézelay and its beautiful surrounding countryside, in spite of the hour's motor run from the Loire.

* In religious symbolism a combination of the nimbus and the aureole.

6

LA CHARITE
AND BOURGES

It was Aldous Huxley who once wrote that an author reading his old prose after a lapse of time lost on the swings and again on the roundabout; if he read something bad he was ashamed that such poor prose should have seen the light of day, but if it was good he had a feeling of despair that what he was now writing was not all that much better. How humbly do I agree.

The reverse of losing on the swings, etc., is to be experienced by those who take a guide-book (preferably two or three) with them on a trip; for whether you study it before or after you visit a town you benefit. If you study it before, you know what to look for and admire; while the joy of dipping into it afterwards is that if you have been enchanted with some small place and its monuments and then refer to the guide-books and find they have been equally enthusiastic, there is a tremendous kick in finding your judgement upheld.

This happened to me with La Charité-sur-Loire, as did another incident which pleased me no end.

At this point the Loire is at one of its widest (before Orleans) and perhaps most beautiful stretches, and is crossed by a splendid 'ass's back', as the French call its sixteenth-century bridge, made so harmoniously of local sandstone. I stood looking at it in open-mouthed admiration and thinking, as the sun was shining so brightly, what a fine photograph it would make from the other side of the town.

The shops are right on the river bank here and I was in a café having a glass of the new season's white wine when a man who must have been reading my thoughts came up and said:

'You get a wonderful picture from the other side of the bridge, for you can walk down some steps there to the water's edge.'

That decided me to make the effort, and I walked over and did just what he had said.

A few days later, when the roll of film had been developed, I was looking at it with the *Guide Michelin* open by my side at the La Charité page, and there was a drawing entitled:

THE PORT OF LA CHARITE IN 1830
After a drawing by Deroy

Nothing had changed!

Or rather nothing of the old town had changed and we both had decided to depict it from exactly the same spot. If Deroy had worked from my snap he couldn't have got closer to his own drawing.

In the foreground, however, the 1830 scene shows all the boats and barges on the river I described in the previous chapter.

*

This little town was originally called Seyr, which meant 'Sun Town' in what was probably Phoenician.

In the eighth century the whole town was converted to Christianity, which seems to have either caused or coincided with an era of tremendous prosperity which was, alas, set at naught by subsequent Arab invasions.

Later, in the eleventh century, a church was built and the abbey reorganized. These two events started an influx of travellers, of pilgrims, and above all of the poor and needy. These latter, hearing of the kindness of the monks, became more and more numerous; they went to seek 'the charity of the kind fathers', and so 'to go to charity' passed into the language. That is how the town got its present name.

Life there was prosperous and without tumultuous affrays from the eleventh to the fourteenth century. At the beginning of the fifteenth things woke up with a bang, the monks being subjected to maltreatment and the citizens to siege. Treason also reared its head.

It started when Philippe le Bon, Duke of Burgundy, specially ordered the capture of the town, as it was 'an important strategic place on account of its passage over the Loire'. One of his captains, Perrinet-Gressard, was put in charge of the garrison and it was he who so roughly handled the priests and pillaged the priory. In 1422 Perrinet-Gressard was ousted from La Charité but in 1423 he retook it with the help of the English. 'Thus', as one chronicler put it, 'betraying shamefully and unchristianly his mother country.'

And the treachery here seems to have paid off, for in December 1429 the redoutable St Joan, acting under instructions from King Charles VII of France, laid siege upon the town. But the rigours of a terribly cold winter and an insufficiency of men caused her to abandon it, leaving Perrinet-Gressard with his ill-gotten gains until 1440 when, in exchange for a princely ransom, he ceded it to the French throne.

*

Founded in the second half of the eleventh century and consecrated in 1107 by Pope Pascal II, the church of the Benedictine Priory of La Charité was capable of holding five thousand worshippers at a time and was thus, after Cluny, the largest church in all France. For this reason it was given the title: 'The Eldest Daughter of Cluny'.

Going round the place is a little confusing because the church is cut off from the other remaining old buildings as a result of a disastrous fire in the middle of the sixteenth century.

But the inside is a 'must' on account of the marvellous mellow stained-glass windows by Max Ingrand. These are very unusual in an ultra-modern way and the two dominating colours are a mellow red claret and a soft yellow.

Lunch was now the order of the day and I was quite ravenous. From various people I had talked to I knew that it was market day, but I did not expect to find so many people in what I had noticed was the best restaurant in the town.

After this bout of sightseeing, I was ready for a good lunch. Unfortunately I have a real 'thing' about waiting at the table for food in restaurants and it is something I have been quite unable to conquer. This is why I do not like to go out to a restaurant as a guest, which role precludes one giving the staff a good stir-up if necessary.

If the situation appears likely to arise when I am alone, as clearly was going to happen that day, I can cope quite easily by giving an order, stating that I am going out and the exact time I will be back. Nine times out of ten this works excellently, because it gives the waiter or waitress time to lay up the table neatly and so on. This, however, was the tenth time; I espied a nice, recently vacated table in the corner and explained what I wanted. But no, the girl insisted that I sit at a central communal table, where about half a dozen bucolic farmers were finishing a lunch over potent cigars and more potent Cognac.

I stormed out and marched up the road to a small hotel, where I had noticed a simple *Prix Fixe* meal earlier on.

Disaster again struck.

All this makes me look as though I am an exceptionally fussy eater but another thing I cannot abide is to sit down in a restaurant and not make my own choice. However good the place is, it annoys me greatly if the angle or gimmick of the place is that no menu is needed, because they pretend the chef has taken care of your wants and will bring you what he thinks you ought to like.

In this instance I had rubbed my nose against the menu outside and seen vaguely that I liked what was on but had not taken in anything.

Much was my anger then when hardly had I sat down before a pitcher of red wine, crusty fresh French bread and some lovely curled butter were set before me, together with diced beetroot in oil and vinegar (which I adore in France because they get the proportion right), half an egg with real mayonnaise and a great fat sardine—my perfect hors d'œuvres.

'What's this?' I said grumpily.

'The first course', said the waiter morosely.

'Well I want to choose from the menu', I replied. 'I want to know what I am going to get.'

'Well, there is no choice', said the man and then, realizing he had a genuine grievance, added with venom: 'And besides, you know what is for lunch because I saw you pushing your little red face almost into the outside menu.'

'Oh! Go to blazes!' I said and again stamped out.

It was only when I got back to the quayside and was munching a horrible sandwich that I recalled that the main course was one of my favourite dishes—fried calves' liver.

*

The drive from La Charité to Bourges was dull and flat, the sun went in and a blustery rain started, and my stomach was now cursing me for not having given it a decent lunch; these may have been the reasons why I wasn't all that enthusiastic about the town, although the *Guide Michelin* gives it top-entry marks from a visit-worthiness point of view.

By far the most important thing to be seen there is the cathedral or, rather, the west front of it. This is a truly majestic sight, for not only are the five arches themselves supremely imposing, but this is accentuated by the fact that to reach them you are obliged to ascend a wide stone, fifteen-step stairway.

Bourges' other architectural treasure is the palace of that multimillionaire Jacques Cœur, the celebrated silversmith to King Charles VII. Started in 1443, the whole immense place was completely finished in under nine years and cost a hundred thousand golden crowns. Poor Jacques, though, hardly spent any time there for he fell into disgrace in 1451.

The interest in the palace lies not so much in the outside for once but in the indoor rooms; these give one a fascinating insight into the fantastic luxury with which a rich bourgeois could surround himself in the middle of the fifteenth century.

The two most interesting things of this particular establishment are the remarkably ingenious devices for the central heating and an indoor dove-cote, planned by Cœur to house the many carrier pigeons he used to keep himself informed of the financial trends of the world's silver markets.

But his pigeons by now did not interest me; I wanted one braised, preferably in red wine, for dinner that night.

So I went on.

7

THE WINES OF SANCERRE AND POUILLY-SUR-LOIRE

WE ARE STILL ON THE RIVER LOIRE, though we have moved up to the very centre of France, to the old provinces of Berry, Nivernais and Bourbonnais. This is an area much lamented by the propagandists of French tourism—lamented as a part where no travellers ever go.

Everyone, who travels from Paris to the Pyrenees, from Brittany to the Alps or Paris to the Riviera, must cross these regions. However, most of us see little more of them than the façade of a country town at the end of an avenue of trees or a little lake amid the heather. Most of us scarcely glance at the ducal palace of Nevers, at the house of Jacques-Coeur in Bourges and at the astounding cathedral, like a giant upon a solitary height, the shrine that a poet has compared with Bayard upon his richly caparisoned horse.

Nevertheless, if the traveller will slacken his pace a little, he will find himself presented with a wealth of scenery and of mountains, about which he had scarcely an idea. At Quincy, Sancerre, Pouilly and St-Pourcain-sur-Sioule he will drink grateful wine.

And to reward him under a sky of which it has been written that 'with a narrow strip of landscape a great painter would make of it a picture as eloquent as those of the old Dutch Masters' the wanderer will have found in these three provinces what are most precious in this world—serenity and peace.

Thus Henri Gillet, whose piece takes us straight to the heart of the region, the quite extraordinary little town of Sancerre. To me, and I know them both well, this place always strikes me as a miniature Carcassonne, but without the latter's walls. The other resemblance is the impression that both give of being far larger than they really are. When, after a walk round Sancerre I got back to my excellent hotel room, I was amazed to see in the *Guide Michelin* that the place had only two and a half thousand souls. The reason must be a psychological one to do with the hilliness of the streets; if they were flattened out they would come down in one's mind to normal proportions.

The chief hotel of the place goes by the odd name of the Hôtel du Point du Jour et de l'Écu—The Dawn and Shield—and is in a commanding position. The first time I went there it was being renovated, and I felt how nice it would be when finished; the next time central heating was being installed (this was many years ago), and I felt how nice it would be when finished; this time when I went, really big extensions, which entailed bricks and so forth in the reception entrance, were under way. By the time you read this, The Dawn and Shield should be a first-rate hotel.

Sancerre's moment of history came during the Hundred Years' War, for it became the focal point where Charles VII, King of Bourges, assembled an army of twenty thousand to combat a combined force of Burgundians and English.

In the middle of the sixteenth century, Sancerre became one of the most important of Protestant strongholds, and even the historic St Bartholomew massacre of 1572 did not bring the inhabitants to heel. So intransigent were they that on 3 January 1573 Marshal La Châtre was, with a force of eighteen thousand men, ordered to lay siege to the place. A tremendous artillery-pounding was rained on the small town (as I suppose it was then) and three breaches in the defence walls were achieved. But that was all; the Sancerrois remained in control. Marshal La Châtre then decided to starve the place out by siege. There followed one of the blackest famines in the annals of war; the inhabitants were reduced to eating not only all the leather and skin they could find, but also slate which was looted.* This resistance lasted nine whole months.

Sancerre is one of the most wanderable-round places in all France; at each turn is an attractive street. One comes, too, across several houses of great historical interest whose walls display commemorative plaques.

On the edge of the town is a fifteenth-century dungeon, all that remains of the castle of the counts of Sancerre and the only reminder of the terrible struggle just referred to. From here is *the* view; what a little word to describe a panorama of such sky-devouring amplitude! It is so vast, so all encircling, that it would take an hour to take in every detail.

* '. . . famine, mangent de l'ardoise filée et tout . . .' This is from the *Guide Michelin* history of the place. Could there be a mistake?

The cheeses of the locality are delicious, and you should not be put off because they are made of goat's milk; they are tiny and round and bear the curious name of *crottins*—sheep (or horse's) dung.

It was while I was finishing my meal in the Hôtel de l'Écu that the young man in the English car, to whom I referred earlier on, came in. Seeing that I was the only person who could have fitted my English car outside, he came up and spoke to me.

'Hello, Mr Layton; and how is your Aquitaine selling?' he asked.

This caused me considerable surprise. Not being recognized but the enquiry about Aquitaine! This was a name I had thought was clever for a cheap claret and had had registered. Few people choose it from my list—preferring usually to go for cheaper or more expensive lines.

My interrogator had been—and in a big way—looking upon the wine when it was red and what he had been imbibing would have been very young and green, for his lips looked as though he had smeared them with mulberry juice. As for his tongue, it called to mind that of a chow. The saying that the Lord protects the drunk was certainly true here, for a little banal conversation told me that he had motored upwards of two hundred and fifty miles since midday. But he was not very interested in what he had done and I, though too proud to ask, was dying to know why he was interested in my house claret, so conversation dried up.

'I see you have changed the bin of your Oppenheimer', he eventually said.

This was stupefying!

Anyone could have known all about the red wine, but this statement meant that he had access to information which was confidential; I'm afraid I immediately and disloyally thought that he was a friend of one of my staff.

I had indeed changed the bin of this cheap hock by going to another supplier who I thought was offering a wine with more style and finesse than the former, albeit with less body. The former wine had been getting too coarse, though there were no complaints; but I like my customers to have what I consider typical of the region, and not what *they* like—admittedly not a good way to build up sales. Only an exceptionally regular customer, and with a professional palate to boot, could possibly have noticed the change.

'You seem to know a lot about my affairs', I said, still somewhat guarded in my approach.

'I buy quite a lot from your Wine Bar', he said. 'I come in regularly once a week.'

'How then is it we have never met?'

'I don't know', he replied; 'I come in of a morning.'

'On Wednesdays?'

'Yes.'

'And you always buy, in half bottles, two of the same wines at a time.'

'Correct.'

'And you ask my barman a devil of a lot of questions.'

'That's right', he said, now clearly as curious as I had been.

'And quite recently he has been drying up with answers.'

'Yes, about a month ago.'

'Six weeks from tomorrow, to be accurate.'

So here in front of me was our Mystery Customer. I should explain that for some three months he had been coming in on the dot of opening hour, and systematically buying two half bottles of every wine on my list. Never once did he buy himself a glass of wine but he invariably fired off a number of highly inquisitive questions aimed in a roundabout way at finding out who were my suppliers. What intrigued us far and away more than anything was that the questions he posed were not ones he had dreamt up himself; in fact, once my barman had seen him take out a scrap of paper before he came into the bar and look at it as if to memorize the contents. I had always meant to run up and see who it was but never quite got round to it.

And now, here he was in front of me at the Hôtel de l'Écu at Sancerre.

One of the funniest stories I know is of a man whose name was Guy Fawkes and whose birthday was on 5 November. He was in a pub early one evening, on that very day of the year, with a friend, when another man came in who knew the friend but not Guy Fawkes, to whom he was naturally introduced. The friend then left, leaving the birthday man with the newcomer.

But the inevitable did not happen and so poor Mr Fawkes had to draw attention to the coincidence before midnight, so that he could add that it was also *his* birthday.

Mine was the role of the newcomer above. Although I was now consumed with curiosity, I had at least a shrewd idea that the young man's job was a confidential one and that any undue interest in his job would shut him up.

I also sensed that, normally a very sober type of person and now well in his cups, he was dying to say what his work was.

It didn't need much intelligence to realize that a little more alcohol would do the trick and, once I had made doubly sure that he had no intention whatsoever of driving his car again that evening, I felt he was fair game.

The end came after the second *Marc*.

He was, of all things, a Confidential Wine Shopper for a group of successful—financially—but not very distinguished wine and spirit shippers, who had recently bought up a chain of retail shops.

We parted that night and the next day I had forgotten his existence in the excitement of bacchic peregrinations around the local vineyards.

With a tiny output of well under a quarter of a million gallons annually and on extremely chalky soil similar to that of Pouilly-sur-Loire and Chablis, some thirteen communes have vineyards which have the right to call their wines Sancerre. Actually this statement does not give an accurate picture for of the above some, such as Vinon, Montigny, Bannay and Veaugues, only have a very small number of growers; the relatively large production being in the communes of Bué, Verdigny, Sury-en-Vaux, Crézancy, St-Satur, Ménétréol and around the villages of Chavignol, Champtin and Reigny.

In this region the Sauvignon grape reigns supreme.

If you are going to wander around this lovely district, you must call upon the establishment of Monsieur Octave Crochet, which is to the west of Sancerre.

His wine, called Clos de la Poussie, is excellent. You can get it in all the better restaurants of the district and, apart from the usual label, there is another, smaller one on the back with a beautifully printed little map showing how to get to the property. It also tells you how to drink this white wine.

This Sancerre is a wine, dry, sprightly and fruity, which should be drunk cool but not iced, with oysters, shellfish and fish.

We are then tempted to visit the property.

The Clos of La Poussie, superbly situated across the picturesque valley, was formerly a monastery. Abandoned during the Revolution it was parcelled up into fifty small properties which we have bought up.

What you will see is the satisfying result of twenty years' fantastically hard work. Stones and rocks, acacias and unwanted weeds had invaded the natural amphitheatre, now so admirable.

Unusual wording but at least it tells its story.

Monsieur Crochet, a former Paris businessman, had not been content to be just picturesque, however. He had revitalized the vineyards of this exceptionally important area.

To see how this was done it is necessary to explain that vines generally produce their best wines on steep slopes (Médoc wines being the one great exception) but that the steeper they are, the harder it is to mechanize the work and that means the more costly things become.

One of the places where the problem was particularly acute was on the northern shores of Lake Léman (more often incorrectly called the Lake of Geneva) around the lovely town of Vevey, also famous for its fabulous *Fêtes des Vignerons* (it has now very little to do with wine) which takes place only four times in each century. Here it was that a small petrol-driven motor placed at the summit of the vineyard hills was attached to a tiny plough at the bottom and winched it up between the furrows for ploughing, and then for weeding. At Vevey it has over the past thirty years greatly helped to arrest the decline of the steep-faced vineyards.

Monsieur Crochet brought not only the contraption to Sancerre but also with it a Swiss expert; soon other abandoned vineyards came back into production.

If you are going tasting in the district here are some other growths:

Commune	Growths
Chavignol	Les Monts Damnés
	Les Bouffants
	Cul de Beaujeu
	Les Chasseignes
Amigny	St Martin
	La Grande Côte
	Beau Regard
	L'Epée
Bué	Chêne Marchand
	Chemarin
	La Poussie
Champtin	Côte de Champtin

Commune	Growths
Verdigny	Les Montachins
	Les Cris
	La Côte
Sury-en-Vaux	Denisottes
	Les Godons
	Démalées

Finally it remains to say that there is a very good, newly formed (in 1936) Cave Coopérative at Sancerre which gives excellent wines. The object was to market a Sancerre which was *suivi*, that is of the same style and quality from one year to the next. These co-operatives are immensely successful in wine regions (and the Sancerre district is perhaps one of the best examples in France) where there are a great number of growers, each with only a tiny parcel of land. Here there are 215 participants, of whom forty give the co-op all their grapes and the balance only a part; but the latter group is tending to give more and more of their harvest to the co-operative.

For information on early Western European wines, the most important source is the author Jullien, who in 1832 published his *Topography of all known Vineyards*.

This is what he has to say of the wines of Pouilly-sur-Loire:

Pouilly-sur-Loire makes white wines which have body and have a bouquet slightly reminiscent of gun flint, and a most pleasant taste They do not turn yellow in the bottle and keep their freshness for a considerable time. Other vineyards in this canton make wines of the same character which are sold under the name 'Vin de Pouilly', although the majority are inferior in quality. The annual harvest is of the order of forty thousand hectolitres, of which the greater part goes to Paris to be purchased for private consumption. The casks used are called puncheons [poinçons] and hold 224 litres. Purchases are made in the vineyards themselves. Pouilly is the landing stage for [boats up and down] the Loire.*

What Jullien, in his rather muddled way, is trying to tell us is that there are two different wines made around Pouilly, one of a less good quality. The better wine, and it is far better, has two Appellation Contrôlée names which are interchangeable. Blanc Fumé de Pouilly-sur-Loire and Pouilly Fumé indicate the same thing: that the wine has been made with the grape that is called Sauvignon in Bordeaux but on the Loire at this spot is called the Blanc Fumé.

* The same as are now called *fûts*. Was this word unknown or just not used in Jullien's time?

The less good wine, though it still is of Appellation Contrôlée (and not VDQS) status, is Pouilly-sur-Loire and is made with the ubiquitous Chasselas grape. This latter wine must be of nine degrees of alcohol, the other eleven.

The three most important communes, with names of some growths following, are:

Commune	Growths
Pouilly-sur-Loire (with the hamlets of Le Bouchot and Les Loges)	Les Chaumes, Les Cornets, La Prée, Les Fouinelles, Corps-Sabots, Les Foltières, Côtes des Nues, Champs des Billons, Champ de la Maison
St-Andelain	La Charnoie, Le Chailloux-St-Andelain, Château de Nozet (very famous), La Renardière, Les Prés, Les Berthiers
Tracy	Château de Tracy (famous), Les Froids, Le Champ Billard

Some other communes are: St-Laurent, St-Martin-sous-Nohain, Garchy, Mesves-sur-Loire and Bulcy, which, however, is not within the delimited areas.

Some good recent years are: 1945 (very fine), 1946 (fine), 1947 (great), 1948 (good), 1949 (good), 1953 (very good), 1955 (good), 1959 (fine), 1961 (great).

Medium years: 1950, 1954 and 1958.

And to drink these vintages, there is a group of wine-lovers called the Confrérie of the Bailiffs of Pouilly-sur-Loire.

*

But what I have written of the wines of the district does not give a good picture of the fascinating problems which beset the growers, of the importance of the age of the vines used, and how great years in minor districts can be not so great as would appear.

To remedy the omission I reprint with his permission an article by the knowledgeable S. P. E. Simon, of L. Rosenheim, the London wine shippers. Simon is a veritable scion of the grape, for he is the great-grandson of founder Rosenheim himself.

POUILLY FUME PARADOXES

Ripeness is all—unless it comes too fast! This is what happened at Pouilly-sur-Loire; in spite of an early harvest, it developed into a race between the vintagers and the 'Pourriture Noble', that over-ripeness which concentrates the juice and spices the wine. The grape-pickers had to hold their picking baskets under the bunches as they snipped through the stalks with secateurs, for the grapes were so mature that many of them dropped at the least touch, and if they fell to the ground, it was impossible to recover them; the skins had become tissue-thin with over-ripeness, so that the grapes burst even at the lightest touch.

In most vintages, it is possible to taste the difference between Pouilly Fumés grown on chalky soils and those from the heavier clay soils; and some times the wines with the most finesse come from the stony soils around St Andelain. In 1964 these distinctions are blurred; the greatest difference in the fully-fermented wines is between wines from ripe grapes, and those which have the spicy flavour of over-ripe grapes.

The small, tight-packed bunches of Blanc-Fumé grapes (the same variety is known in Bordeaux as the Sauvignon) were so sweet this year that many growers have found difficulty in fermenting their wines to the crisp but full dryness which is so much appreciated in Pouilly Fumé. This may well be due to the 'Pourriture Noble'—a micro-organism related to penicillin. It has recently been discovered that it produces a natural antibiotic ('Botryticin'), somewhat like penicillin, which may account for the health-giving reputation of a number of wines (like Bernkasteler 'Doktor'), yet which may also inhibit the normal development of the yeasts which make the wine.

Although 1964 may seem a 'great' vintage as far as the maturity of the grapes is concerned, paradoxically quite a few 1964 Pouilly Fumés may not keep particularly well, because the wines may lack the acidity which gives them crispness and staying-power.

The staying-power of a wine may also depend in part on the age of the vines from which it is made. When vines are newly planted, they do not yield at all during the first three years, but thereafter the yield increases until the vine is in full, vigorous production. Later on it shows a reduction in yield, but the quality of the wine from such a vine continues to get better and better. Therefore, one usually wants to buy wine from the oldest vine in the vineyard. In 1964, however, such vines have yielded great wine with plenty of body but in some cases without the full freshness which the French market seeks. They want to drink wines which have been bottled early and have just had time to get over their bottle sickness. For the French market, therefore, recently planted vineyards will paradoxically produce the best wine in 1964. Thus, careful selection of well-balanced wines becomes of prime importance.

When I phoned Simon and asked if I could reprint his article he said that as it referred to only one vintage he felt it might be too ephemeral for a book. I did not agree; I confess to having learned much from what he had written and felt that, though with different overtones, the same thing could well happen some years hence.

Now it only remains to add that, just a mile north of Pouilly, is one of the best views along the River Loire of its entire great length.

8

GIEN AND
ST-BENOIT

I GOT TO GIEN AROUND MIDDAY on a morning of glorious sunshine and there to welcome me was another old bridge as beautiful as that of La Charité, with a panoramic view along the Loire and another, from the centre of the bridge itself, of the old town.

Gien has one of the largest pottery works in all Europe; it is situated on the outskirts of the town and occupies a site of just fifteen acres. Gien was also one of the worst-bombed towns of the last war. It has a very fine municipal architect.

You may think these facts wildly unrelated but in fact they are not so, for they have all contributed to one of the most excellent reconstructional jobs that any ancient monument can have known.

Let us first go back a few centuries, to the fifteenth, in fact, when Louis XI gave Gien to his eldest daughter, Anne of Beaujeu. Anne must have been quite bright, for Louis once said of her, 'She is the least stupid woman of France, for of wise ones I know none.'

Anne must have enjoyed very happy memories of this town of now ten thousand inhabitants for she built there and bequeathed to the burghers its present splendid bridge, its château and two churches. Also, as a wise precaution, she improved its fortifications.

One of the churches she built was that of Joan of Arc, which in 1940 was so badly hit from the air that only its tower remains. At the end of the war, the pottery firm came on the scene for, whether out of generosity or with an eye to a stupendous publicity effort, they saw to it that the rebuilding was done in a startling pattern of red and white bricks, interspersed with glazed tiles, together with an astonishing portrayal of the stations of the Cross. The effect could have been terrible if a first-rate architect had not been employed.

The other thing to see at Gien is the museum of the history of falconry, installed, with a collection of three centuries of sporting guns, in the old château.

★

Motoring less than fifteen miles northwards down the Loire we come to Sully. Here, grandiosely situated on the banks of the river itself, is a château whose history is the history of France itself. Voltaire, in the eighteenth century having been exiled from Paris for composing too many and too forcefully rich epigrams, stayed there and so impressed the great duke and his duchess that a special theatre was built for him in one of the dungeons.

Three centuries earlier, in 1429, it was here that the Maid of Orleans persuaded Charles VII to bestir himself and go to Rheims to be crowned.

In between these two came a great man who took the name of his well-earned dukedom from the village and château.

Maximilien de Béthune, Duke of Sully, was born in 1560 and died aged eighty-one in 1641, after having worked for his country, and later for himself, about as hard as has any statesman before or since.

One reliable historian says that he started in the service of the King at the age of twelve and it is certain that when he was writing his extraordinary memoirs he himself was up at work at 3 a.m. daily and kept four full-time secretaries hard at it.

The most remarkable thing Sully, who was created a duke in 1606, did was to persuade Henri IV of Navarre to become converted to Roman Catholicism while himself steadfastly refusing to do so.

At the very early age of thirty-six Rosny, as he then was, became a member of the King's council of finance and a year later it seems that he was sole superintendent of the country's fiscal policy. For the next twelve years he achieved near miracles in putting the country's finances to rights. Agriculture was encouraged, swamps drained, canals and roads built, grain and wine were freely exported, and what helped the kingdom most but made him loathed by the nobility was his establishment of courts for the trial of bad cases of peculation and the forbidding of local governors to raise money on their own authority.

Sully was hated in his lifetime with an intensity which was astonishing. Truly evil men have in the past been more loathed but not, surely, many real do-gooders; the Roman Catholics loathed him because he was Protestant, while these latter did so because, in spite of their two different religions, he was always loyal to the King.

After Henry IV had been stabbed to death by the religious madman Ravaillac,* Sully retired to his domain to write the remarkable disjointed memoirs ('Notes on Finance' would be more accurate) which run into five volumes and three-quarters of a million words. Some idea of the size of his retinue can be gathered from the fact that on one occasion the surgeon to the duke made a visit to the castle sick-bay and found eighty persons in bed, 'and no one perceived that the service of the house suffered the least disorder or delay on that account'.

In his later years, Sully became somewhat of an eccentric and he developed a passion for detail which became almost a mania. He also installed a press in one turret of the castle for the printing of his memoirs, because he did not want printed on the title-page that the work was done in Amsterdam. All very confusing and made worse by an account of a wholly fictitious visit to Britain, especially maddening when he did make a genuine visit two years later.

*

The outside of the Château de Sully is majestic, but there is one thing inside which is pure joy. It is the main timbering of the old hall of the dungeon.

This is considered the finest wooden roof still extant in Europe which is over five hundred years old. The reason it has remained in

* An appendix to Sully's memoirs tells posterity to what Ravaillac, after a very long trial, was condemned on 26 May 1610.

'The court doth condemn him to make *amende honorable* before the principal gate of the Church of Paris, whither he shall be drawn on a tumbril in his shirt, bearing a lighted torch of two pounds' weight, and there he shall confess his most despicable parricide. From thence he shall be carried to the scaffold and the flesh shall be torn with red-hot pincers from his breasts, arms and thighs and calves of his legs; his right hand holding the knife wherewith he committed the aforesaid parricide shall be scorched and burned with flaming brimstone and, on the places where the flesh has been torn with pincers, melted lead and boiling oil, scalding pitch with wax and brimstone shall be poured. After this his body shall be torn in pieces by four horses, his limbs and body burnt to ashes and dispersed in the air. It is further ordered that the house in which he was born shall be pulled down to the ground (the owner thereof being previously indemnified) and that no other building shall ever be hereafter erected on the foundation thereof.'

And so on, including the banishment of his mother and father from the kingdom.

such a perfect state is on account of the extraordinary care taken by those carpenters of the Middle Ages. First, only trees between fifty and a hundred years old were selected; second, they were felled in winter; third, they were shaped on the spot; fourth, they only used the heart of the tree; fifth, they were kept in water for several years to take out all the sap; sixth, they were left out in the open for a further span of years; seventh, they were given a disinfectant and, eighth, they were assembled in the roof in such a way that the air was able to get all around them. Result: no rot which attracts flies, so no spiders' webs which follow dead flies, so nothing to rot—perfection.

After a visit to the château, Sully offers the hungry traveller a good restaurant at the Hôtel de la Poste, where you can have either calves' sweetbreads Sullyloise or kidneys flamed in Armagnac.

*

Motoring farther north, and again right on the Loire, and only some six miles from Sully, you come to St-Benoît-sur-Loire.

At this point I feel I must let myself go. Before starting on the trip in order to write the book, I naturally did a fair amount of reading about the churches, monasteries, châteaux and other monuments I was to see on the way.

And oh! those soldiers of the wars of religion and those bloody revolutionaries of the French Revolution! Just because a thing was beautiful, it was to them evil and they had to desecrate it; that is the tragic pattern of nearly every fine building the length of the Loire, from Montélimar to St-Nazaire. I'd like to dig them up from their graves, resurrect them and tweak their noses.

I choose this place for this outburst, because the Monastery of St-Benoît during the Religious Wars had an abbot, one Odil de Châtillon-Coligny, who became converted to Protestantism and then, shame on him, sold off one of the greatest libraries in existence, and to this day the Libraries of Berne, Rome, Moscow and Oxford possess books acquired during this wicked disbandment.

The abbey's origins go back to the seventh century, at which period it was called St-Fleury. It got its present name in an interesting way, for the monks of St-Fleury heard in 672 that the body of St Benedict (St Benoît), founder of the Order of the Benedictines, was interred in Monte Cassino in Italy and that that monastery was being destroyed by the Barbarians.

Vézelay (*Below*) The door
of the narthex

La Charité-sur-Loire. The
remarkable similarity
between my photograph
and one taken a century
ago shows how little the
Loire has changed

The Church of the
Benedictine Priory, La
Charité, which contains
some beautiful stained glass

Sculptures in the
Benedictine Priory,
La Charité

A portable still. A dying
trade frowned on by the
Government, who are
slowly cutting down the
granting of licences to
operators

The Basilica at St.-
Benôit-sur-Loire.
The famous bell is
under the colonnade

One of the famous
eleventh-century
sculptures

Greatly moved by this desecration, the then abbot sent a contingent of his most sturdy monks down to Italy, where they exhumed St Benedict's remains and brought them back to France, with, what was considerably more profitable, a number of precious relics. And like good public relations people they changed the name of the abbey and awaited the inevitable crowd of pilgrims.

All of St-Benoît is lovely, but the thing which people go most to see is the beauty of its vast enclosed entrance porch with its great peal of bells.

*

Three miles to the north of St-Benoît in the messy, little village of Germigny-des-Prés, is one of the oldest churches of France, perhaps the most curious of all to visit and a veritable treasure of Byzantine art.

Except for a tiny part of the church at Aix-la-Chapelle, this church is the only one left that was built in the reign of Charlemagne. The other interesting thing about it is that its design is so intimately linked up with its remarkable creator, Bishop Theodolph, or Theodulph.

Born in the north of Spain, the illustrious and highly intellectual Theodolph, fleeing at length from the terror of Islam, eventually arrived at the court of Charlemagne, where he soon became one of his highest dignitaries and a personal friend of the Emperor. After he became a widower, the bishop was promoted to look after St-Benoît, and St-Germigny was his religious house of retreat; a place where he went to get away from the bustle of the larger church.

In building the church, Bishop Theodolph secured the help of one of the builders of the church at Aix-la-Chapelle, one Odo de Messina, who, be it noted, was of Armenian origin. What a fine team it turned out to be for the result is a gem of a church with a blend of Byzantine, Armenian and Spanish trends which make it unique.

The other thing here are the mosaics.

In the eighteen-thirties the French, probably ashamed of the desecration caused by their fathers during the Revolution, became tremendously interested in their monuments, with the result that a great number were classified as ancient and given priority for repair.

Germigny was such a place, and archaeologists working on the spot came to notice that the local children frequently played with small cubes of glass. On being questioned, they admitted they had taken these from the floor of the church.

That was the clue; the revelation soon followed. Under a thick coat of distemper was discovered a truly wonderful and unique Byzantine mosaic.

The theme is the Ark of the Covenant and recent research has made it clear that Theodolph had almost certainly 'borrowed' the stones from Charlemagne, who in turn had taken them from Ravenna.

9

ORLEANS AND ITS ENVIRONS

A̲t this point I was joined by young Timothy John Hanbury, as courteous a junior travelling companion and as assiduous a
wine trainee as one could ask for. He was to take down notes of what
we saw on the way and savoured by the wayside, and get the car out
of the garage in the morning; I was to show him what to look for in
tasting wines.

Our objective was Orleans and we got there at tea-time, at a time of
year when surely, I thought, hotels would be exceptionally empty. The
first two were full; the third had the reception desk on the first floor,
which is so depressing, and the man asked a very stiff price for the
rooms. Had he given me half a smile or had he offered me the chance
of looking at them I would have stayed, but we went on and got in
easily at the Ste-Catherine Hôtel in the Place du Martroi.

'What is the form tomorrow?' said Hanbury.

'We do Orleans first,' I said, 'and then we set out to look at the
Orleans vineyards. The wines are made with the Gris Meunier grape.'
As it was to be his first day with me, it did not seem wise to add that
the vineyard might not exist and that the wines could well be mediocre
at best.

The next morning the telephone in my bedroom rang at an incredibly early hour.

'I'm packed, paid up and breakfasted, sir', said Hanbury. 'Ready
for the early start, as you said.'

But I was ready for him. 'Go and look at the old bridge,' I said,
'then have a look at the cathedral, and finally take a good look at
Joan of Arc's statue in the Martry Square. And for your information
this is a sixth-century word—the place where the relics of martyrs were
buried.'

Orleans is very much a town of wars. Here it was that in 1428-9

79

the famous siege took place, which was raised by Jean in April 1429. In the last war it suffered a cruel bombardment but never, I think, has a place been better rebuilt; the warm sandstone and the neat arches of the main street, the Rue Royale, leading down to the river, make it one of the pleasantest shopping centres in France.

Two things have contributed to the exceptional affluence of the town; the Americans have their Army Headquarters just outside, and there is a new university. The result is more and better bookshops (both new books and second-hand) than anywhere else in France save Paris and this goes for jewellery and clothing too.

As for the old bridge, it is extremely fine, and I wanted Tim Hanbury to see it. It was rebuilt in 1760 to replace one that had been there since the time of Joan of Arc. One day Madame de Pompadour, that costly favourite of Louis XV, arrived with her entourage to cross the bridge at a time when her extravagances were at their most onerous. In a spirit of revenge the Orleanais are supposed to have said, 'Our bridge is in truth strong, it has just carried the heaviest burden of France.'

On Hanbury's return we foregathered in the foyer and I went up to a man at the cash desk. What made me say something quite so pompous I do not know, but: 'I am a writer here to do a book on Loire wines,' I said, 'and am just going out to buy a camera. When I return, could I ask you to let me have the names of the best communes where Orleans wine is made, and perhaps give me an introduction to some growers?'

Make a stupid request and you get your deserts, I thought, but on my return the man handed me a book and said:

'There are almost no copies of this book left in existence but you may borrow it. I have marked the Orleans' vineyards.'

I was too flabbergasted to say much, but was about to stutter out a few words of thanks when the proprietor, for such he was, continued: 'Perhaps you would like to start your trip with a visit to my own cellars.'

A man stepped forward, introduced himself as the *chef caviste* and off we went.

We descended a flight of immensely old flagstone steps and at the bottom our eyes were arrested by the sight of a huge bottle suspended from the ceiling by two iron bands.

'That', said the head cellarman, 'was the bottle which was laid down for the proprietor's daughter when she was born; it was drunk at her first communion twelve years later.'

'What wine was it?' I said.

'The Gris Meunier of Orleans', he replied.

Good! I thought; if a wine which I had imagined to be on the most minor scale could withstand twelve years in bottle, it would be worth seeking.

'How many bottles does it contain?' I said.

'Six,' said the man, 'a Jeroboam.'

'Wrong', I said to Tim Hanbury, making a quick aside in English. 'If it's six then it's a Rehoboam, or if eight then it's a Methuselah.* A Jeroboam, also called a double magnum, is four bottles.'

'What about the bottling?' said Hanbury.

'Good question. Actually, after magnums, perhaps the Jeroboam would be the best size for maturing wines, but there is the difficulty of getting a suitable cork, and the pressure of the liquid in the bottle and the handling problems all make it a most unwise proposition.'†

The cellarman now conducted us into the cellar proper and then stopped at a place where four alleyways met.

Now the Hôtel Ste-Catherine abuts on to some of the very oldest buildings in Orleans and so what the *chef caviste* next said was probably true.

'These arches', he said, 'held up an old monastery which was here long before the time of Joan of Arc.'

We looked at them with awe for they were graceful and indubitably authentic.

As we walked round the rows of bins I remarked to the man that he must be kept fairly busy bottling and binning.

'No, I do not do any bottling', he replied.

I said I was surprised at this for it was unusual that so much wine should have come in both unlabelled and uncapsuled.

'We have a bottler who comes in to us to bottle the hogsheads when we receive them.'

'Is this a common practice?' said Hanbury.

---

* Other sizes are Salmanazar 12, Balthazar 16, Nebuchadnezzar 20. But only the Jeroboam occurs in the *O.E.D.*

† Champagne drinkers should know that this wine is only matured in magnums, bottles and half-bottles. Champagne is fermented in these bottle sizes, the sediment thrown down on to the first cork, which is then extracted, and a little dollop of further Champagne is added to replace that lost, and another better-quality cork is put in. If quarter-bottles are needed these are filled as and when required.

'No, it is not. The man is a true craftsman and there are very very few self-employed itinerant bottlers left in France.'

Upstairs I thanked the proprietor with the utmost sincerity, saying too that I was interested to learn that a wine made with the Gris Meunier grape should have held together for twelve years.

'What wine?' he said.

'The big bottle down the steps', I replied.

'That wasn't from here,' he said, 'it was Clos de Vougeot!'

'Well, anyhow,' I said, 'the visit made a wonderful send-off for our wine tour; perhaps you will tell me the name of your cordial cellarman.'

'It's André Simon.'

'! !'

'And yours?' I said.

'Le Blanc.'

'Ah!' I said. 'Monsieur Blanc de Blanc! What a vinous hotel.'

At that moment the *chef caviste*—André Simon—returned, with the name and address of the local home bottler, whom I thereupon decided we must visit forthwith.

As we drove along Hanbury said:

'What was so odd about Blanc de Blancs?'

'It is a type of wine', I replied. 'Most people think that Champagne is made with white grapes, but in fact there are only forty per cent of them to sixty per cent red. The white grapes give the wine its bouquet and sprightliness, while the red give the body. But sometimes a Champagne is made with *all* white grapes and then it is called blanc de blancs. Actually, I find it a little thin.'

At long last we found Monsieur Camille Guillemeau. I was so excited to get there that I called at 54 Faubourg Bannier, where they had never heard of him. I looked at the piece of paper again and saw that there was a squiggle in front of the five which could have been a two, three or five.

'Never mind,' I said, 'the street is numbered odd one side and even the other. We shall be there in no time', and I pointed to a garage sign a few hundred yards up where I thought the spot would be.

Not on your life! Though it was true that the numbering was as I said, and even though the buildings were tiny slum houses, nearly every number was followed by an 'A' 'bis' or even 'C', so that in fact four houses were passed before the next number came up, and it seemed to me that garages and factories were not in the numbering at all; our destination was miles away.

Monsieur Guillemeau turned out to be rather more of a Master Cask Repairer than anything else and attached to his house was a large shed with butts, casks, hogsheads, firkins and *fuders* of every description awaiting repair. When we asked him to show us around I can understand why many, many of his customers may well have been waiting for rather a long time for their casks to be returned. For out of sheer Christian goodness this kindly little peasant dropped everything at once to answer our questions.

Yes; he did do the occasional bottling for people; mainly lawyers and magistrates and dentists. No; he had not got a car to transport his bottling gear; he put it on to a carrier which he attached to his bicycle. No; he did not have to fine the wine or supply corks, the customers did that. Bottles? Generally there was a stack of these lying about in a yard and in this case he undertook to wash them with his bottle-washing machine of which he was very proud.

We went out in the yard to look at it—a comic little Emmet affair of great antiquity. It could be picked up by a child and was clamped to the rim of a sawn-off, upturned half butt filled with water. The turning of the handle does two things; it sucks up water through a pipe and it also rotates a wire brush, which sticks out through a tube. The dirty bottles are placed downwards and are drenched with water while the brush scours out sediment which has collected in the inner part of the punt, which is the protuberance in most table-wine bottles.

We mentioned that we were just about to set off to look for growers in the region and the old man asked us to come into his workshop, where there might be the names of a few growers.

This presented a remarkable sight. Cask-making is still a real and complicated craft which apart from machines for cutting and shaping the staves allows for very little mechanization. A great number of different tools are needed. The most unwieldy and dangerous-looking are those which are used to shape the inside of the staves, while the most ingenious is that used for grooving the staves and fitting the cask ends into them.

Naturally each generation thinks it can improve on the design of tools of the past and as this man was the third in his line there must have been upwards of a hundred and fifty implements there.

The old man dived into a box and eventually produced a handful of terribly old labels presumably from days when his grandfather had supplied them and when Orleans wines were more made than they are now.

There were several names of growers on the bottom of the labels which all pointed to St-Jean-de-Braye being the most important area, and as it was virtually a suburb of Orleans, we got to it in no time.

We stopped along the main road by a group of scruffy little shops and I pulled in at a garage.

'Look,' I said, 'you buy five litres of petrol and while you are doing so ask the chap whereabouts the vineyards might be. I will go and buy a box of matches at the grocer's and do the same.'

'Actually the tank will easily take fifteen litres.'

'I know,' I replied, 'but when abroad never fill up to the top. You might suddenly find yourself caught short, or with a sagging tyre, or in need of water for the windscreen cleaning gadget. So you must always be in a position to make a purchase, which will get you better service.'

So I bought matches at the first place, where they looked blank when I asked where the vineyards were, and a chocolate bar at the next, where a couple of chattering women ceased their flow to say that the vineyards were definitely . . . and they waved their hands due north.

The garage man had given the same advice only with more precise directions. We followed the directions with care and just about at the end of the stated distance we did indeed come to pretty undulating countryside planted almost entirely with plots of tiny trees of apples and pears.

Actually at a distance these tiny trees can look *very* like old vines and at first I kept pointing to the distance and exclaiming that we were coming to what we were seeking; but on getting nearer I was always wrong. We twisted and turned through dozens of little lanes but never a vineyard did we see.

'I'm going to turn back into the main road and call on that big firm of wholesale wine merchants we passed; they may be able to help us. It will not be as good as a small grower; still, we can but try.'

The offices were shut when we drove into the courtyard and, judging by the many different types of bottles stacked up and of the mineral water and beer crates as well, I felt sure that they specialized in supplying local cafés in Orleans.

I was turning the car round to leave when I saw a movement behind a glass-panelled door which seemed to be holding up a most ramshackle shed; a man's face, his cheeks stuffed full of food, peered out. And if a face so suffused, and through a filthy pane of glass, can say something this one said, 'I wonder who you are? But it's not worth while interrupting my lunch to find out.'

My reaction to this was damn you! and I got out, and went to the shed and explained my mission.

'You are wrong', said the man to whom *inter alia* I had explained that I had tried the office door. 'It is not locked but it gets stuck; you must turn the handle the wrong way.'

'Let's go and try together', I said, and along we went.

The door refused to budge; and infuriated, the man, who now wanted to make his point, was pummelling away like one possessed.

This brought slow ponderous footsteps along what sounded like a long corridor.

'Ah! That will be the boss', said the man, at the same time giving the door another savage kick with his boot. 'He will be coming from lunch.'

I had time to think: 'Lunch or no lunch, he is not going to get out of talking to me.'

The person inside gave an immense tug from the inside, which caused the wrought-iron to rattle against the glass panes; but at last it finally opened to reveal a man in a pair of carpet slippers with his mouth equally full of food. The peasant, now immensely relieved that the door had not in fact been locked, moved back to his shanty.

To the waiting man I summoned up my best French and put my case. By this time he had finished his mouthful, and he now stood wavering.

This, I thought, is the moment of truth; I must persuade him to ask me in. But at this moment there came down the passage the smell of the lunch he had forsaken. It must have been a *bœuf bourguignon* or a *coq au vin*, and what an excellent wine must have been used, for what assailed the nostrils was rich and rare beyond compare. To keep a man from such ambrosia was torture. I now wavered; he now stiffened.

'Will you come back at two o'clock', he said.

One is never wanted in France at lunch-time, and so we stopped off at a place farther down the road to see what we could forage. This turned out to be the smallest self-service place I have ever seen and attached to it was an even smaller bar—it cannot have been more than four feet long; but behind it was a superb coffee-making machine. We ordered a couple of cups and stretched a hand out to the self-service department for a bun and a bar of chocolate, but while munching these noticed that on shelves behind the bar were rows of bottles of Orleans wine—and from the very man we had just left to lunch in peace.

'Do you sell any of these wines by the glass?' I said.

'No', said the man.

'Then why do you display them?' said Hanbury.

'To remind people to take away a bottle; you will find them in the self-service shop.'

We moved three and a half feet from the bar to the 'Wine Department' of the shop and sandwiched in between help-yourself detergents and a display of fruit and vegetables was a huge rack of wines from every part of France.

The one I selected to take back to England was labelled:

La Maison

OCTAVE CHAMPILOU

garantit la pureté
de ce vin de terroir
exclusivement issu de

CEPAGE GRIS MEUNIER
DE L'ORLEANAIS

Mis en bouteilles par ses soins

The lettering was in unusual but excellent taste; indeed, what one would expect from a man whose household could produce such exquisite food smells.

We were now becoming quite good customers, and as Hanbury was copying down the wording of other labels in his little black book the owner engaged us in questing conversation; whereupon we told him of our peregrination among the pear plots.

'Not surprising,' said the man; 'there used to be sixty-five growers in this region; now there are barely a baker's dozen.'

But now production is going up again; the reason could be that the tourist likes to think he is drinking a little local wine and will try anything once. The future of the region, viticulturally speaking, is in the balance.

The extraordinary thing is that in the Middle Ages and earlier Orleans wines were equal to the greatest in France. In A.D. 560 that prolific historian of the Franks Georgius Floretius, usually known as Gregory of Tours, made special mention of the good wines of the region, and three hundred years later another chronicler wrote, 'It is with the Orleaner (grape) planted at Rüdesheim that on Charlemagne's orders the vineyards of Johannisberger were created.' To think that one of the greatest white wines in the world had its origin in this region is indeed extraordinary.

In 1865 the grapes were so full and fat, so golden-yellow and so ripe that the saying was, 'The hare has piddled upon them', and amateurs paid almost any price that growers cared to charge.

One reason possibly that the wines from here have not had a good press in the past half-century is that just as in England Sheffield is known for its cutlery and Grimsby for its fish, so in France Limoges is renowned for its china, and so on; perhaps regrettably for the wine, Orleans is reputed for its vinegar.

But as I say all is not lost, and for those who would like to follow my footsteps here are some communes of the Loiret Department which certainly were making wines twenty-five years ago. The comments are from the French book given to me in Orleans.

Baule	Good quality Gris Meunier and a pleasant Auvergnat— grape name
Pont aux Moines	
St-Ay	Pleasant wines to drink after healthy exercise
St-Jean-de-Braye	'Aimable' wine, especially suitable for consumption with copious meals
Saran	Pleasant wine if it is not blended with others
Semoy	Welcomed by those who want to quench vast thirst or when ravenous
Tavers	Splendid wine for expectant mothers
Olivet	To the south of Orleans and intimately connected with Joan of Arc

★

After a couple more coffees it dawned upon us that the proprietor had been no fool in keeping his *service libre* so miniscule. When it came to settling up, I found that I had picked up for purchase a packet of drawing-pins, a khaki handkerchief and a comb, although I had at least six of the latter in reserve in the car; while Hanbury among other acquisitions had got a pair of hefty brown leather boot laces which looked more like leather straps.

A BIBULOUS DAY

WE NOW HAD TO GO BACK AGAIN through Orleans to get to Beaugency, a small local wine centre where, judging by several labels I had seen during the morning, there was a reliable wholesaler who dealt in regional wines.

At Meung, a village west of Orleans and east of Beaugency, we stopped at a café which had a large 'Vin du Pays' sign outside. It was indescribably scruffy, bare of furniture and people, save a very old wizened woman dressed entirely in voluminous drapes of thin black wool.

She was standing in front of a closed coal stove in the middle of the room and helping herself with an immense ladle to soup from a steaming tureen, which I am sure contained not only bones but fish-heads as well.

'Two glasses of wine, please', I said.

She went round to the counter and got out a huge bottle of dull-looking white wine, which I felt sure was not of the locality, and so I queried its origin.

'Then why do you have a sign outside saying wines of the region?' I said when I had indeed been proved right.

'We only sell it in bottles', replied the old witch; 'there is not enough made to sell it by the glass. The bottles cost seven shillings and six-pence.' This was nearly half as much again as we had just paid and for the same wine so we left.

The next café did not say anything whatever outside but once through the door we found it packed and every man jack of the customers was drinking wine. On making enquiries I found out that we had come across that rarity of a very small owner-grower, and rarer still for that particular district, a man making a white wine with the Sauvignon grape.

'What do you think of it?' I said to Hanbury after we had tasted a couple of glasses.

The wine was good; full and clean on the palate but very acid and *diurétique*, or urine-promoting, as the French peasant loves to say when he wants to praise such a wine. I now waited, as I have done with all the first vinous pronouncements of my wine trainees, to hear what adjectives would be used.

'It's rather sour', said the young man.

'You have picked out the flavour correctly', I said, 'but you have used the wrong word; that is if you want to convey your meaning to another person who is used to a certain specialized jargon. Sour means exceptionally thin and weak and perhaps verging on the *piqué*, or pricked in English.'

Hanbury smelt and sipped the wine again. 'I do not dislike the wine, and, therefore, I thought to call it acid was being a bit too unkind.'

'That is where you are wrong', I said. 'All the great wines of the world, red perhaps less than white, have a certain amount of acidity in their make-up which the Germans call *Fruchtsäure* or fruity acidity. When it loses all traces of it, the wine tastes flat and insipid and then afterwards dies.'

This state would, perhaps, be called *flasqué* (flabby) by one *vigneron*, or *plat* (flat) by another, but the question of translating the vast number of adjectives and nouns used in the various wine districts of France presents many difficulties.

France being a wine country with so many more varieties of great wines than *all* the other wine-growing countries of the world put together, the number of official descriptive words is vast. By official I mean words which are known, accepted and understood to convey flavours, smells and colours to all experts in all wine-growing parts of France.

But over and above these words different localities have almost different wine languages of their own. I do not mean only dialect words but ordinary everyday French words which take on a quite different meaning when applied to wine. Lastly, there are picturesque words which amateur French writers seem to invent almost as they go along.

Translating some of these words into English is a nightmare because, of say four adjectives describing one wine, only one of them when translated into English will have any meaning so far as wine is concerned. Take, for instance, the following six uncomplimentary words used to denote a wine with the opposite characteristics of finesse:

commun, grossier, frivole, à fanfreluches, un plébéien, un rustre, which translated mean common, gross, shallow, with fallals, plebeian and loutish. All with different shades of meaning to the *vigneron* but, surely, in English the distinctions are too fine.

Another difficulty is that a large number of words used to praise the general constitution—apart that is from the colour and bouquet—of a wine like *corsé, étoffé, vigoureux, capiteux, généreux* and *charnu* all mean that, as well as being full-bodied, full of stuffing, vigorous, heady, generous and fleshy, they are also high in alcoholic strength. But this attribute is being more and more avoided in conversation in French wine circles.

This sounds curious but I feel it can be explained.

1. The French Government have for a half century been trying to improve the quality of wine made or, rather, sold and consumed in France.
2. One of the things they would like to see less of is the *vinage* of (mostly red) wine which represents a large proportion of what is consumed by the populace daily. *Vinage*, which is highly illegal unless done with permission, is the addition of alcohol to wine, and if you look at placards in grocers' shops you will see Vin 9°, Vin 10°, Vin 11° and even up I think to 13° of alcohol. The wine tastes flabby and mawkish, and is unpleasant and unhealthy to drink.
3. The Government's energetic anti-drink-and-drive propaganda is having its effect.
4. A great deal of very fine wine is in fact quite low in alcohol.

But there is a certain amount of confusion over this last point. A lot of great wines may be low in alcohol in relation to cheaper wines which have been *viné* but, other things (balance of acidity, sugar and tannin in red wines) being equal they would be that amount greater if they were, perhaps, a degree of alcohol stronger. Of course, if they were two degrees higher, they would taste spirity and would not be so pleasant.

Taking all these points into account I am certain that there is a climate of opinion, an unwritten conspiracy in French viticultural circles, to look on *alcoolisé* as a 'dirty' word, just as sports cars are given every epithet connected with speed except 'fast'.

One of the more picturesque French phrases for denoting a fine bouquet is to say that it 'makes a peacock's tail', where the opposite, where a wine has a bouquet which is dull, is to say that it 'has its hat over its ear' or that it is a 'tumbled-down bonnet'.

These two latter phrases have a curious origin. Most of the buying and selling of wine in France is done through the good services of the *courtier*, or commission agent, a most respected profession with very strict rules of conduct. Occasionally, he will take his purchasing customer round with him to growers' cellars. If any wine tasted were a little doubtful, he would signify this by a secret sign of pushing his hat on to the side of his head.

But wine merchants in England have their own pet phrases.

'Blotting-paper' is one. After the war, I am certain that the quality of the asbestos sheets used in filtering wines was poor and certain cheap clarets definitely took on a nose, as though they had been pressed through blotting-paper.

'Dog Sick'. This is a horrible smell we only notice on cheap white wines. It cannot be all that noticeable to the public, because some years ago I sent twelve dozen Graves with this smell to an institution's common-room with great regularity and never had a complaint. I myself can pick it out a mile away.

*

The sharpness of the wine we had drunk gave us the whale of an appetite, but we felt that we should just cast our eyes over the co-operative wine cellars at Baule. So we took a turning off the main road, which was sign-posted 'Route des Pommiers'. I had never seen an Apple Blossom Road in France before though those around Marden in Kent, which attract loads of char-a-banc trippers from the London area in springtime, are breathtakingly beautiful.

The premises of the Baule Co-op were a sorry sight; so tumble-down and decrepit that, on reflection, I now wonder if it is still in use in the season.

'Are you sure this is the place?' said Hanbury, as we surveyed the rotting garbage, tin canisters and piles of unwanted tyres.

'It must be', I said, 'for there is the weighbridge for the members' grapes. Each one brings along what he has picked at vintage time and when they are ripe. His lorry, the weight of which is known, goes on to the weighbridge, where the grapes are weighed and also tested for sugar content. He is given a docket for what he has brought along, the contents of the lorry are then tipped out ready to be crushed along with other growers' grapes, and off he goes for another load. A record is naturally kept of what he supplies and when the wine is sold the following year he gets cash in proportion.'

At Beaugency we decided that food in our bellies would replace the fiery pangs there and that anyway it would be dangerous to taste further without sustenance.

'I'll go for butter and pâté,' I said, 'and since you have talked so much about the joys of French bread you can buy that.'

Hanbury locked the back of the car and I the doors—one should never travel around without a duplicate car key—and we set off towards opposite sides of the delightful little square, which is perched at the top end of the tiny town.

Beaugency I feel is the place along the Loire where the Middle Ages give way to the Renaissance. Of the ancient, the vast eleventh-century *donjon* known as the Tour de César still looms high above the town. It is one of the hugest keeps in France and serves to remind us that only five miles away the burglar-poet François Villon was imprisoned all the summer of 1461 in a dungeon overrun with rats, until King Louis XI visited the place, and to mark the occasion ordered the release of all prisoners. This was the King who declared that literature was detrimental to those following the career of arms and was to be despised; and yet just half a century later, François I and his gentle wife Queen Claude, surrounded by their gay court, had reversed the situation and what Michelet called 'the discovery by man of himself and of the world' was in full swing.

In the eleventh century Beaugency was a fief of the bishopric of Amiens and its great château was the home of the barons of Landry, the last of whom died without children in the thirteenth century. Philippe IV (usually called le-Bel) bought the fief and united it with that of the Count of Blois, but later it became attached to Orleans.

So much for the Middle Ages. Of the Renaissance period, a charming edifice of the very best in building of the period is the Town Hall built in 1526, but restored with skill in the last years of the nineteenth century.

The winding old streets of Beaugency contain a dazzling medley of old houses in wood and stone and the old Maison des Templiers is well worth a visit.

It was not long before we were both back at the café we had selected;

Hanbury with one of those poker-thin, yard-long loaves which are all hard crust and no dough.

'Delicious', said the young man, contentedly chewing; 'how I love these really hard loaves.'

'Deli . . .' I said and crack! half a back tooth came away, stopping and all.

We were some time getting to our next wine contact, because our car was held up in a tiny street by the slowest funeral I have ever come across, even in France. Six magnificent black horses were carrying the hearse while for the flowers they must have bought up half the market. But Monsieur Pierre Goujon's establishment was not hard to find after we had got out of this bottleneck; he was the largest dealer in Beaugency.

The premises were in an attractive open courtyard with a neat garden and flowering shrubs in the centre. Several workmen were about and there was plenty of activity.

'Whatever is that thing?' said Hanbury.

He was pointing to a cask-rinsing machine. It consists of a metal revolving stand in the centre of which is a spout. The empty cask is placed on this stand in such a way that the spout goes through the bung. A powerful jet of water is then turned on and the cask rotated. After that, great chains are put inside it and it is vigorously rolled to and fro and finally it has sulphur burned in it. For this a stick of sulphur is suspended from a footlong iron hook which is attached to a wooden bung which, after the sulphur is lit, hermetically seals the cask.

As is usual with this sort of business, the office was tucked away in a corner of the courtyard and adjacent to the living quarters of the owner. Sometimes the offices are difficult to locate, but it is strictly etiquette to call there before looking at any bottling, capsuling or cellar work; any snooping before being introduced to the proprietor is definitely not done.

One can get some idea of the general set-up, and even the quality of the wine sold, in this sort of establishment by an appraisal of the garden in the courtyard. This one was tidy and, when a workman had taken us to the front door of the house, Madame Goujon appeared, the picture of neatness, and showed us into an office of the same calibre.

I explained my mission to Madame Goujon, but confess to dropping one or two untruthful hints about possible large purchases if I liked the quality. This was important; sometimes you will get more information if your host believes there is a sale forthcoming. Often, however, with small peasant growers who have a real passion for the flavour of the wine they make, the thought of a sale or rather all the *paperasserie* (red tape) in the form of documents needed* to export to a foreign country will make them dry up. It is a matter of judgement.

In this case I had played my cards correctly for a half-bottle of wine quickly made its appearance and we sat down to taste and wait . . . and wait and wait. Poor Madame Goujon after a while lost a little of her *sang-froid* and explained that her husband would not be along quite yet.

'You see', she said, 'he has gone to a funeral.'

'Someone has swallowed the gudgeon, Madame', I said.

The kind lady gave a wan smile and ordered another bottle.

'That, my dear sir,' I said as an aside to Hanbury, 'is one of my better puns, though admittedly in shocking taste. *Goujon* is French for gudgeon, and *avaler le goujon* is slang for 'push up the daisies', or 'hop the twig'.

'Ha!' said he weakly.

What a godsend that funeral was!

For while waiting for Monsieur, we tasted the following ten wines.

Gris Meunier de L'Orléanais Rouge
Gris Meunier de l'Orléanais Rosé
Mont Près Chambord Cour-Cheverny
Cépage Sauvignon
Coteaux du Layon
Muscadet
Anjou Rosé de Cabernet
Vouvray
Rosé de Touraine
Bourgueil

Of these, of course, only the first four were specialities of the immediate district.

* Some parts of France are well served by *transitaires* (forwarding agents) who can cope easily with the formalities; other parts are backward. But let me give the amateur buyer one tip: *never* buy a wine ex the grower's cellars, but always F.O.B. (free on board) the nearest port. If not, you can get badly caught; as I did later on this trip to the tune of paying as much per bottle for road delivery from Angers to Nantes, as the wine cost itself. Remember, too, there is a substantial charge for the *verre* (bottle) itself.

At last, changed back into ordinary clothes, Monsieur Goujon appeared. A most pleasant man but with the most remarkable habit of pulling his hand right down over his face every few minutes. It was like one of those character actors on the music-halls who used this gesture to put on a completely new face.

It was most disconcerting to start with because there we were waiting for something different to appear behind the hand but Monsieur Goujon's features remained exactly as before.

'Who told you about me?' he said.

'No one', I replied. 'I have seen your name on various bottles in cafés during the day and you struck me as being the most honourable merchant in Beaugency.' That I thought would be good for at least a half dozen free samples, and it was indeed the case. Slowly the sombre effect of the funeral wore off and older bottles were trotted up from the cellar.

'Tell me,' I said, 'why is it your red Orleans are so pale in colour?'

'Because we make it in the same way as they do in the Beaujolais district', said Monsieur Goujon; 'that is we only *cuve* it for some four to five days, whereas farther down the river at Chinon they *cuve* it for up to ten days and an absolute minimum of six.'

To *cuve* a wine, a red one, that is, is to vat it, and this means to leave the crushed grape-skins in an open wooden vat with the juice. To do this for only a few days produces a lighter, fresher-tasting, faster-maturing wine, but one with less guts and with a shorter lifetime in bottle.

Another bottle of wine arrived.

We had long ago given up spitting the wines out, not from any special urge to imbibe but because it meant that as no spittoon had been provided we had to go through the french-windows each time and spit on the flowers. This seemed to have caused immense amusement to Monsieur Goujon's cellar staff, for after some dozen appearances quite a crowd had collected and I think some thought we were putting on a comic act. So we started swallowing, and as the scale of quality ascended, so not spitting out became more and more enjoyable.

*

How much table wine can a normal person drink with sobriety and without injury to health?

French writers avoid the subject like the plague, and in thirty-five years of reading everything that country offers in vinous literature, I have only come across one person who has had the courage to make a definite statement on the subject; and that, by a coincidence, is the man but for whom I should never have gone into the wine trade.

I had failed to get into Eton, St. Paul's, Westminster and Merchant Taylors, and after I had been accepted for Bradfield I stayed second bottom boy of the second from bottom class until my second year, and then failed to answer a single question in a Common Entrance exam. My father, a throat surgeon, was, to put it mildly, hard-pressed to know what to do with me.

This coincided with an international congress of medical men in London, where my father saw a lot of a younger group of colleagues, also otorhinolaryngologists. Among them was Professor Georges Portmann, of the Faculty of Medicine of Bordeaux. My father told Professor Portmann about me, whereupon this kind man arranged to take me under his wing in Bordeaux, and got me a job, unpaid, in the cellars of Messrs. Hanappier Peyrelongue, the shippers. Today, as Senator for the Gironde, he is the Deputy Leader of the French equivalent to the House of Lords, but in addition he has been for the last thirty years the President of the Medical Society of the Friends of Wine, and as such he has written as many introductions to French wine books as have those kings of introducers Baron le Roy of the Office International du Vin and the Institut National des Appellations d'Origine and the Marquis de Lur-Saluces, the proprietor of that most famous, most visited vineyard in the world, Château Yquem.

The dose will vary according to the profession and type of life lived by a consumer. We feel that the consumption can be fixed at a litre and a half for outdoor manual workers; one litre for indoor manual workers, and 75 centilitres for a sedentary office worker. We feel that this intake can lead to no ailments in a sound body.

Thus Professor Georges Portmann, himself a very abstemious man; but I could have been almost certain that in an earlier work he put the heavy manual workers' allowance at two litres a day.

But even here there is no mention as to whether this quantity is with *meals alone* and does not take into account an aperitif before lunch, one or two before dinner and a brandy or so after both meals. It also gives no indication of the alcoholic strength of the wine to be consumed.

If a wine of 10° is envisaged and a sum total of a half-bottle of, say,

Graves, Muscadet, Bourgogne Aligoté, Hock or Moselle for lunch and another half-bottle (the two making 75 centilitres) of claret, Beaujolais or red Rioja for dinner, then I am positive the amount has been pitched too low.

*

Another half-bottle came along, which I noticed Madame Goujon handled with much greater care than usual; she also went to a cupboard and got out a set of more elegant glasses. Monsieur Goujon took a cloth to wipe clean the top of the bottle before he applied the corkscrew. I became very silent and took a long hard look at the cork.

Reverently the wine was poured out and we lifted it to the light. Its colour was of pale amber, but of a brilliance which only those superb old white wines still in impeccable condition can display. It seemed to have the power to attract to within itself the sun's rays, though no sun shone. And as one rotated the glass gently, sparkles of light were thrown off as though some bidden spotlight were being played upon it. And little beads of glycerine denoting that it would be *moelleux*, or luscious or sweet, fell down the side of the glass.

We stood reverently and then Monsieur Goujon said:

'The wine is not from here but farther down the Loire, a Quarts de Chaume; but would you care to guess what year it is?'

By its deep colour it could have gone back to the very early twenties and again by the colour it could not have been more recent than 1953, giving a possible choice, allowing for complete failure years, of some twenty different vintages.

I was, however, pretty certain which it was.

'It's a . . .' then I reflected.

What a pity to spoil these kind people's fun so soon. So I sniffed, I twirled, I sipped; I hinted at 1921 and 1926, both great years, and then said it could even be the great 1911. Then I shot forward and wondered if it could be a 1947. This I retracted. Then I edged nearer to the vintage I was pretty certain it was, so that it would not appear to be a guess. I mumbled something about its affinity to the great 1945 and then became silent.

The atmosphere was now as taut as a bow-string.

'I think it is a 1942', I said.

Hanbury looked at me; then at the man. The man looked quickly at

his wife; she looked at me, and there was only one thing her face said:
'Spot on!'

Monsieur Goujon was unashamedly astonished. He went outside and
came back a few moments later with five bottles beautifully wrapped.

'Samples,' he said, 'with my compliments.'

'Quite definitely not', I replied, producing my wallet.

*

'How did you manage it?' said Hanbury, as we were bowling
along towards Blois.

'Deduction', I replied. 'Did you notice the condition of the glass of
the bottle? It was in a shocking state. It looked as if it had been re-used
dozens of times. There was a terrible shortage of bottles during the
German Occupation during the war and any bottles were better than
none. In ordinary times, no one would have bottled a fine vintage year
in such bottles. But the cork confirmed my point. These were in even
scarcer supply than bottles during this time and what Monsieur
Goujon pulled out was a squinny little thing, utterly unacceptable in
normal times. That left me with six years, of which 1940, 1941 and
1944 were pretty mediocre and would not have lasted. 1945 was a
"comet"* year, but with a tiny harvest, and 1943 was nearly as fine.
That left 1942, a good year and plenty of it.

'Now I can understand a man getting a good bottle up for a couple
of English people he has never seen before but hardly go to the extent
of producing a "divine" bottle, as the French call a 1945 or a 1943; so
1942 it had to be.'

I paused. 'And that is enough of wine for a bit, let's do some
châteaux.'

---

* A wine made in a comet year was popularly reputed to have a specially fine
flavour. It started, I think, with one in 1811.

11

BLOIS, CHAMBORD, CHEVERNY

In the tenth and eleventh centuries castles were little more than dungeon-keeps, and life was rudely tough. The entire family lived, cooked, ate and dossed down in a room on the first floor which was reached by a moving, retractable ladder.

Life was deadly boring and the day interminably long. The main object of the master or seigneur was to get away from a room which was in twilight even on a bright day. Any pretext would do, but hunting, an excuse to quarrel or war with a neighbour were the best diversions. And when wandering minstrels or some jugglers passed—and how rarely that happened—it was an excuse for a real party.

Things improved in the thirteenth century and this was mainly because of new ideas of comfort brought back from the Orient on the Crusades. Bedrooms appeared; the food was cooked in a separate kitchen. The peasants took baths once a week while the seigneurs had one once a day. It was quite an occasion; barbers cut hair, guests were received, and even meals were taken in the water. From these beginnings stemmed the *petites* and *grandes levées* of Louis XIV.

Entertainments changed too in the thirteenth century. Jugglers were considered old-fashioned and dwarfs became the popular distraction of the women, while the men played chess.

Outdoors they played tennis, wrestled and indulged in archery. But *la chasse* was still the supreme sport.

The design of the outside of the buildings changed too, and the towers and turrets instead of being square became rounded mainly in order that grappling-irons and other engines of war should be able to grip less easily. Then again the bases of the buildings were greatly enlarged; the better to withstand mining work and the battering-ram.

In the sixteenth century came the superb domestic buildings of the Renaissance. By the seventeenth century the castles, or châteaux as they were becoming, had come down from the hilltops into the plain. True they were still built with moats, dungeons, drawbridges and towers, but these were added only for decoration.

In the seventeenth century these vast mansions or palaces were nothing but country retreats and all military reminders had completely disappeared; splendid ornamental gardens replaced them.

The marvel of the Loire is that on the short stretch from Orleans down to Nantes one can study the entire history of the building of castles from the dungeon-keep, through the fortified city like Loches, Amboise and Angers, on to the châteaux of the various counts— Blois—and down to the glories of the Renaissance such as Chambord, Chenonceaux and Azay-le-Rideau.

Perhaps the most visited, the most written about and most interesting is Blois. But it is *not* the most beautiful.

Here is what was said about it just sixty years ago by Francis Miltoun in his travel book on the region.

Much has been written of Blois, its counts, its château, by writers of all opinion including those critics of art and architecture who have discovered that Da Vinci designed the famous spiral staircase. From this one may well gather that Blois is the foremost château in all the Loire in popularity and theatrical effect. Truly this is so, but it is by no manner of means the most lovable; indeed it is the least lovable of all that great galaxy which begins at Blois and ends at Nantes.

It is a show place and not much more and partakes in every form and feature—as one sees it today—of the attributes of a museum and such it really is.

But although it is far from beautiful the siting is superb; built on an inclined rock which towers above the roof tops of the town, the Château de Blois is quite fairy-like in its setting.

Actually it is composed of no less than four quite separate and distinct foundations. It was first occupied by the aged Count de Châtillon who in 1391 was forced to sell it to the brother of King Charles VI, the amatory Louis d'Orléans who at the same time as he made the purchase seduced the count's wife.

In the sixteenth century Blois became a royal residence and Louis XII liked it so much that he not only added a wing but surrounded the place with vast gardens (now disappeared) in the Italian style, and the château became the Versailles of the Renaissance.

François I, who was born at Cognac under an oak-tree in the castle grounds there because his mother could not get back indoors in time, came there next and he added by far the most beautiful part of the building.*

Finally the last, most ambitious and least attractive building was undertaken in 1626 by Gaston d'Orléans in amusing circumstances. He was the brother of Louis XIII and the most assiduous conspirator of all time. In order to get him out of the way and keep him occupied, the King gave him Blois and also advanced him money to rebuild it. Gaston threw himself into the work with a will and for three years there was a feverish amount of rebuilding done.

But unexpectedly,† the future Louis XIV was born and Richelieu, seeing Gaston's chances of coming to the throne diminished, cut Gaston's subsidies.

Such is the history of the château of Blois and we could leave it at that if it were not for that splendiferous eye-catching beauty, the François I staircase.

That it is the most photographed piece of architecture in all Blois is certain; that it was the prototype of many others is also sure. Seen from the vast courtyard its beauty is undeniable.

Actually the stairway is not right in the middle of the François I wing, because architect François Mansard (it was he whose roofs made attics habitable) took down a part of it to erect the newer one for Gaston d'Orléans.

This marvellous openwork stairway which, incidentally, in its ascent turns not as most *escaliers* do clockwise but counterclockwise, served a dual purpose, for apart from giving ample room for the hundreds of people—it is estimated that, when the court was in residence, some 15,000 people were directly or indirectly employed there—who must have been using it to get to and from the various floors, it served as a grandstand when there was any ceremony going on in the huge courtyard below.

For this reason the stairway had an octagonal framework, three sides of which were let into the masonry, leaving five giving a frontage on to the courtyard. The construction is very open in design and cut away to leave pillars at each exterior angle. The effect was that at each

* It is noteworthy that only twelve years elapsed between the rebuilding of Louis XII and François I, but the difference in style is enormous—a revolution in taste and ideas had taken place.

† Louis XIII was on the way to visit his mistress when a terrible storm obliged him to take refuge in his wife's establishment.

opening there was space for a rostrum, where the members of the Royal Court could welcome guests or where guards could be in attendance.

Historically the other thing of interest about Blois is the constant recurrence of emblems, a reminder that in spite of the Renaissance the inhabitants still partially thought in terms of the Middle Ages.

François had the salamander which was supposed to live in, or to feed on fire; his mother had a swan pierced by an arrow, but the most attractive of all was that of Louis XII—the porcupine. In those days people believed that the *porcus spinosus*, or spiny pig, could stand aloof from the enemy and dart its spines at them, and on drawings of the animal done in the Middle Ages you will see that a number of its quills are free of the animal. On masonry, however, this was too difficult to depict.

Actually Blois specializes in an attractive kind of glazed earthenware pottery, and an ashtray with one of these emblems is one of the least revolting of souvenirs, especially as there is a raised groove for cigars, so essential for civilized cigar-smoking.

*

I hate retracing my steps but in this instance it was necessary, for we had heard that at the Château de Talcy, which was on the way back to Orleans, there was an interesting wine-press over four hundred years old.

The château was built on the site of a small fortress of the twelfth century by an Italian, Bernard Salviati, a cousin of Catherine de' Medici. But what on earth decided this gentle Italian to construct his residence, so utterly Italian in style, where he did? Only a few miles away he could have had the magnificent setting of the river, whereas instead he chose the dull flat plain of Beauce, surrounded by meres and moorland, where every pond and stream abounds in pike and other freshwater fish.

Talcy is the château of poetry, for here was born Cassandra—daughter of Salviati—to whom Ronsard addressed so many sonnets, and it is possible that they were composed actually at the château.

The wine-press was a great sight, for despite its age, the mechanism is so wonderfully balanced that two men only can to this day get ten casks of juice from one pressing.

But by far the greatest sight at Talcy is the sixteenth-century giant dove-cote, probably built at the same time as the main building and certainly contemporary in style. There are no less than 1,500 pigeon holes or *alvéoles* as the French call them, in the building and the construction is in a very good state of repair.

As well as wine another thing that was beginning to interest us was the names that people from various towns called themselves. It had cropped up back at Beaugency with Monsieur Goujon, after our tongues had been well and truly loosened and the business part of our visit was over.

'With this wine', Hanbury had said gallantly as his glass again was charged with the famous 1942, 'you must be the happiest of all Beaugenciens.' This sounded good.

'No, we call ourselves Balgentiens,' said Madame, 'but I am from Blois, a Blaisois or Blésois.'

'And I am from Sully, a Sullinois', said Monsieur.

'What does a man call himself if he comes from Bauge?' said I in an undertone.

But after this we did a bit of research into the subject by asking people in cafés and at filling stations. The way to get the information was not to ask people what they called themselves, as this brought no reply, but to have a shot at it and hope to get it *wrong*.

Amboise. 'Are you an Amboisien?'

'No! No! I am an Ambacien.'

Illiers. 'Are you an Illiérois?'

'We are Isleriéns!'

By this technique, especially in cafés where people were chatting at a bar, we collected a large number of names. Note that Illiers has a population of only 3,250; it seemed to us extraordinary that places so tiny should have created their own words for their inhabitants.

Here are some more places	*Inhabitants*
La Flèche	Fléchois
Cholet	Choletais
Pontlevoy	Pontiléviens
Vouvray	Les Vouvrillons
Troo	Les Troiens
Tours	Les Tourangeaux
Angers	Les Angevins
Montoire-sur-Loire	Les Montoiriens
Châteauneuf-sur-Loire	Les Castelneuviens

Here are some more places	*Inhabitants*
Château-Renault	Les Castelrenaudins
Châteaudun	Les Dunois
Bourges	Les Berruyers
Solesmes	Les Solesmois
Romorantin	Les Romorantinois

*

'Blast and damn', we both said at the same time. For now upon looking at the map we saw that to get to mighty Chambord there was no bridge over the river except at Blois and it meant doing that stretch yet a third time.

When you run the treasury dry; when you ransack the gold of your kingdom's churches, melt down the silver ornaments of your subjects; when you do not even pay the ransom to Spain for your own two sons, and when you wish to turn the course of a mighty river . . . what is the result?

Chambord!

A hundred and seventy yards long and 120 yards wide, with 440 rooms, and 365 chimneys of feudal-cum-Renaissance fantasy, set in a 13,000-acre park and surrounded by the longest wall, of twenty-one miles, in France.

The most curious thing about Chambord is the difference in looks of the ground and first floors to that of the roof. The former are straightforward and severe in design, while the latter is of a fantastic exuberance. The author Vivian Rowe has the best description of it and one can hardly blame him when he confesses that he had saved up his *bon mot* for his travelling companion for weeks.

'My God', says his friend, who never uses strong language. 'What is that?'

Rowe replies, 'The skyline of Constantinople on a single building.'

That amorous, amoral, charming and not unsuccessful King François I started building it in 1519, first having razed to the ground a small fortress which had been erected previously by the counts of Blois. And in this case the otherwise mercurial monarch stuck ruthlessly to his appointed task of employing on an average 1,700 men over a period of fifteen years.

The design was possibly that of Dominici de Cortone, who had come to France from Italy as one result of the King's foreign campaigns.

But the French architects Denis Sourdeau, Jean Goberau and Pierre Neveu certainly had some sort of a hand in it, and the man in over-all charge of the work was François de Pontbriant, the governor of Blois and the fortified city of Loches.

But François I was intensely interested in architecture and some credit must go to him for the over-all conception, even though much is perhaps legend. One is that he meddled so much with the architects that they left and that when it came to finishing the building he called all the masons together and told each one to do a part of the roof as best he could, and at all events to show up the Italian architects.

But whatever made the king choose this spot? It was the most seemingly unsuitable location, having no decent road up to it and being surrounded by marshland. As with Talcy, one is amazed that such a site was chosen rather than one at Blois or Amboise. Three theories have been postulated: one that François I simply wanted, like Louis XIV later at Versailles, to create something beautiful out of a wilderness; secondly that it was merely his passion for the chase; while the third is that he was at that time enamoured of a lady in the vicinity.

Chambord is much the largest of the châteaux of the Loire and certainly has had its share of history. In 1539, when it was newly finished, perhaps the greatest event of all occurred there when the King received by far the most powerful man in the western world, Emperor Charles V of Spain and the Netherlands.

As soon as he saw the building he exclaimed, 'Chambord is the sum total of human endeavour.' Was this compliment accorded solely because of the size of the place; or possibly because on arrival he was greeted by a great bevy of young maidens scantily dressed as Bacchantes, who strewed spring flowers in front of his retinue and the royal carriage?

Chambord was not finished when François I died, but Henri II, who married Catherine de' Medici, continued the construction, and it was here that in 1552 was signed the treaty with the German princes which gave France the bishoprics of Metz, Toul and Verdun.

After François II (who married Mary Queen of Scots) and Charles IX, who both brought a gay hunt-loving court there, the château passed through a quiet time for nearly a hundred years until the Sun King Louis XIV reanimated it and brought down a huge retinue of courtiers with their appendages which stretched for miles. So great, in fact, were the numbers that the King (who loved the châteaus) had to make many internal alterations to accommodate them.

Here it was that in 1670 Molière wrote, in the space of a few days, and first performed *Le Bourgeois Gentilhomme*, and underwent one of the most agonizing moments of his life. For Louis seems to have been unable to make up his mind whether he liked the play or not. The courtiers all thought he did not care for it and were all bent on tearing the author to pieces verbally. But the king decided on a second performance, during which he laughed; Molière was saved.

In 1748 the château became the property of the violent, proud, eccentric Marshal de Saxe, who brought with him two regiments of cavalry which included Tartars and Negroes imported from Martinique, and also six cannon captured at the battle of Fontenoy. It was in gratitude for this victory that he was given the château.

The Marshal directed that when he died the six cannon, which he had placed in the courtyard, should fire every quarter of an hour for sixteen days as a mourning salvo.

After that the great days of glory were over. Uncared for after the death of Marshal de Saxe and pillaged during the Revolution, the château was eventually given by Napoleon to the loyal Berthier, Prince of Wagram, and all he did was to sell the timber while his wife later put the property on the market.

It was finally bought by the state in 1932.

★

Although only a very few miles separate Chambord from Cheverny, the difference between the two is startling. For whereas you can detect the styles of three centuries in the former building, Cheverny was started in 1634 (much later than most of the neighbouring châteaux) and finished in one fell swoop by the Count de Cheverny, Henri Hurault, whose direct descendant, the Marquis de Vibraye, owns it today. It sits in the midst of a lovely wooded park and the great avenue which leads up to the main entrance extends for very nearly five miles, perhaps longer than any private roadway elsewhere in Europe.

But if Blois and Chambord are architectural muddles, at times pleasing and at times ugly, Cheverny, built by the architect Boyer, is in about as severely symmetrical and classical a style as you can get. At each corner are pavilions with the domes and lanterns so customary in the heyday of the Louis XIV style.

The outside is by no means exceptionally pleasing but the inside compensates in an astonishing way; for while Blois is empty and Chambord nearly so (and what is there is of extreme banality), Cheverny is furnished in the style of the seventeenth century.

'The luxuriance of the interior is an object lesson to Hollywood in sheer magnificence', says Vivian Rowe in his *Châteaux of the Loire*, and he continues: 'It is the very kind of thing that decorators try to achieve in film sets when they only succeed in producing masterpieces of bad taste. Cheverny is a masterpiece of good taste, too rich for my liking, but impeccable of its kind. The superbly painted ceilings, the decorated chimney pieces, the Gobelins tapestries, all dealing with classical subjects, rival Versailles in all but sheer size and quantity.'

Most of the decorated work was done by Jean Mosnier, who was born at Blois in 1600 and came from a family who were artists to their fingertips, for both his father and grandfather had been notable painters on glass. Young Mosnier was first taught by his father and then so impressed Marie de' Medici that she defrayed the cost of his education for eight years in Italy. I like best the dining-room panels representing scenes in the life of Don Quixote.

Other decorations of interest are those in Cordovan leather, but the *pièce de résistance* is the King's bedroom, together with the Salles des Gardes, both magnificent sights.

In one of the outbuildings, the Bâtiment des Communs as the French call it, is the famous Museum of the Hunt, decorated with no less than two thousand heads of stag, while in the kennel-house is a pack of seventy hounds.

*

'That is enough of châteaux for the day,' I said as we left Cheverny. 'I can assimilate no more.'

The castles had gained a hold on Hanbury too, but in another way. Shortly afterwards we again stopped for one of our innumerable cups of coffee and this time Hanbury went on from a second to yet a third cup. But he seemed more interested in putting in lumps of sugar than in drinking the stuff; he also had developed a habit of peering at the debris scattered around the bar counter and then swooping down to pick up some object too small for me to see what it was. I had hoped to have found out what he was collecting without asking him, but curiosity won.

'It's the papers the sugar is wrapped in', he answered. 'They have pictures of châteaux on them.'

So that was it! He had not done badly for one day, having got seven different ones; Azay-le-Rideau, Blois, Chambord, Chaumont, Cheverny, Chenonceaux (why so many beginning with Ch?) and Langeais. In addition to the picture of the building there was also an appropriate coat of arms and the words *Châteaux de Lumière*, so I suppose that only those which were floodlit formed part of the series. How many more there were we never got round to finding out.

We had decided that Montrichard was our best bet for a hotel for the night, but at Pontlevoy we saw a most attractive place which went by the name of the Hôtel d'École, named after the ancient college which used to be there. This formed part of the eleventh century abbey which can still be seen. It was founded by Gelduin de Chaumont as a thank-you token to the Virgin Mary, who had saved him from a shipwreck, and he handed it over to the Benedictine monks who later set up the school.

The hotel was very spacious downstairs, well furnished but also out-of-season empty. There was a slick American bar on the right with tall stools, which often denotes that the place is too grand to serve simple glasses of local wine. But a very pretty, ultra buxom young woman came in and said yes she could do, and while she served us we both looked with unconcealed amusement and admiration at her stockings. They were fine, black wool, clearly hand-knitted, with dozens of holes of various sizes and shapes, each one sewn round with different-coloured silk thread.

We asked about a couple of single rooms for the night, which request brought along another woman who seemed thrown into an inexplicable state of indecision. She mumbled something vaguely about the central heating not working and dust being everywhere, and then spoke as though she did not expect me to be at all satisfied.

'Would you care to come up and see the rooms?'

I could not back out of things now and so followed her, but as I left said to Tim Hanbury:

'You had better tell that girl how much we admire her stockings.'

'Yes, sir', said he seriously.

Upstairs I inspected five rooms which were spotless and cosily warm. The woman turned down the bedspread to reveal virgin white linen sheets and I turned on the bedside light, which worked—an important thing to me.

We went downstairs back to the bar and I said I would take two rooms.

This again made the woman shuffle from foot to foot in an agony of indecision.

At last she said:

'Er—they are not really available. You see, we are not open for the season until next week and the upstairs staff have not all arrived.'

'Then why on earth did you take me upstairs?' I said.

'Well, I did not want you to go away with a bad impression.'

How utterly sensible!

As we drove away, I said to Hanbury jokingly:

'Did you tell the girl about her stockings?'

'Yes, sir.' His tone implied that he was surprised I doubted it.

'Well done,' I said, 'but did you say they were pretty, amusing, sexy, attractive, exciting or what?'

'I said they were *très gais*', he replied.

Montrichard is on the River Cher. From the old bridge you get a fine view of the ruins of the medieval dungeon which dominates the small town of only three thousand souls, which, however, is very well placed for hotels.

By far the best is the Croix Blanche with an extremely inviting front, but in one of the narrowest, longest-way-round one-way streets ever. One always feels that this is bad luck on the hotel concerned when this happens in a town, but on reflection, as bookings are ninety per cent through the grape-vine or guide-book, or having-been-there-before, one wonders if off the beaten track may not be a positive advantage, from the point of view of bedroom noise.

The Croix Blanche had another thing to its credit, namely a restaurant with a single star in the *Guide Michelin* for good food. With the star (or two or three—but there are only twelve of the latter in the whole of France) the guide prints alongside the restaurant a couple of its specialities and also if, but only if, it is a wine-making region, two local wines.

Here they were Oisly and Mareuil.

Odd, I thought. Because I imagined that I knew the name of every wine in France.

So after dinner I sought out the proprietor, who was behind the cash desk smoking a very Sherlock Holmes type of pipe.

'Oh', he said in very good English. 'The *Guide Michelin* send you a form and I put down two villages around here.'

'You have done well', I said, 'and I must congratulate you on your English. For a Frenchman,' I continued, 'it is wonderful; and may I ask your name?'

The proprietor did not answer but instead picked up a small rubber stamp. 'Edmond L. Krawczyk.'

'It's easier this way', he said.

We went to bed.

12

COUR-CHEVERNY
TO CHENONCEAUX

❧

THE ELDERLY CASK-MAKER HAD GIVEN ME A VERY OLD, tattered label with Cour-Cheverny on it and so that is where we wandered back to the next morning. The village, sleepy though it is, has one of the prettiest little churches set in an adorably tiny square, which to all intents and purposes *is* the village, but nestling right up against the church in such a way that it appears to almost form part of it is the Trois Marchands Hotel, which also has earned its good-food star from the *Guide Michelin*. The wines chosen are extraordinarily unimaginative, but the three dishes recommended would make just about the most perfect meal one could imagine; terrine of pigeon, pike au beurre blanc, and medallions of Charolles beef *aux délices de Sologne*, whatever that may mean.

I suppose that when filling in the form stating what dishes they would like to see written up in the *Guide Michelin*, restaurateurs have played for safety, for only that can account for the real lack of imagination shown. Chicken and lobster appear with the utmost regularity, and the number of dishes 'with cream' is endless.

The other day I went through the near thousand pages of the *Guide* to see if there were any places that had got any bright ideas.

Aix-en-Provence. Roi René (hotel): Thrush paté made with gin.
Anglet (near Biarritz). Relais de Parme (restaurant): Sole with foie gras.
Beaulieu-sur-Mer (near Nice). La Réserve: Red mullet braised with fennel.
Bordeaux. Château Trompette (restaurant): Lamprey à la Bordelaise.
Cannes. Reine Pédauque (restaurant): Fillet of lamb in pastry.
Castres. La Caravelle (restaurant): Châteaubriand steak grilled over vine wood prunings.
Chablis. Etoile-Bergerand (small hotel): Hot ham, fondue of game, orange soufflé. [Sounds a good place.]
Château-Arnoux (near Digne). Bonne Etape (small hotel): Lièvre à la Royale. [An extremely expensive, elaborate and lengthy way of cooking hare.]

Feurs (north of Lyons). Chapeau Rouge (restaurant): *Morilles* in cream.

Fontaine-de-Vaucluse (near Avignon). Château (restaurant): Trout au Porto and à la crème. [Sounds scrumptious!]

Grenoble. Poularde Bressane (restaurant . . . chef Piccinini): Kidneys sauté with fois gras sauce.

Illhaeusern (in the foie gras country). Auberge de l'Ill: Brioche of fresh foie gras. Soufflé of salmon.

Limoges. Taverne Lion D'Or (restaurant): A gratin of langoustine tails.

Lyons. [If the proportion of stars for good food in relation to its size is any guide, then this town far outstrips any other in France for gastronomy. It is the only place, including Paris, where there are six places starred for good food in succession.] Mère Brazier (restaurant): Artichoke hearts with foie gras.

Marseilles. Caribou (restaurant): Loup (sea perch) grilled with fennel.

Paris. Tante Louise (restaurant): Fresh duck liver with raisins.

Quimper (Finistère). Pascal and Terminus (restaurant): Casserolette de filets de sole.

St-Nectaire (near Clermont-Ferrand). Modern Hotel (small hotel): Quail souvaroff.

Strasbourg. Valentin-Sorg (restaurant): Hot foie gras à l'Alsacienne [November to March only].

Tain L'Hermitage. Chabert (restaurant): Young guinea-fowl with bananas.

Tancarville (bridge of, near Le Havre). Marine (restaurant): Ham éclair.

Val d'Isère (Alps). Edelweiss (hotel): Lavaret du Lac d'Annecy.

Some of the less common wines listed in the *Guide* are:

Apremont	From the Jura.
Pierrefeu	A Rosé wine made in Provence.
Carianne	Provence Rosé.
Montagnieu	Sold in Bourg-en-Bresse. Probably a Jura wine.
Corent	
Buzet	A curious, spirituous, strong, white Sauternes type wine made in the Lot-et-Garonne department, south of Bordeaux. The wines are called (with pride) *Vins Pourris*—'Rotten wines'—and with age take on a good bouquet.
Chanturgue	
Taradeau	A red Provence wine from the Valley of the Argens.
Irancy	A red wine from the Chablis district. Unusual.
Ripaille	From the Jura.
La-Croix-Valmer	A red Provence wine with quite a reputation among the *nouveaux riches* in Nice.

So there you have it; the *Guide* gives information on 'nearly 4,000 towns', it tells its readers, but does not say how many eating places are listed in each.

Actually, when they say 'towns' they must mean this as distinct from villages, for there are on an average some six *places* mentioned on every page, and most have three or four restaurants mentioned, say 20,000 in all. Of these 575 have one star, sixty-four two stars, and twelve three stars, of which Paris claims five.

And in all these not one mention of Scotch smoked salmon, gulls' eggs, fresh asparagus, smoked eel, smoked cod's roe, sturgeon as a hot dish (not caviar), veal chops, hot marrow bones, or grouse, which are some of the world's greatest dishes.

*

Having got to Cour-Cheverny it now behoved us to dig out the name of a grower and we were just going into a café as usual, when young Hanbury pointed to a shop a few yards up the road.

'A taxidermist', he said.

'Right first time', I said.

It was an extraordinary place to come across in such a sleepy hamlet, and it was the more unusual in that it was not a shop but a private house in the main street, into which had been let an immense and beautiful bay window.

The animals on show had been stuffed superbly and the specimens were very fine indeed. Pride of place had been given to a great badger but the one I liked best was a dear little hedgehog, who was placed as if coming out of a hole in a bank.

We pushed open the door, which jangled like mad, and found ourselves in a room much larger than it appeared from the outside. On the walls were the stuffed heads of not only the usual deer, stag and wild boar, but horses, cats, dogs, and even sheep, pigs and cows.

There were some lovely antique tables on show and on these were innumerable stuffed animals and birds not in cases but on little wooden plinths.

But nobody came to see us. So I let out a polite call which brought along in due course a pleasant quiet woman who asked us what we wanted.

'We have been here quite some while', I said as apologetically as I could in explanation of my call.

'You could have rung', said the woman and pointed to a wall we had not got round to looking at yet. On it was a large sign. 'We shall leave you in peace to look around *but* if you want us RING.'

'I'm sorry,' I said, 'but aren't you afraid of light-fingered persons?'

'Not really,' replied the woman, 'my husband is pretty good at other things besides stuffing animals.'

She pointed to one of the tables and turned to Hanbury, asking him to pick up any of the animals at random.

Tim Hanbury obliged and picked up a pine marten. As he lifted the plinth off the table, an alarm went off that would wake the dead.

'It also bolts the door', said the woman placidly, adding: 'And now what can I do for you?'

It was rather a come-down for us to have to now explain that we were not prospective purchasers, but had come for information concerning Cour-Cheverny vineyards. Unfortunately Madame was new to the district and so it meant a visit to a café after all. Eventually we were bowling along to a hamlet called Les Huards with a choice of two introductions. One of these was to a Monsieur Gendrier, into whose farmyard we shortly drove.

Several children were playing around in the tractor shed as we got out of the car, and the eldest, a pretty little thing of some ten summers, came up to me almost at once; one of these people who do not know what shyness means.

'Where is your father?' I said.

'He is out in the vineyards', she replied. 'But I'll go and get Mother.'

Almost immediately Madame Gendrier came out and equally quickly did I sense that this was going to be an easy session; it was plain to see where the little girl had got her absence of shyness from. Sometimes, when the man is absent, these visits can be purgatory. Often the wife may not understand why you should want to come and buy wine from a small peasant, but when at last she does she is frightened of sending someone off to fetch her husband, who may be miles away and working in his vineyards and annoyed at having to return.

I have recently formed a theory concerning people's level of intelligence and their understanding of foreigners speaking their language. The lower their I.Q., the less *willing* are they to understand. I have asked questions of people in the street or in a shop in France, Spain and Germany many, many times when the person addressed has said he could not understand, while bystanders have understood perfectly.

It is not in the slightest that they are anti foreigners. You can prove that, in fact, they have understood but have not wished to take it in by a simple experiment.

You select a perfectly straightforward question, to which the person *must* be able to give an answer, and one which you are absolutely certain you can say with perfect clarity.

Do you sell oranges, please?

Could you kindly tell me the time?

Have you any cold milk?

The super unintelligent person will either say, 'What?' or 'Don't understand,' or shake his head negatively.

You ask again to make quite certain and give the person a chance. If after this they give the same response, you say (if you are in France) slowly, 'Do you speak French?'

What they think you have asked them is, 'Do you speak English?', and often they will say vehemently 'No', when you have only got as far as saying 'Do you speak . . .'

Then the penny drops. They do not like the idea of your thinking that they are a foreigner in their own country and they reply 'Yes! Yes!' *Of course* they speak French.

And more often than not they answer the question you have just put to them without it being posed again.

But Madame Gendrier summed up the situation in a trice and said to her daughter:

'Get on your bicycle and fetch your father and tell him to come back.'

The little minx set off straight away in the pouring rain and we settled down banality-talking to wait in the farmyard.

After what seemed an age the girl returned, her face as brimful of smiles as heretofore.

'No', was the reply. 'He says he's got too much to do, and won't be back until the evening.'

'Did you tell him that an English wine-merchant has come specially along to see us and wants to buy some wine?'

'No', said the child.

The mother was quite unperturbed. 'Well, go back again and tell him that', she said.

The girl turned round her bicycle and started to set off, but I restrained her, saying, 'No, that will take too long. I will go and see him.'

The woman described where he was and then said, 'He will be working in the vineyard. He will not be able to come on to the road but you can shout to him.'

What frightful cheek, I thought angrily, but I contented myself by saying, 'To save time while I am away, could you draw off the two cask samples you promised me? Perhaps my young trainee could see over your cellars, and could you allow him to use your corking machine on the samples so that he can learn something?' It was that sort of place.

When I got to the vineyard Madame's remarks became clear, for between the road and the first vines was the most unusual, immense dry ditch, deep and wide and far too steep to cross, running alongside the road as far as the eye could see.

Monsieur Gendrier and three of his men were busy cutting down a row of trees which, he explained, were not so much obstructing the sun as taking too much nourishment from the soil. What with the wind and driving rain conversation was not easy, but after a tremendous yelling match I managed to find out a bit about the wines of the region.

The interest in these wines, which were accorded Controlled Appellation status (quite an achievement for a small district like this) in 1953, lies in the fact that the wines are made with a grape uniquely used* in this district called the Romorantin, presumably after the town farther south. It was in this delightful medieval town that François I started to grow his famous beard, after his doctors had insisted on shaving his head when a lighted candle thrown from a window had fallen upon it.

The other two grapes used to make these wines are the Chenin and the Sauvignon, which result in a dry, fruity, light wine of some charm.

The vineyard area is tiny, only twelve hundred acres, making some million bottles of wine in all, most of which is made at the local Caves Coopératives. The wine is made in four communes: Mont-près-Chambord, Cour-Cheverny, Cheverny and Huisseau-sur-Cosson.

★

* This is an over-simplification; the *name* of the grape is not found elsewhere, but I should be amazed if the grape itself was not to be found, though with a different nomenclature.

This visit had taken us the best part of the morning and our next stop was the Château de Chaumont, too far to do before lunch, so I suggested that we stop at a *café des routiers* when and if we saw one. The quality of service and cuisine in these places is, as I have said, terribly patchy; I have eaten superbly in several and also been treated to disdain, squalor and vile food in others. They are, after all, only good-pull-up-for-carmen types of 'caffs' and so far as I know have not been graded. One should be pleased then if one eats well and not complain if high standards are often lacking. The one we found was bad by any standards and worse if one was averse to garlic, which I am not; but this was carrying things too far, by jove!

The hors d'oeuvres had garlic sausage and also little bits of cold, fried garlic bread, and this was followed by hot garlic mutton, from which I pulled two pieces of raw garlic the size of a small sugar lump. How I wish I had not gone for the table d'hôte but had had a plain cheese omelette like Hanbury, who was not to be doubled up with indigestion later that day. And the wine was revolting.

Chaumont is a meandering little village slap on the Loire; the castle is above it and from the park a stupendous view of the valley spreads in all directions.

The building itself is a cross between a fortress and a residence, and is all tall chimneys, steep roofs, and what I personally always fall for, *round* towers—how I love the sight of Kent oast-houses!

Actually it is amazing that Chaumont does look as much of a piece as it does, for the number of different owners it has had is surprising. Its history is mostly one of faction, and it had been twice razed to the ground before Pierre of Amboise, the eldest son of the seventeen children of Charles I of Amboise, rebuilt it in 1465, completing the whole work forty-five years later.

In 1560 Catherine de' Medici bought the castle to have her revenge on poor Diane de Poitiers, the mistress of Catherine's dim-witted French husband, Henri II. This purchase shows how terribly history can get falsified by popular imagination. One has been brought up to think that Catherine de' Medici was all that was evil and yet when she at last had her dreaded rival at her mercy, what did she do?

François I had more or less chosen Diane as a mistress for his son, who soon became so infatuated with her that he chose as his own colours the black and white mourning (she had previously been married) that the widow wore for the rest of her life. Diane, twenty years older than Henri, advised the King in matters of state, mothered and brought up his legitimate children, and generally made herself indispensable, with the result, and quite rightly, that when Henri II died in 1559 this placid woman was not only the possessor of most of the crown jewels but also of Chenonceaux. This château was, and is, far more beautiful than Chaumont.

Catherine de' Medici was now all-powerful for although Diane had virtually brought up her children they obeyed their mother completely. So the Queen, threatening to revoke the gifts of François I and Henri II, forced a swop of châteaux and ordered the return of the jewels—which anyway in those days really belonged to the state. Surely not a very cruel revenge.

Chaumont comes from *Chaud Mont*, hot or burning mountain, and it certainly has seen sparks fly. In the early years of the nineteenth century there arrived that turbulent character Madame de Staël after one of her quarrels with Napoleon, who had ordered her 'to separate herself from Paris by at least forty leagues'. She had hovered around the capital like a moth about a candle flame; Auxerre, Orleans, Blois, Rouen had all been tried and then one day she was going by *poste chaise* from Tours to Saumur when she saw Chaumont rising high above the river-bed. She 'installed herself in the affection of the then proprietor, M. Leray, and made the court there for many years'.

Those interested in horses will probably want to visit the stables; the size and luxury of which give some idea of the esteem with which this animal was regarded by our ancestors.

*

François I on Chenonceaux:

'The castle is a fine palace on the River Cher, in a fine and pleasant country.'

Henri II:

'The castle is one of the best and most beautiful in our kingdom.'

Chenonceaux is unique among the castles of the Loire in that it is built right over a river.

It is not as vast as many of the others but it is quite perfect; purely feminine in style, it has been variously called 'the maiden most perfect; the Lady of Light; the White Lady of Touraine', and she deserves every compliment.

The land first belonged to the seigneur of Chenonceaux, who owned the fortified mill built on the banks of the Cher, which incidentally joins the Loire just twelve miles downstream. This mill had a very valuable feudal right attached to it, for all the corn had to be ground there. This affluence caused seigneur Jean Marques to decide around A.D. 1432 to rebuild the derelict fortress near by.

After that things did not go so well, for either the mill ceased to be so profitable or Jean Marques was over-extravagant; so much so that he was obliged to start selling some of the surrounding land. Thus arose a situation so bizarre that it belongs more to the realms of novels than of fact.

A certain Thomas Bohier, who was not of the nobility himself but had married well into the rich Semblançay family, the financiers, obviously became deeply attached to and desirous of possessing Chenonceaux, or rather, as you will see, the site, so each time that Marques was obliged to sell a piece of surrounding land, Bohier quietly purchased it, but always through the agency of nominees.

Came the day when the former owner found he could not get to his mill and home without passing over the other man's land. At this moment, Thomas Bohier claimed that he had in fact also bought the buildings, which started a twenty-year long legal battle, at the end of which Marques admitted defeat.

Almost as soon as the property changed hands and the demolition squads were in Bohier went abroad in the service of Francois I (whose Receiver-General of Finances he was—did all the money go to the King?) and his wife Katherine started to direct the rebuilding.

Chenonceaux, apart from its other complimentary names, is also called 'The Château of Six Women.'

They were:

Katherine Bohier

Diane de Poitiers. She had time to build there a splendid garden, still called the 'Jardin de Diane de Poitiers'.

Catherine de' Medici. Some accounts say that she had wanted Chenonceaux long before it had been given to 'That old hag Diane de Poitiers, Duchesse de Valentinois'.

It is said that after her husband, Henri II, had crossed lances at the tournament with Montgomery and lay dying of his wound, Catherine's eagerness to drive Diane from the court was so great that, no sooner had her husband fallen (though he did not actually die for some days), she sent word to the mistress 'who sat weeping alone'—to quit the court at once.

Diane paid no heed to the command. She simply asked the messenger, 'Is the King yet dead?'

'No, Madame,' he is supposed to have replied, 'but his wound is mortal; he cannot live the day.'

'Tell the Queen then', replied Diane, 'that her reign is not yet come; that I am mistress over her and the kingdom as long as the King breathes the breath of life.'

Poor messenger.

Catherine, once installed, built a garden on the opposite side of the château to that of her rival and she also commissioned Philippe Delorme to build the immense gallery on its five arches over the Cher. It is this which is the most striking part of the whole place.

Louise of Lorraine. Also called Louise de Vaudémont, this simple, unaffected and supremely faithful wife of Henri III had the most tragic life of all the Six Women of Chenonceaux.

She had been left the château—and its debts—by Catherine, and she was passing the heat of the summer there when she heard of her unpleasant husband's being knifed by the monk Jacques Clément. Henri III in fact was not killed outright and thought he might live, so he wrote Louise a charming letter asking her to wait for him at Chenonceaux, or words to that effect. The Queen seems to have taken him at his word, and so, for eleven long years taking on the white mourning (La Dame Blanche they called her), she prayed, sewed and finally died.

Louise left no garden by the Cher and did no building, but you can still see her bedroom with the bed, the velvet curtains, everything draped in black velour.

Madame Dupin. When Louise died in 1601, she left the property to her niece, Françoise of Lorraine, the Duchess of Mercoeur; it then passed rapidly, deteriorating all the while, through several royal hands until it was bought in 1733 by the Chief Tax Collector, Monsieur Dupin.

This rich gentleman had a wife who was a bit of a social climber. How she liked to have literary lions to her receptions! And how she succeeded! The food was good, and so they all gathered around—Fontenelle, Buffon, Montesquieu, Marivaux, the mighty Voltaire and Jean-Jacques Rousseau. This last had been the tutor to the only son of the Dupins and had been happier at the château than anywhere else in his life. So happy indeed that in his *Confessions* he wrote:

'We amused ourselves greatly in this fine spot; the living was of the best and I became as fat as a monk.'

Madame Pelouze. In 1864 the chemist Théophile Pelouze purchased the place and his wife 'made the restoration of the château her life's work', says the *Guide Michelin*. She put the building back to the way it was in the time of Thomas Bohier. It is also not generally known that the young Debussy spent several months there with other chamber musicians engaged to play for the family during the summer vacation.

Then it was bought by a wealthy Cuban called Terry, and now it is owned by the Menier family, to whom the visitor must be sincerely grateful for the vast sums they have spent to keep the place in splendid repair.

Chenonceaux has more enthusiasts for its beauty among architects and those who ought to know than any other castle of the Loire. Vivian Rowe considers it to be 'the most beautiful domestic building of any age, that I have ever seen'. The operative word, I suppose, is 'domestic'.

I like to feel that the helpful and tasteful patronage of rich industrialists, through pills, rum and chocolate in this case, can save our great buildings for future generations.

13

VOUVRAY WINES

THERE IS NO DOUBT THAT certain wines and wine districts suffer in popularity from the fact that their names are veritable tongue-twisters. Wachauer Schluck (white Austrian), Pedro Ximénez (sweet brown Sherry), Vosne-Romanée (fine red Burgundy), Quincy (white French), Yquem (sweet, great white Sauternes), and Monbazillac (very sweet, white Dordogne) are all bad enough, but the worst is Echezeaux, which sounds like someone in an advanced stage of inebriation trying to say *is that so?* The sales of this fine red Burgundy have indubitably been hit by such a tongue-twister.

Then there are wine places where sales have soared because their names have captured popular imagination. The great example here is Liebfraumilch, which derives its name from a very small vineyard of only twenty-five acres, in the northern part of the district of Worms, where there is the famous Liebfrauenkirche, or church of Our Lady.

To order a bottle of the milk of Our Lady must have been tremendous fun for the hordes of English tourists who visited the Rhine in the middle of the nineteenth century. By 1875 wine writer James Denman was able to write: 'The attraction evidently lies in the name which with one exception, that of the renowned Johannisberger, is commercially speaking the most popular among the copious Rhine nomenclature.'

In other words, even then the demand far outstripped the tiny amount of true Liebfraumilch that could be produced from the vineyard that begat it all, and by 1910 the German Chamber of Commerce of Worms allowed Liebfraumilch legally to become a fancy name, which meant that it could virtually come from anywhere along the Rhine.

Another wine which may go this way is Vouvray. An attractive little town of three thousand inhabitants lying on a busy main thoroughfare; near a large tourist centre, Tours; easy to pronounce; a semi-sweet flavour easy to understand; what more can a wine need to get it on its feet and away to a flying start?

Although the region is small and only a million gallons of real Vouvray are produced each year, there are no less than a thousand small growers, most of whom sell their wine to the large producers of Vouvray Mousseux, which wine is made to sparkle in the *méthode champenoise* way.

You can get a wine to fizz by two means. One is by pumping in bubbles under pressure which results in a very gassy drink that goes rapidly flat once the bottle has been broached, while the other is a costly process under which the bubbles get smaller as the years pass and the wine gets finer.

This latter 'champagne way' consists of getting the wine to sparkle in bottle in the spring after the vintage. The bottles are later placed upside down in *pupitres*, or specially constructed racks, and over the course of some three months the sediment is shaken down on to the cork. When the shaking or *remuage* (a highly skilled job) is finished the bottles are stacked vertically, cork downwards, for anything from six months to a comfortable six years to mature. When the wine is needed for shipment the old cork with all the lees on it is extracted and a new cork is put in.

You may wonder what happens to the lees which have settled on the first cork. The bottle goes upside down into a refrigerating unit which freezes just one inch of the neck. The *agrafe*, or metal clip, which holds in the first cork, is then undone and the cork blows out, together with a pellet of ice in which is embedded the lees. This is replaced by a *dosage* of wine (sweetened or not according to the tastes of the importing country) and the new cork is inserted. As I have said, with the passing of years the bubbles seem to break up and with Champagne especially an extraordinarily pleasant bouquet becomes noticeable.

Vouvray wines themselves (which by the way are usually classed as wines of the Touraine) have been upgraded by the relevant French ministry for nearly sixty years to Appellation Contrôlée status, though records of the quality of the vintages go very much further back, to 1811 in fact, which with 1834 as an equal was the best year of the century. Other fine years of the nineteenth century were 1848, 1865, 1871, 1887, 1893 and 1900. Really bad years were 1890, 1892, 1894, 1896 and (into the twentieth century) 1910 as everywhere.*

I said that a large proportion of Vouvray wine went to the manufacturers, a situation which produces exceptionally severe shortages in

* But 1910 for Vintage Port was superb.

The Château of Loches

Twelfth century cellars in which some of the great wines of the Coteaux du Layon are kept

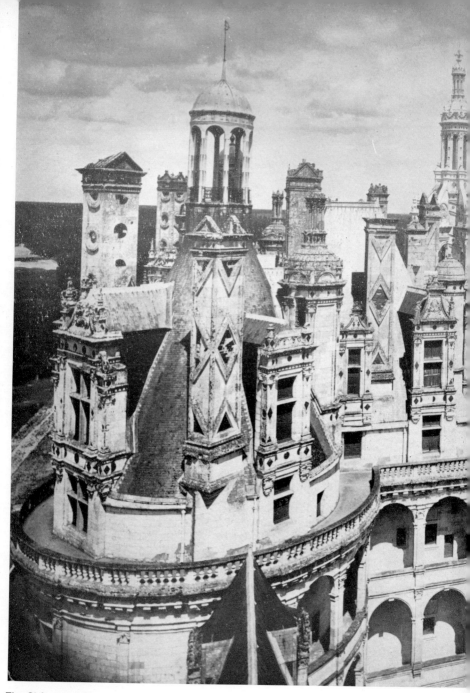

The Château of Chambord,
showing the fantastic
detail of the roof

The Château of Chinon
overlooking the beautiful
promenade alongside the
River Vienne

The Tour d'Evrault,
Fontevrault. Inside is the
famous kitchen

fine small harvest years. The reason has some connection with La Fontaine's delightful fable of the grasshopper and the ants.

Just as in the Cognac and Champagne areas so in the Vouvray districts there is a tradition that certain growers always supply certain producers. Nothing is legally binding; all is done on trust, but if the big sparkling wine makers relieve the peasant of his thin plentiful years they naturally expect their whack of the fine short-fall vintages, and the over-greedy grower listens to the moral of the fable. I had an example of this some years ago when the wines were fine but in terribly short supply. Tastings were laid on for me galore, but when it came to buying it was no go.

All Vouvray is white, no red is made, and the most important communes are Rochecorbon, Vernou, Noizay, Chançay, Reugny, Ste-Radegonde, and of course Vouvray, where in the two valleys of Coquette and Chartier are the following best growths:

Les Bois Turmaux	Clos le Mont
Clos de Cosson	Les Barguins
Marigny	Clos Bel Air
Clos de Nouis	Le Gaimont
La Chatterie	Clos le Paradis
Le Haut Lieu	L'Epinay
Clos Dubois	Le Gué d'Amant
Clos Vaufuget	Clos Auberdière

At Rochecorbon some vineyards are:

Clos Martin	Clos de la Chasse Royale
Clos des Bâtonnières	Clos des Amuseries
Clos du Pouvray	Clos de la Tainerie

The first place Tim Hanbury and I got to in this area was Noizay, where we saw a neat café and a 'New Wine of the Season' sign hanging outside. That got us immediately inside; but not before noticing that we had drawn up beside a large, new, immaculate English van which, however, of its business told us nothing.

I have seen some funny things in my travels but this, I think, beat the lot. We opened the door to find a counter on the left completely deserted, but packed solid with dirty glasses, and judging by the colour and smell I was certain it was in fact the new wine that was being advertised.

In the far corner was a very wiry group of Frenchmen all in a high state of inebriety and all trying to put what looked like half-crowns into a gleaming brand-new one-armed bandit.

Seated round this gambling machine were three very English-looking Englishmen, by no means sober but nothing like as tight as were the locals. As we approached the crowd, one of the Englishmen espied us and called out in the most atrocious French:

'Would you like to have a go?' And offered us some discs.

I thought we looked pretty English ourselves even if alcohol was blurring the vision, and was just about to say something to that effect when it dawned on me that once they knew that we were from Great Britain they would dry up like clams.

I jabbed Hanbury in the arm, which caused him to reply in the affirmative in French, and I stretched out my hands too. To my amazement the discs which looked like half-crowns were real ones. We were both handed ten each and got into the noisy queue.

The machine, when we got near enough to see its detail, turned out to be a marvel of engineering and it looked like a 'precision job' throughout. There were four revolving drums instead of three and, instead of a lever handle, they were sent spinning round by pressing an electrically operated knob.

'I wonder they don't make off with the half-crowns', I whispered to Hanbury, 'or is it that they don't know they are real coins?'

'I think they are playing for drinks', he replied and nodded to the far corner.

And indeed that was it and as I watched Hanbury playing I was able to piece together something of the motifs behind this weird operation. In the first place the utmost secrecy was the order of the day and the name of the makers had been covered over with a strip of black adhesive tape. Then, too, the pictures on the metal drums had all been covered over with paper and on this were very rough amateurish sketches of various drinks, interspersed sometimes with the name of the café, sometimes that of the proprietor, and occasionally Noizay, the village we were in, and Vouvray.

The improvised paper was not all that thick and I asked Hanbury to have a good look and see what was underneath. He thereupon paused before inserting his next half-crown and stared closely at the face of the machine. This caused one of the three Englishmen who was seated to say to his colleagues in an alarmed way:

'Hey! what is that fellow peering at?'

'Oh, he is just curious', said the other.

'Oh, I thought the —— might be English.'

Hanbury went on peering as if he had not understood, whereupon the Englishman said in his atrocious French:

'Hurry up there, you are keeping the others waiting.'

'Sorry', said Hanbury in reasonable French and put in another coin and pressed the knob. The revolving wheels spun round as usual but when they came to rest, a loud electric bell started clanging and a great pile of half-crowns clattered into the container. A second later the bell clanged again and the voice of the Englishman with the terrible French called out in French:

'Attention please! Attention please! Attention please! I have a special announcement to make.'

Then the bell clanged again.

All this got eventual silence in the café.

Then the voice continued.

'You are at the Café du Coin, and the lucky winner has won a coupon towards winning a car in the Dupont Competition. Please get it from the side of the machine.'

The bell clanged again. Then a huge red arrow appeared, lit up on the face of the machine and pointed to the left. We both looked and there waiting was a gay ticket with the name of the café at the top and details of a competition following it.

Suddenly Hanbury gripped my arm and piloted me away from the crowd.

'I think I have got it!' he said. 'This is a try-out for a sort of advertising kind of fruit machine, which is hired out to pubs on a rental basis by some large firm. I'm sure now that under the paper on the drums there were pictures of packets of cornflakes and tins of soup.'

At that moment one of the three Englishmen came up to us and, in French, asked Hanbury for the half-crowns which he had just won.

'I'm terribly sorry', he said . . . in English.

The game was up so I added:

'Can we keep the ticket as a souvenir?'

The man snatched it from me.

'You royal ——'s', he said. We left as fast as we could.

★

Noizay, which we then left, is the beginning of the Route du Vin of Vouvray and is so proud of its beautiful houses and of its wine that it has for a slogan: 'Once you stop, you will return'.

Here, as for the whole of this little region, the grape variety for the white wines, of course, is the Pineau de la Loire. There are several sub-divisions but for precocity and regularity of production it is the 'red-stalked, round-leafed' Pineau which is the most important.

A further description of it is that 'The bunches are fairly large, and in the form of a feathered pyramid. The grapes are close together, oblong, medium large, and the skin gets thinner towards the end of the season, while at the same time the colour deepens to a golden yellow. The colour darkens when the grape is attacked by the fungus which starts off the "noble rot".'

This *pourriture noble*, as it is officially called, is a condition which causes the skins to shrivel and the moisture to evaporate, so that when the grape is pressed a very sweet luscious wine is the result.

The grape I have just described is one of the hardest to manage in the Loire, and for the most successful results cultivation very close to the ground is the best. Moreover, the pruning of the Pineau needs exceptional skill for the work cannot be in any way standardized, and the vigour of the American-grafted root-stock, the general condition of the vine and the nature of the soil all have to be taken into account when it is being done in the spring.

Vouvray vineyards are harvested as late as any in northern Europe, and it is interesting to note that just as with many wine-growing areas in Germany, records concerning the proclamation of the vintage (which have been preserved in the Vouvray Town Hall) go back to 1800. These records show that, during the first quarter of the last century, the first day of the grape harvest took place as early as 30 September, the latest commencing day was 18 November, while the average was 26 October.

And today things are much the same for, in spite of a slightly earlier average harvest date through the breeding of grape varieties which mature sooner, the vintage in average years still starts around the end of October.

The next place on the wine route is Vernou, which has six vineyards of considerable repute: Clos du Pouvray, Clos de Vaux, Clos Cosson, Clos du Fougeray, Clos de Chaillemont and Clos des Thierrières. Here the limestone caves used both as dwellings and as vast cellars are very much in evidence, of which more in a moment.

On leaving Vernou I saw for the first time in my life a mobile or travelling distillery, such as is more common in the brandy-making district of Condom in Armagnac.

We both goggled at it. There on a lay-by in a tiny lane with a little stream running at right angles was the most Rowland Emmett of machines you could imagine. The spirit that comes from this conversion is called *eau de vie de marc*, which word means residual husks, or grout. In other words, when the vintage is well and truly over and the grape skins have been pressed a second or even a third time to give a little wine (illegal to sell) for the workmen, water is added, the mixture is re-fermented and from this a spirit is distilled.

The actual cost of making such a rot gut (compared with Cognac) is infinitesimal and between the two wars when the excise duty was so much less than now, a first rate Marc de Bourgogne could be so much cheaper than a Cognac that if one was counting costs it was worth looking for. It was always less good but not necessarily twenty-five per cent less good. Now that the duty has pushed the total cost up so high, the percentage saving on a bottle is so fractional it is nonsensical to choose the cheaper spirit.

Vouvray is the last place on the vine circuit and, before you get to the main road, it is charming. Here, as all around in this region, are habitable dwellings cut into the rock, as they have been for generations and certainly since Balzac wrote about them in 1831.

There are often three stages of houses dug out of the rock and united by dangerous steps cut equally out of the same rock. The smoke from the chimneys can be seen wafting into the air, and small farmers can be seen labouring in perpendicular fields, while the hammers of the cask-makers ring with a clanging sound in aerial caves. Nowhere along the whole course of the Loire is the panorama so richly rewarding as in this spot along the Touraine.

Thus Honoré de B. and I agree.

*

Leaving the Vouvrillions to their wine we arrive some eight miles farther on, and crossing the mighty Loire, at the town of Tours, where the bustling Tourangeaux are so well supplied with little restaurants that I always imagine them permanently guzzling.

Tours is the home of that delightful and eccentric 'soldier-saint' of the end of the fourth century A.D., St Martin, Bishop of Tours. He gets the epithet of 'soldier-saint' from a curious incident which occurred when he was only fifteen years old at Amiens. His father (the family came from Sabaria, a town in Pannonia) was a pagan; an officer in the army who had risen from the ranks. Martin was forced into the army against his will and, says one biographer, 'For some years though not formally a Christian lived more like a monk than a soldier'.

One winter's day during a terrible frost, at the gates of the city (of Amiens), the young soldier saw a poor shivering beggar asking for alms from passersby. Nobody was heeding his plight, and so Martin, drawing his sword, cut his cloak in two pieces, gave one-half to the beggar and kept the other half for himself. Actually those who have sneered at this act and have wondered why he did not give up his whole cloak do not realize that the gesture was far more generous than it appeared; the Roman soldier was strictly forbidden to part with his clothing; hence the division.

Our word 'chapel' derives almost certainly from this incident, for the oratory where the alleged cloak of St Martin was preserved was called in Latin *cappella*, a Latin diminutive of *cappa* a cloak, and in Old French *chapele*.

As the years passed, Martin became more and more attracted to Christianity and more and more fractious in the army. The authorities would surely have called him a 'bloody-minded' soldier and, indeed, he was probably one of the first 'conscientious objectors' in history.

Things came to a head when with his comrades he was ordered to appear before Caesar, not to get a reprimand but actually to be given a war bounty for service rendered in repulsing a barbarian invasion of Gaul. Martin told Caesar what he could do with his money and promptly got put into prison.

In spite of his eccentricities and in spite of the fact that his tatterdemalion clothing and unkempt hair caused neighbouring bishops to consider him unfit for the appointment, in A.D. 371 the people of Tours demanded Martin for their bishop. He was, however, unwilling to accept the office so a trick was devised to call him to the city to visit a sick person, whither he was then conveyed to the local church.

St Martin died in 397 and, forthwith, his tomb became the object of a pilgrimage. In 470 a splendid basilica was erected around his sarcophagus. It was destroyed by the Normans but reconstructed magnificently in the eleventh century, and part of it can still be seen.

The early Tourangeaux must have been exceptionally forceful in their religious demands; first they get St Martin to become their bishop by a trick and then, in 573, they go down to Clermont-Ferrand to seek and bring back a bishop who later becomes the great Gregory of Tours, known to future generations as the Father of French History. Under Gregory, and sustained by efficient propaganda, Tours becomes the Lourdes of the Middle Ages and pilgrims who flock to the 'soldier saint's' tomb receive a potted history of the town, together with accounts of miraculous cures. The abbey and the town, needless to say, both become very rich.

Today, Tours is a pleasant city with no single great monument to visit but with a host of minor architectural attractions, which makes it all the more enjoyable to wander round, especially in the old town, which is a little enclave of exceptional charm.

One most unusual aspect of this Ville de Luxe, as writer Francis Miltoun called it in 1907, has been its population fluctuation. There are today only some ten per cent more inhabitants than there were in the fifteenth century, when the number of souls stood at nearly eighty thousand; and yet, in the first years of the nineteenth century, the number had fallen to twenty thousand.

The reason for the high figure of Louis XI's time was that this King, finding that the workers of Lyons were (so stupidly) not too enthusiastic about the manufacture of gold cloth, moved the industry up to Tours, thus creating employment there for some twenty-five thousand textile workers.

But, after we have looked in at the Hôtel de l'Univers so beloved by Henry James, and after we have seen the Cathedral of St Gatien, with its marvellous stained-glass, we always come back to that grand old eccentric, St Martin. 'Oh mihi, beate Martine' began the Latin invocation to the saint, which it is said got corrupted to 'All my eye and Betty Martin'. The occasional spell of warm weather experienced around Martinmas on 11 November and called the *Été de Saint Martin* has nothing to do with his cloak and sword act at Amiens, but with a struggle for his body after he had died at Candes-St-Martin. Both the people of Tours and of Poitou wanted his body, but the Tourangeaux finally won when the monks of Marmoutier stole his body, and as they hastily bore it back, spring flowers began to blossom along the route.

★

The most famous food of Tours and indeed one which has spread to the whole of the Loire Valley is Rillettes de Tours and its close cousin, Rillons.

The latter is hardly worthy of a second's serious gastronomic consideration. According to one French dictionary it is 'Fat obtained by melting the left-over parts of pork or goose'. Translated from French to English the word becomes 'greaves', for which the *Oxford English Dictionary* has this entry: 'The fibrous matter of skin found in animal fat which forms a sediment on melting and is pressed into cakes to serve as meat for dogs or hogs; fish bait; the refuse of tallow; cracklings.'

The word, we are told, was originally a term of the whale fisheries.

Rillettes are a very different matter, being a spiced, pounded combination of raw shredded pork and lard. As a first course and washed down by a glass of chilled Vouvray, I know of nothing more delicious. None the less, I have hardly ever eaten *rillettes*, though, when my fellow-travellers note that I am abstaining and ask the reason why, I become embarrassed. I love good food far too dearly to tell a lie and pretend they are not good, but I am loth to say the real reason and so, perhaps, spoil someone else's luncheon.

Anyway my fear of eating roast pork is probably over-exaggerated because of the hygiene precautions taken, though they were not less than half a century ago when a serious disease, Trichinosis, caused by the introduction of trichinae (a tiny worm) into the alimentary canal, and the migration of their larvae into the muscular tissue, was prevalent and now is still a possibility.

14

LOCHES AND FONTEVRAULT

A<small>T THIS POINT IT WAS NECESSARY FOR</small> T<small>IM</small> H<small>ANBURY</small> to go back to London to give a hand with my small wine business. A large consignment of Chinon and Baumard's Rochefort had arrived all at once, due to a hold-up at the docks, and it all had to be labelled, capsuled and cased to go out as part of one of my Dazzling Dozens.

In spite of the incredible efficiency of modern labelling machines, there are still a number of wine firms who like to do their labelling by hand; like me they think it looks nicer and anyway the machines are totally uneconomical when only a small number of bottles have to be dealt with.

It is a pretty simple operation. A person who is deft with his hands can label at a fast speed and also have the glass around the label shining, whereas a clumsy man will go at a quarter of the speed and leave most of the glue on the bottle.

Wine labels, incidentally, are not pre-gummed, but all the equipment you need is a smooth, three-foot-square board, a brush and a solution of paste. You put your labels print-side downwards on the board, slap the paste on with your paper-hanger's brush, peel the labels off from a corner, put onto the bottle, press it firmly on and also wipe away the remaining paste with a clean cloth. This is the hardest part because often the label tends to slither about on the glass.

Alternatively you can use a tiny all-brass hand-labelling machine, which is only some ten inches long and half that height, and consists of two rollers, a handle and a well for the paste. You put the paste in the well, the label on a roller, give half a turn and the label is covered with paste. It is not all that much quicker, but you don't get the paste on the front of the label, as with labelling from the board.

Hand-capsuling nowadays is very easy; there is a thin foil capsule which you pop on top of the neck and then tighten with a rubber-ringed contraption.

So Hanbury went back to give a hand and another trainee came out; a youngster whom I had only seen very briefly through his father's contacting one of my best friends in the trade; a practice which I detest.

For some fifteen years now I have taken on annual trainees. I should like to think that I have helped them as well as they have helped me, but all the successful ones have been those who made the original applications off their own bat. If only fond parents would not write applying for jobs on behalf of their sons.

Grandmothers are worse; many a letter have I had:

Dear Mr. Layton, [and they have never met me]
My charming grandson is at . . . [name of a smart public school] and I
think he might like to join the wine trade. He cannot himself answer as he
is just now skiing at St. Moritz, but perhaps he could come and see you
when he returns if he has time. We have always dealt with . . . [name of a
West End 'By Appointment' firm] and I expect you know . . .

Everything about this letter makes my blood boil and especially the last sentence. If they deal with X, the West End firm, why in the name of Bacchus don't they write and get their grandson placed there instead of with me? There is only one type of letter that infuriates me more; when women (usually) write: 'Mrs Chuffington-Wylde would like to etc., etc.' Letters like this, even if they are from potential customers, go straight into the W.P.B.

But one always sees youths whose parents write in for them because, being soft-hearted, you don't see why the stupidity of the fathers should be visited upon the next generation. The extraordinary thing is that, when they come for an interview, they always turn out to be the type that you feel would need mollycoddling.

But this young man had seemed quite amiable when I gave him a brief interview. He was to come on different terms to Hanbury for I suggested paying his expenses and fare and said that in return I expected him to make himself generally useful and, especially, to help me with notes on the way.

Anyway, we rendezvous-ed successfully at Tours and set off for the medieval city of Loches which I had heard so much about.

After a few minutes the young man without a word of by-your-leave turned on the heater.

'My feet get damp', he said.

I wondered.

Travel guides have been wont to compare Loches with the sensational town of Carcassonne in the very south of France. True, they are both medieval cities of great historic interest, but there all other resemblances end. The Carcassonne that is a tourist draw the world over is completely on its own, outside a ghastly modern town of the same name with a population of nearly forty thousand inhabitants. The old *cité* was beautifully restored in the twenties and a walk around the ancient battlements is an exhilarating experience. But, apart from the St Nazaire basilica, there are few buildings to study, and you will do well to rest your feet at the sumptuous Hôtel de la Cité, the only one built within the old precincts. Here, if you spend the night in one of the sixty rooms, you can have trout braised in Blanquette de Limoux, the local Vin Mousseux made around the town of that name, followed by Chartreuse de Perdrix, and then the next morning see the sun rising over the Pyrences. And dull would you be if you could forget a sight so touching in its majesty, to misquote Wordsworth.

With Loches, instead of approaching the place from a barren plain, you first see it after crossing a great forest of splendid trees. And instead of seeing an almost complete circle of fortress walls it is impossible at Loches to tell where the old town ends and the new one begins; indeed, some new streets are inside the old fortifications, while others are outside it.

Loches was the Luccae of the Romans; of this we can be certain and it has been said that no town in central France has seen more history than has Loches, and this may well be true. In the fifth century a monastery was founded here by St Ours, which ultimately gave its name to the collegiate church which exists today. In the sixth century a fortress was built. This in 742 was sacked by Pepin, and later Charles the Bald made it the headquarters of his government.

The medieval importance of Loches came about when it was found to be the perfect fortress guarding the ancient Roman highway from the Blois area to southern Aquitaine.

Then it became a royal residence, to which Charles VII often returned with his lovely mistress Agnès Sorel, called the Dame de Beauté, not only because of her looks but because the infatuated Charles gave her a property, Beauté-sur-Mer near Paris. One does not think of them being punsters in the Middle Ages, but there is another one perpetrated in connection with Agnès, which concerns her tomb on the ground floor of the King's palace itself. It is an exquisite piece of work by an unknown sculptor of the fifteenth century, and there she is stretched out full length on her death-bed. But at the feet of Agnès are two lambs—*agneaux*.

She was only a country girl and as the daughter of a minor noble she could not marry Charles VII. None the less she bore him children, was utterly devoted to him, and gave him, so history tells us, the wisest of advice.

But what a spendthrift she was! Though her extravagance was legendary, the money she got through did not all go on personal luxuries and the old church at Loches benefited greatly from her gifts. They were not entirely without thought for the future, since being terribly aware of her own sin, she wanted to be certain that when she died (which she did at only twenty-eight) her mortal remains would be assured of a resting-place in a spot she had been so fond of. But she knew that the clergy disliked so notorious a sinner, so she bribed them. When Agnès died, the dean and chapter did nothing about her tomb; but, when Charles VII died, they suddenly became very pious and suggested to Louis XI that her remains be removed from so holy a spot. They obviously hoped that by this scandalous piece of toadying they would please the King. However, they had overlooked that they were dealing with one of the meanest men who ever wore a crown.

'Agreed,' Louis is reported to have said, 'but also let me have the treasures she showered upon you.'

Agnès stayed where she was.

I have briefly mentioned the collegiate church of St Ours, but I feel it deserves a more detailed description for, when a devout Frenchman describes a holy place as 'not so much like an elephant but rather like a camel with two humps', it surely cannot be anything but curious. Described also as 'bizarre, but not unchurchly', this freakish but beautiful Romanesque building has between two magnificent towers a couple of eight-sided pyramids, which form the vaults of the nave. Unique in the world of church building, it was the inspiration of one Thomas Pactius, a former prior of the church. The other thing to see here is the remains of a little Roman altar, now used as a font.

The dungeons are generally considered to be the most important of the many sights of this medieval city and if you like macabre magnificence they are certainly impressive, especially when given the *son et lumière* treatment.

In these gruesome cells, to give only one example of the details of hundreds of incarcerations, did Louis XII confine the Duke of Milan, Ludovico il Moro. For eight years he was in captivity, but on the day of his release the sun shone too brightly, and the poor man died on the spot.

Loches is not a place for wandering around by car. We did it on foot, at least I did; the young man got weary and went back to wait in the car.

Eventually I got back to the parking square, getting lost twice en route, for, in spite of its only six thousand inhabitants, Loches is one of those places which reminds you of the Hampton Court maze. Incidentally, Loches had a population of nearly four thousand in the Middle Ages, which goes to show . . .

I found the young man in the car at the driver's seat with the engine on and fairly racing.

'What in the name of thunder is happening?' I said.

'It is the only way to get the heater going,' replied the youngster; 'my feet were damp.'

*

The next stop should by rights have been Azay-le-Rideau but as I had an appointment with a grower to the south of Chinon, I decided to do Fontevrault, which was much nearer.

I confess to having been quite excited about going to this vast abbey, not only because of its historical connections with our island history, not only because of its curious kitchen, not only because it had always been governed by an abbess, but because I had heard it was still a prison with an inmate population of eight hundred to a thousand.

Fontevrault was begun in the eleventh century by a Breton priest named Robert d'Arbrissel, an exceptionally devout man who outlined his ideas to the world and gathered together a community of monks. What was unique, and I suppose was startlingly modern at the time, was that he started both a monastery and a nunnery around the abbey, and that when he died (in 1117) he handed over the reins, not to the abbot, but to the abbess Pétronille de Craon-Chemillé, who acquitted herself so well that thereafter for six centuries it was always an abbess who was in charge (the greatest, called the *reine des abbesses*, was

Gabrielle de Mortmart, sister of Madame de Montespan), and this, it has been claimed, is unique in Christendom.

From the start Fontevrault was a tremendous success story. Popular from its inception with the counts of Anjou, it gained an immense reputation when the family became Kings of England, and one of the most emotional sights an Englishman can see anywhere abroad is here, where under one roof there lie the tombs of Henry II of England, his wife Eleanor of Aquitaine (the divorced wife of Louis VII of France) and their son Richard Cœur de Lion. The fourth tomb is that of Isabella of Angoulême, wife of the pathetic King John Lackland.

In the very first years of the nineteenth century the abbey, ransacked by the Huguenots and then by the Revolutionaries, was turned into a state prison, and so it had remained until recently.

Judging by what one can discover by reading between the lines of successive guide-books, it has taken just sixty years for Fontevrault to be won back as a tourist's delight by the Beaux Arts Department from that of the French Prison Commissioners. In 1905 precious little was to be visited. As Francis Miltoun says:

'The nave of the church of the old abbey has been cut in two, and a part is now used as a dormitory of the prison, but the choir, the transepts and the towers remain to illustrate the simple and beautiful style of their age.'

He also refers to the most important sight (of which more in a few paragraphs) of Fontevrault. 'This curious, bizarre, kilnlike pyramid known as the Tour d'Evrault is like the church of St Ours at Loches one of those edifices which defy architectural classification. The architect played with his art when he let all the light in this curious *tour* enter by the roof. . . . It is a most surprising effect, but one that is wholly lost today since the Tour d'Evrault has been turned into the kitchen for the *maison de détention* of which it forms a part.'

In view, too, of the fact that the 'chapter house is now used by the director of the prison' it would seem that the visitor of those days saw very little.

Writing in almost the same year, Frederick Lees in his *A Summer In Touraine* records his disappointment at seeing so little. He records the fact that the Tour d'Evrault, 'a building of three stories; the first an octagon, the second a square, the third an octagon, and these surmounted by a sort of pyramidal structure', was for a long time supposed to have been not a kitchen but a chapel, and incidentally when you have seen the building you will not think this so silly after all.

Lees continues:

'Two other churches both of the twelfth century were connected with the Abbey of Fontevrault; the church of St Lazarus and the church of St Benedict. But the prison regulations forbid either these or a curious building of the same period which we chanced to get a glimpse of on leaving, to be visited.'

And eleven years ago Vivian Rowe in his book on the Loire said: 'It is as you approach the heavy entrance door that you get your first surprise. It is a gaoler who opens it for you. As he takes you round there is a great noise of clattering keys and the opening and closing of iron doors and gates.'

No château or prison for that matter could possibly have been more 'open' than was Fontevrault when we visited it that early afternoon. We drove into a courtyard which seemed about as large as Trafalgar Square deserted save for a half a dozen or so children romping about with an enormous red plastic ball. But of course it was lunchtime.

The children came up to gape at us and the little car, so I took the opportunity to ask them where the caretaker was and a door was pointed out to me on the far side of the courtyard. I dashed over there, for by now time was really pressing, and knocked on the door, which was immediately opened by a youngish man very much in déshabillé: braces, open-neck shirt and carpet slippers.

'Are you the caretaker and is it from you I buy tickets to see the old kitchens?' I said.

'Correct', said the man.

I explained my mission with as much fluency and urgency as I could, but frankly did not expect anything very startling to happen during a French lunch-hour.

But the fact that I was writing a book had an electrical effect. The man said he was only too pleased to help me; but to my bewilderment promptly turned his back on us and walked back into the house.

'Hi!' I said, 'where are you going? I thought you were going to show me around now.'

'I am', he replied disappearing through the door. 'But I want to change into uniform', and the door slammed.

'Damn and blast', I said to 'Damp Feet', as I walked back to the car, 'I suppose that means he has gone back to finish his . . .'

I heard the click of the door opening.

'Here I am, sir. All present and correct.' He had completely changed, and he had donned a smart hat too. The fastest quick-change I have ever seen.

The tickets were as quickly purchased and to show the guide my appreciation, apart from tipping him, I bought a little excellently produced guide to the place which gives a clue as to how the famous Romanesque kitchen got the name of Evrault's Tower.

'Legend has it that a robber of that name had his lair there (hence the name Fontevrault). He used to light a beacon after dark to lure on travellers benighted in the forest and strip them of their belongings. . . . This is the only intact specimen of a Romanesque kitchen.'

This last is almost certainly not true.

The cathedral at Pamplona is not visited much, probably because it has one of the most hideous façades that the eye can be affronted by. But adjoining it is a cloister where, incidentally, is a lovely old fountain at which pilgrims on their way to Santiago used to refresh themselves.

Off the cloister is a sixteenth-century refectory, one of the most graceful and beautiful rooms I have ever seen, and here the pilgrims were fed. Leading from this room is a many-flued kitchen, very similar indeed to that at Fontevrault.

But to return to Fontevrault: close to this beautiful architectural freak lie the great cloisters, whose role was to draw all walks of life towards the spiritual centre of gravity—the church.

By far the most unusual thing in this haven of peace are the flag-stones of the cloister walk, for here are chiselled the various arms of those royal Bourbon abbesses, who succeeded one another at the head of the abbey.

Yes, as the guide said, this was 'the Queen of all the Abbeys of France'.

15

THE RED WINES OF THE LOIRE

THE CRAFT OF THE SOMMELIER OR WINE BUTLER is dying out apace in France. Recently I dined at one of the best hotels in Lisieux. After giving the food part of my order I asked for a bottle of really good wine from a little girl waitress. When she brought the bottle and started to cope with the cork extractor in a very bad way, I protested angrily.

'I had better fetch the *sommelier* then', she said.

But 'he' turned out to be a girl who, I am sure, was not yet eighteen.

Still, this is nothing to the ignorance that will eventually be shown by French *sommeliers* in the future, for the Ministry of Education there has for the past few years been reducing the time allocated to oenological studies in the curriculum of the state-run Hotel School. The worst blow was struck in 1964 when wine classes were declared to be non-obligatory for boys and out of the question for girls, who were required to take shorthand and typing instead.

This has all been done as part of a tremendous anti-alcoholism drive which is taking place in French official quarters, and teachers, it appears, strongly object to seeing youth taking minute sips of wine for sampling purposes at eleven o'clock in the morning.

These restrictions have naturally made the editorial board of France's premier wine journal, *Revue du Vin de France*, very angry.

They attack the Ministry of Education as a body addicted to 'puerile thinking, the outcome of a timid mind daunted by dreams of the perfect world which would bore us all so quickly'. These words are not my translation; they come from a special English edition.

It will be argued by the English anti-snobbery-about-wine clique that too much buttling at a restaurant puts people off, and no one would agree more fervently than I; but that applies to nine-tenths of the wine we drink annually and not to that one-tenth of great wine which deserves all the care we can possibly give it.

There are of course some wines which are a bit of an enigma; can you fairly call them great or not? In this category come the wines of Chinon and St-Nicolas-de-Bourgueil.

The wines of Chinon and St-Nicolas-de-Bourgueil are made with that little blue-black, world-famous Médoc grape, the Cabernet Franc, which if you saw it in a greengrocer's shop you wouldn't give twopence for.

But how did this small variety, which must not be confused with the Cabernet Sauvignon, come to travel up to Touraine?

There are many theories.

An attractive one concerns Cardinal Richelieu. According to the Cartulary, or place where the registers are kept, of the Château de Chenonceaux, it is known that the Abbot Breton, Richelieu's financial superintendent, ordered in 1631 several thousand vine plants from Guyenne for a vineyard which the Cardinal wanted to create in his Duchy. This variety of the Abbot Breton's replaced the Pinot Noir.

But those who object to this theory are quick to point out that the word 'Breton' for the red wines of Touraine was in use long before the seventeenth century, Rabelais having already used it.

Actually it seems likely that the 'Breton' (i.e. Cabernet Franc) variety got established along the Loire in A.D. 1152, at the time of the political union between Anjou and Aquitaine. Now in the Middle Ages wine was known as *breton* because it was the Bretons who principally drank it and it was transported to them by barges sailing along the Loire. This, then, may well be the story of the 'good breton wine which does not grow in Brittany'.

The Cabernet Franc, as grown in Bourgueil and Chinon, is pruned in a special way, known as the *'taille longue'*. A long pruned branch of last year's wood is the fruit-bearing limb and is called the *vinée*. A further spur is left by the *vigneron* to grow on as next year's *vinée* and is known as the *poussier*. The annual yield from each vine is reasonably steady; the bunches are elongated, the grapes small and round, with a pleasant flavour. As this vine is not susceptible to rot, the fruit can be harvested late—end of September or early October—when the grapes are at full maturity.

This would appear to have been the time of the vintage for four centuries. If you check this by studying your Rabelais you should remember one interesting thing; namely that this author was writing some thirty years before 1582, when the ten days' difference between the civil and astronomical calendars was brought once and for all into line.

On my wine labels there is printed, under the word Chinon, 'the slightly scented wine that Rabelais loved', which short phrase calls for more comment than you would imagine.

Rabelais first; Chinon was first and foremost his very own beloved town but he was not, as recent researches show, born there but at La Devinière in the commune of Seuilly, a few miles to the south. There is a Rabelais museum here with a fascinating collection of documents illustrating his life and times.

It is known that he spent his youth in Chinon, where his father was the local lawyer; and happy times for him they clearly were.

> Chinon, trois fois Chinon;
> Petite ville, grand renom,
> Assise sur pierre ancienne,
> Au haut le bois, au pied la Vienne,

> Chinon, three cheers for Chinon.
> Little town but with the big reputation,
> Situated above ancient ruins,
> Above are the woods, below flows the Vienne.

I wonder if there is more in that 'little town, big reputation' remark than meets the eye, and whether it has anything to do with wine?

All over Europe there are places known for certain products, where the larger town has scooped the reputation, leaving the poor little village some few miles away, where it is really made, unknown and out in the cold. Tarragona, for example, is known for that ghastly, port-type red, sweet wine but it is actually all made around Reus, in the hinterland. And in many smaller wine-growing places in France this is especially noticeable; so much so that a little jingle has grown up, of which one of many examples is:

> Arbois le renom,
> Pupillin le bon.

Arbois being the attractive Jura town of three thousand souls, whereas

Pupillin is a hamlet a few miles away where they think, and I agree, they make better wines.

Now Rabelais' father, as well as being a lawyer, was also the owner of a small amount of property in the region, which he let out on a particularly French system called *métairie* (it is still popular), and which consisted of sharing out the crops. It is known that the land contained several vineyards and what is more likely than that when he went round to collect his dues, he should have taken his young son with him and that young Rabelais should have become fond of wine? And perhaps there was some other district more famous for wine than Chinon which was hogging the limelight.

François Rabelais never returned to Chinon again after those early childhood days. But they have put a plaque at 15 Rue de la Lampoire in the town, for they are now pretty certain that that is where he lived.

We know very little of this jovial man and are not even certain of the date of his birth, which some authorities have put as early as 1483 and others as late as 1494. As he was a younger son there was not enough money to set him up as a gentleman and so he went into the Church. First the Benedictines educated him, then two other religious bodies, and finally he took holy orders and became a Franciscan. To this order he took an instant and violent dislike, so much so that he even went to appeal to the Pope for a dispensation to change and become a Benedictine. This order pleased him no better, so off he went to Montpellier to study medicine. There, he seems to have had a rumbustious time but to have also taken a degree and made a good reputation for himself.

As the years passed he must have discovered that the monastic life was not for him, and around 1536 he took himself off to Rome and persuaded Pope Paul III to release him from his monastic vows and also to grant him a licence to practise medicine. When he did practise we do not know; probably soon after he published his *Fourth Book of Pantagruel* in 1547.

Rabelais loved wine and is continually making his characters talk about it.

Thus Pantagruel says, 'Je sçai où est Chinon et la cave paincte aussi; j'y ai bu maints verres de vin bon et frais—'. 'I know where good Chinon wine is and the painted cellars as well; I have drunk many a glass of it there excellent and cool.'

Which brings us to a nice point; should real Chinon be drunk at room temperature as are clarets and Burgundies, or should they come under the white-wine banner and be drunk at cellar temperature?

By the beard of Bacchus! I think you can do both. An extremely simple experiment will prove my case; pour half of a full bottle of Chinon or Bourgueil into a decanter and let it get nice and warm, and put the other half left in the bottle in the refrigerator. Try the latter with your first course of smoked trout, *hors d'œuvre variés* or melon, and then have the *chambré* Chinon with your roast chicken or grilled veal chop. You will be surprised how both taste appropriate to the relevant course.

Which brings us to the 'slightly scented' part of my wine label.

'What scent?' you will ask.

Surprisingly, sometimes violets, sometimes raspberries (that is official), but more often a bouquet blend of both; that is my own personal experience.

Actually, it is the wine of Bourgueil which has the raspberry smell and that of Chinon the violet.

Bourgueil is a little townlet of three thousand inhabitants, prosperous, affluent-looking, attractive, and neat and, although not given a mention in the *Guide Michelin*, has a small hotel, the Etoile, where I have eaten in the spacious restaurant as well as anywhere in France.

> In this good-looking place of Touraine,
> Yes! Here does Madame Charpentier reign;
> Nor will I keep you longer in the dark,
> The Star Hotel has made its mark;
> In winter it is so warm and cosy,
> In summer there is the garden with many a scented posy.

If you think this jingle bad, I can tell you it is not quite so bad as the French from which I have translated it; but the food is really good.

Bourgueil has also a tourist cellar drinking place, of which the inhabitants and the local growers are inordinately proud. They call it:

THE CURIOUS TOURISTIC CELLAR OF THE DIVINE BOTTLE

Where while savouring them, the most 'gulpworthy' of red wines will afford you true delight.

Here in miniature and by the aid of splendid illuminated photos, you can without leaving your seat 'do' our 'wine route' which is so famous—

St-Patrice, Restigné, Benais, Saint-Nicolas-de-Bourgueil, Chouzé-sur-Loire, La Chapelle-sur-Loire and Bourgueil.

Then in another gallery you will find the Wine Museum.

Here is every sort of vinous material under the sun, a collection of old presses, an unusual oval oak vat and the pièce de résistance of the collection, an immense and majestic sixteenth-century wooden press which in 1893 performed the remarkable feat of pressing 43 casks of wine in one single go.

Your visit ended, it only remains for you to taste our wine of Bourgueil.

Noble visitors, be doubly welcome; you are here in a sanctuary devoted to our 'Breton' wine. It is so good and so pleasant that you will be bound to agree with our slogan:

DRINK BOURGUEIL, WALK STRAIGHT AND KEEP YOUR EYE IN

P.S. And only three miles away is France's premier nuclear power station E.D.F.I.

The establishment is open from April to October and the entrance charge is one franc and twenty centimes.

*

For those who may contemplate a tasting tour of the region, I must stress that the difference between Chinon and Bourgueil is very marginal, and that two very distinguished French writers on wine state that only those who are of the country can detect the difference.

By and large, it may be Bourgueil wines keep a little longer than do those of Chinon whereas the latter have, perhaps, more finesse.

With very rare exceptions, four to five years is sufficient for them to reach full maturity in cask and then in bottle and, as I understand it, once a wine reaches full maturity it starts slowly, and in proportion to the time it has taken to mature, to go downhill.

There are a number of communes which form the Côte de Bourgueil, the most important of which I give hereunder, together with a selection of some vineyards or *clos*.

BOURGUEIL

Vineyards

Les Geslets	Les Galluches
Le Grand Gibet	Les Perrières
La Salpèterie	L'Ormeau du Maure
La Mutte Pesque	Les Pins

SAINT-NICOLAS-DE-BOURGUEIL

(Generally considered to make the finest wine)

Vineyards

Le Fondis	La Contrie
Clos du Guiet	Clos de la Torillière
Clos de L'Epaisse	La Martellière

RESTIGNE

Vineyards

Les Brosses	Grands Champs
Les Vinaudières	Clos de la Plâterie

BENAIS

Vineyards

Les Raguenières	Les Beauvais

INGRANDES DE TOURAINE

Vineyards

Les Blottières	Les Evois
Clos des Baresmes	

The communes mentioned above are in three areas. A valley; a plain some five miles wide; and the hillside, which is of clay or *tuffeau* soil, and it is here that are the best wines.

*

The Chinon vineyards cover both sides of the River Vienne. The communes with some vineyards and *clos* are:

CHINON

Vineyards

L'Olive	Les Aubuis
Clos du Palis	Château de la Guille
Clos de L'Echo	Clos Testu
Clos du Pin	Château Noiré
Les Quinquenets	Les Closeaux

BEAUMONT-EN-VERON

Vineyards

Les Picasses
Les Grésilles
Clos Pineaux

La Roche-Honneur
Le Perré-Souris

LIGRE

Vineyards

Le Paradis
La Hégronnière
Le Vau Breton

Sassay
Saute-aux-Loups

CRAVANT LES COTEAUX

Vineyards

Pallu
Les Galluches
Les Coutoures

La Grésille
Les Cornuelles
La Semellerie

LA ROCHE CLERMAULT

Vineyards

Les Aiguillons
Les Rosettes

Les Bessardières
La Butte à Néron

PANZOULT

Vineyards

Roncé
La Galippe

Clos Quéron
Le Pressoir

In the Middle Ages, Ligré used to be very well known and highly thought of, but what wine they then made was white. Rabelais thought a lot of it and called it a wine of 'taffetas'.

What exact flavour did he mean to convey to his readers by the use of this word? In England, apart from meaning the material, it came to mean figuratively dainty or fastidious, and this seems to have stood for a sort of sweetmeat. Did taffeta in sixteenth-century France mean a dainty light wine or a rich velvety one? Or did the incomparable Rabelais just invent it on the spur of the moment? He was a veritable James Joyce of a writer.

Practically no white Ligré (made with the Chenin Blanc grape) is produced today.

16

CHINON AND SAUMUR

ONE OF THE MANY EXCELLENT PUBLICITY IDEAS of France's various wine regions is to have wine glasses with supposedly traditional shapes. This is seen at its best along the Loire where there is first the Anjou-Saumur glass on a longish stem with the bowl having straight sides, or with an almost imperceptible curve inwards. It is the most dignified of the three. Second is the Vouvray glass, usually on a somewhat longer stem, but here the sides of the bowl curve out rather steeply at the top, rather like those long tumblers used for lager which tend, if you do not watch it, to throw most of the contents over your face; a stupid design and quite useless, above all, from the point of view of the retention of the bouquet.

Third is the Chinon glass, really rather elegant if a bit gimmicky. The bowl looks like a round dumpy tulip but with a tiny, sudden outward curve at the top. You can buy them very cheaply in the many glass shops in Chinon and for good measure engraved on the bowl is a picture of Rabelais with that floppy hat he is always wearing with the motto:

> Beuvez tousjours,
> Ne mourrais jamais
> (Always drinking,
> Never dying)*

Which brings us to the point: just how much did this famous son of Chinon know and care about wine?

In the first place, we must remember that the fifth and last book of Gargantua and Pantagruel is to obtain the verdict of the bottle; the securing of which was the whole purpose of this long voyage. And indeed the whole of the last thirty pages of the work are devoted to

* This is in fact a quotation from Rabelais' 'Drunkard's Conversation'.

wine and wine-drinking. From then on it is drinking, drinking and carousing all the way and there is an amusing chapter called 'How the water of the fountain tasted of different wines according to the imagination of the drinkers'.

Here Friar John talks of a Graves wine gay and sparkling and asks his lady how it is made. This is interesting; in the past two hundred years Bordeaux Graves has been full and rather flabby and certainly not as described by Rabelais. But recently they have been experimenting in Bordeaux with making a white wine just as is here described.

HOW WE APPROACHED THE TEMPLE OF THE BOTTLE BY AN UNDERGROUND WAY AND WHY CHINON IS THE FINEST CITY IN THE WORLD

Then we went underground, through a plaster-lined vault, roughly painted at the entrance with a daub of women and satyrs around an old laughing Silenus on his ass.

'This entrance reminds me of the painted cellar in the first city in the world', said I to Pantagruel. 'There are paintings like these there and they are just as fresh as these.'

'Where is the first city you refer to?' asked Pantagruel, 'and which city can it be?'

'Chinon—or Carnon', said I, 'in the Touraine.'

'But how can it be the first city in the world? Where did you find that written?'

'I find it in the Holy Writ', I replied, 'that Cain was the first builder of cities. Now it is very probable that he called the first one of all after his own name Cainon as all other founders and restorers of cities have done since his time, in imitation of him.'*

But where did Rabelais get this information?

Or did he start it?

There are still many eighteenth- and nineteenth-century historical books where the theory is, but only half-heartedly, advanced that Cain, fleeing from paternal malediction, took refuge in Chinon and that at first it was called Caynon.

But a more likely explanation is that it was called Caino, from the Celtic word meaning an excavation, which came to be adopted because

---

* From J. M. Cohen's wonderful translation in the Penguin Classics of over a quarter of a million words.

of the subterranean quarries from which the stone was drawn for the building of the town.

Chinon was certainly a pre-Roman town and under the Romans was *Castrum-Caino*. Then under Clovis it became one of the principal fortified towns of the kingdom. Then it passed to the house of Blois and on to the counts of Anjou.

Here in 1189 Henry II, King of England, died and it is believed, though by no means certain, that this was where Richard Cœur de Lion also died; at any rate he is buried, as I have said, with his father at Fontevrault nearby.

In 1361, the town witnessed a tragedy so unpleasant that it must have sent shivers of fear down the spines of its inhabitants for generations; on an island in the River Vienne there were burned alive a hundred and sixty Jews, accused of having poisoned the wells in the district.

An historic town even then, but its greatest day was yet to come, for it was at the castle of Chinon that Charles VII met the Maid of Orleans. Here I think occurred one of the most moving events of all history. Bernard Shaw has dramatized it marvellously, but it was all true and came out at St Joan's trial and then again at her canonization.

Dressed like a man in black tunic, long boots and spurs, the Maid arrived outside Chinon at Ste-Catherine-de-Fierbois. Here she sent a letter to Charles saying that she had come four hundred miles to see him and adding amongst other things that she was sure she could pick him out of a crowd. It was an odd remark to make and foreshadowed the famous episode in the castle.

At first the lazy Dauphin could not be bothered even to see her but after two long days he gathered up enough energy at least to send a couple of messengers to her with the request that she should say what exactly her mission was. Haughty Joan of Arc sent them packing; she would only deal with Charles personally. The messengers went away but returned shortly to say that they were the personal emissaries of the Dauphin, and that she could tell them everything with complete confidence. Joan capitulated. 'Heaven has sent me with a double mission', she said; 'to lead Charles to Rheims Cathedral for anointing as King but first to raise the siege of Orleans.'

Still they shilly-shallied and it was another forty-eight hours before she was invited to the castle.

Though there is little left today, we know what the Great Hall into which Joan was ushered was like. It was nearly twenty-five yards long, with at one end an enormous hooded fireplace and along both sides windows, some of which looked out on to the courtyard while others, the smaller ones, gave a view of town and river below.

What Joan had said in her letter had obviously put thoughts into the Dauphin's mind; it could hardly have done otherwise.

'Look!' he may well have said to some young knights in his train. 'This crazy girl thinks she can recognize me by a sort of second sight. Let us change costumes. You ascend my throne. I will mingle with the crowd.'

But Joan was not to be bamboozled. Indignantly telling the courtier not to make fun of her, she turned away from the throne, mingled with the crowd and went unfalteringly to the man (and *how* unworthy he was!) for whom she was looking.

'Gentle Dauphin! They call me Joan the Maid. I am sent by the King of Heaven to see that you shall be crowned and anointed in the city of Rheims, and that you shall be Lieutenant of the King of Heaven, who is the King of France.'

But Charles still kept up the pretence and said, 'It is not I, Joan. There [pointing to the throne] is the King.'

Whereupon the Maid said, 'In God's name, noble prince, it is you and none other.'

There was still doubt in everyone's mind about Joan's abilities. She was sent to Poitiers to be thoroughly tested by the doctors of law and other learned men of the day, for there was general agreement that either she was a sorceress or was inspired by Heaven.

What impressed her judges was her obvious piety, her inner confidence and above all her witty, forceful answers. Also, it must be cynically admitted there was Orleans; the people there were starving, and every remedy must be tried, even to employing a youthful country bumpkin of a virgin as a war-leader. Joan won and she returned to Chinon to be equipped for the fray; it was her last visit there.

Seventy years later Chinon castle and town, sleeping tranquilly after that tornado of a Pucelle, was to know another fine moment of glory.

This was in 1498. In that year Charles VIII died, and obligingly made it a condition of allowing a distant cousin (later known as Louis XII) to come to the throne that he marry his wife and widow, Queen Anne of Brittany. Louis XII was nothing loth; he obviously found her attractive, especially as his own poor wife, Jeanne of France, was a hunchback with oxalgia (a disease of the hip joint) and had an unusually simian appearance. But to get a divorce it was necessary to consult the Pope and obtain his permission. The result was probably a foregone conclusion but, none the less, the rules had to be observed and, when it was known that no less a person than the Pope's famous legate, Cesare Borgia, was on his way with the answer, it behoved the King to make a show. Chinon castle was the venue and it was well and truly *en fête*. Rare tapestries were hung up to hide the grey walls, the countryside was plundered for delicacies, and thousands of torches were lit every evening. Then the Pope's answer was given; poor Jeanne of France was to be Queen no longer. After this Chinon lapsed into obscurity.

The Château de Chinon, as it is called, is worth a special visit, for it differs greatly from the usual Loire châteaux and is more like a castle as we know it in England. In fact, it is three castles and each, so far as the remains are concerned, is distinct and separate.

The oldest is the Château de St Georges and is an enlargement by Henry Plantagenet of a still older fortress. Then comes the Château du Milieu, which dates from the eleventh, twelfth and thirteenth centuries, and was built on the ruins of the *castrum romanum*, of which vestiges are still visible. The third part is the *Grand Logis*, of which very little is left, and it was here that all the great events took place. Near by in a field is the famous echo, so perfect that it is mentioned in most guide-books.

*

One now descends into Chinon town proper. I think I have spent more odd nights here than in any other town on the Loire and still the place enchants. In the first place the town stretches along the River Vienne, which is here so wide and swiftly flowing that many a bet has been lost by people asserting it is the Loire. The result is an attractive promenade which in the summer months is as gay as a Paris boulevard. In the Rue Voltaire the street is so narrow that the old wood-beamed houses appear to be at almost handshake distance from one side to the other.

But it is the Grand Carroi (literally the Great Crossroads) which is the quintessence of Chinon. Of this spot the *Michelin Guide* speaks with restrained enthusiasm.

This was the town's centre of activity in the Middle Ages. Here is a unique assemblage of ancient houses and a perfect back view of what the town was like in former times. One has the feeling that nothing has changed since those days when Richard Coeur de Lion, wounded at the siege of Chalus-en-Limousin, came here to die in one of the houses (now a bakery).

It is easy, too, for us to picture Joan of Arc arriving at the hostelry of the Grand Carroi. In order to descend from her horse, she placed her feet on the curb stone of the well at the corner of the Rue Voltaire.

★

On the way from Chinon to Saumur we come to the tiny hamlet, at the confluence of the rivers Loire and Vienne, of Candes-St-Martin where, as I have said, St Martin of Tours died. Here above the cell in which the saint died they erected in the twelfth and thirteenth centuries one of the most beautiful and interesting churches in France. Its size in such a small place is astonishing.

Candes is a Gallic name meaning confluent, which disappointed me because I thought I had made a tremendous philological discovery.

Apart from the church, which, by the way, was fortified in the fifteenth century and thus is doubly interesting, this hamlet is also famous for its dried fruit industry. If they had a dried fruit industry in the area, I thought, then surely more than likely they had a crystallized one as well. Candied fruits! First the place was called St Martin; then the industry became so important that the inhabitants felt it would be good for trade to call it Candy-St-Martin! just as they have done at Puligny-Montrachet, Gevrey-Chambertin, Nuits-St-Georges and Vosne-Romanée.

But alas! a search in the dictionary showed me that the word came from the Persian *Qand*, the crystallized juice of the sugar cane.

★

Saumur the sophisticated! Its shopping centre, its huge open air cafés, its all-imposing castle, its unique horse museum, its cavalry school, its sparkling wine but, above all, its striking on-the-Loireness.

The derivation of the name is curious—Salmurium or Salvus Murus ('safety walls' or 'walls of our salvation')—and this because of the fortifications which were put round the town by the monk Absalom after it had been pillaged in the tenth century.

In the seventeenth century the population was seven thousand more than the twenty-two thousand today. It was the bloodshed caused by the revocation of the Edict of Nantes which cut down the inhabitants so drastically. This, of course, has meant that this town is far more

155

spacious than Nantes or Angers, and great houses dating from centuries ago line Saumur's principal streets which, somehow, pleasantly give the appearance of being oversized for the population.

Saumur—called formerly the Rome of the Huguenots—houses one of the most famous cavalry schools of Western Europe and it has been there for just over two hundred years. It was in 1763 that the élite regiment of Carabineers belonging to 'Monsieur' (brother of the French King) were sent there to garrison the town; this was the foundation of the cavalry school.

To see them in action your best time to go is at the end of July, when the school's famous Equestrian and Motorized *Carrousels* take place and their famous Black Squadron thrills an immense crowd.

The château of Saumur can probably be seen by the motorist from farther away than any other along the Loire and, for this reason and the way it stands out so starkly against the skyline, it is the best remembered. It also figures in one of the most colourful and famous miniatures in the world, 'Les Tres Riches Heures du Duc de Berry', whose vineyard scene is described on page 164.

There has been many a fortress built upon this Tom Thumb mountain in the town, but the one we see at present was built by Louis I of Anjou, who left the finishing of it to his son, Louis II, at the end of the fourteenth century.

The whole of the inside was completely recast in the fifteenth century and then, in the sixteenth, it was fortified by that great soldier, *littérateur* and reformer, Duplessis-Mornay, whom the Catholics of the period called 'The Pope of the Huguenots'. It was he who founded in the town a Protestant Academy, which soon gave Saumur a great reputation.

Inside the château are two museums, one with a fine collection of Renaissance works of art and the other claimed to be unique in the world—but this is probably exaggerated—the Museum of the Horse, though it has, indeed, a fine collection of saddles, bits, stirrups and engravings.

*

And now we come to the most famous thing of all: Saumur's sparkling wine.

As usual it isn't made in the town at all, but at two twin villages bordering the Loire, St-Hilaire and St-Florent.

Here is the home of one of the fifteen Appellation Contrôlée sparkling wines in France. These are:

South	West (Loire)
Gaillac Mousseux	Anjou Mousseux
Clairette de Die	Montlouis Mousseux
Bordeaux Mousseux	Vouvray Mousseux
Blanquette de Limoux	Touraine Mousseux
	Saumur Mousseux

Central	East
Bourgogne Mousseux	Arbois Mousseux
St-Péray Mousseux	Seyssel Mousseux
	L'Etoile Mousseux
	Côte du Jura Mousseux

Then there is one VDQS* sparkling wine, which goes by the name either of Mousseux de Savoie or Vin de Savoie Mousseux.

Of all these above, the highest minimum permitted alcoholic strength is Bordeaux, 11°, followed by Burgundy, Gaillac, Anjou, Saumur and Touraine, 10½° and oddly enough Seyssel, 8½°, which is so low that I at first wondered if it was a misprint, which it was not.

In the above categories Appellation Contrôlée Rosé can come from Anjou, Arbois, Burgundy, Jura and Touraine.

The only red Appellation Contrôlée wines are Arbois, Burgundy and Touraine.

And now, in order to try and explain about Saumur sparkling wines, you must hear a dissertation on the actual word sparkling, on Champagne and on the French anti-wine-fraud laws!

*

Recently I asked a wine trainee, who said he had got an 'A' level in French, to translate into French for one of my French shippers a letter that I had lazily written in English.

It thanked them *inter alia* for the safe arrival of fifty cases of sparkling wine and the young man had called them *vins étincelants*.

It should have been *mousseux*; frothy or mossy. The Germans actually call their sparkling wines *schaum*; foaming, frothy.

* Vin Délimité de Qualité Supérieure. Not quite as good as A.C. wines.

Who then was the genius who first translated *mousseux* into English as sparkling? Was he a dictionary compiler with a touch of the poet about him? What a public relations man!

I said that there were fifteen top-flight sparkling wine districts but with Champagne, which is legally a sparkling wine, there are sixteen.

Champagne, from the labelling point of view, is unique in France, being the only wine (notwithstanding Yquem, Margaux, Montrachet and Richebourg) which need not have the two famous words Appellation Contrôlée printed upon the label.

This is merely one rule amongst a jungle of them designed by the French Government to see that when Champagne is Champagne everyone knows about it and gets the best and when it is not, they are aware of that too.

The only vines permitted in the Champagne area vineyards are the Pinot Noir, Pinot Meunier, Arbanne, Chardonnay and Petit Meslier and the permitted growing is mostly in the Department of the Marne.

One may not transport the grapes, however fine, out of the region; Champagne must be made in the old province of Champagne. And, as well as on the label and the wrapper, cases of Champagne destined for delivery by road and rail must have this magic word thereon very clearly.*

As a protection against substitution at the table, the word Champagne has to be branded on the cork 'on the side where it touches the neck of the bottle'. An immense tome of 800 pages, which I have in my possession and which sets out to explain and comment on the French Code du Vin, says: 'this is very useful as a means of telling if a *vin mousseux* has been substituted and clients of certain 'dancings', buffet bars and 'boîtes de nuit' would do well if they had the inspiration to examine the cork when the bottle was opened.'

With respect to non-sparkling or still Champagne, which would-be connoisseurs affected to like and wanted us wine merchants to get for them in the 'thirties, the position is that the available supplies are negligible and that the law makers, by the very phraseology that must be used on the label, are obviously out to discourage sales.

The term 'champagne nature' may no longer be used; nor may any derivative of the word 'Champagne' be employed. The only phrase

---

* This regulation was relaxed at the worst period of the last war on account of the number of thefts which were taking place.

permitted for such a still wine is 'Wine originating from the Champagne Viticultural Area'.

★

When we come to wines, other than Champagne, that fizz, foam or sparkle after the cork has been drawn there are four categories:

1. *Vins Mousseux* (a). Made the Champagne way, i.e. the fermentation has taken place naturally inside the bottle.
2. *Vins Mousseux* (b). Wines made *mousseux* by a fermentation in enormous glass-lined tanks, after which the wine under pressure goes straight into the *expédition* bottle.
3. *Vins Gazéfiés.* When the effervescence is obtained by the addition of carbonic acid.
4. *Pétillants.* This word I have found the hardest to translate in all the Bacchic vocabulary. *Pétiller* means the crackling of a fire, the sparkling of eyes and the effervescence of a wine. But to the English wine merchant, a *vin pétillant* means one where the sparkle is rather weak in an ordinary bottle and with an ordinary (i.e. not usually wired down) cork.

I will deal with (2) and (3) first, and I think these points will be useful for my readers who will be wining and dining in France. If a wine has been made in what is termed *Cuves Closes* (sealed vats), then the words *produit en cuve close* must be placed under the words *Vin Mousseux,* in such a way that the typography shall all be the same and the words must be at least one-third the size of the largest letters on the label.

As for gassy wines, the words *Vin Mousseux Gazéfié* must be very apparent. They must be of the same typographical appearance and at least half as large as the largest type on the label.

Dealing with Vin Mousseux in category (1a) the regulations here are devised to ensure that while the wine is made in the Champagne way it is not passed off as Champagne. To this end the words *méthode champenoise* (which words are not obligatory) if they are to appear are not permitted to be in a type larger than half the largest size on the label; note the difference here.

Also, the phrases *crémant* and *grand crémant* are forbidden since, being synonymous in Champagne with *méthode champenoise,* they would cause confusion.

Finally, the most anti-deception regulation of all; it is not permitted to put a wired Champagne-type cork on to a bottle of *pétillant* wine.

*

Sparkling Saumur then is made like Champagne, and all other similar French wines, in the following way:

1. The grapes are picked and crushed. They ferment.
2. The wine goes into the cask till spring, when it is racked off its lees.
3. The wine is blended to produce a standard quality. A little pure cane sugar, dissolved in old wine, is mixed into the blend. This is then bottled, the Champagne type cork being secured by an *agrafe*, a strong metal clip.

   Fermentation now starts in each bottle and is completed in about three months. A sediment forms along the underside of the bottles.
4. The bottles go into a *pupitre*, a board with holes in it. When they start they are nearly horizontal, but each day a *remueur* or shaker (a specialized job) shakes the sediment downwards and on to the bottle cork, till the bottles are almost vertical but upside down. A skilled *remueur* can deal with 40,000 bottles a day.
5. Still in this position the wine goes, *sur pointes*, to be stored in the cool, underground cellars to mature.
6. After the maturing period comes the most interesting operation of all, the *dégorgement* or the extraction of the old cork.
7. The wine comes up from the cellars again to have its gold- or silver-coloured lead foil put round the cork; a label is affixed and away it goes. The total time that can elapse, starting from operation one, will be from five to seven years, according to the quality of the vintage.

*

At St-Hilaire you can visit a tiny Romanesque twelfth and thirteenth century church; at St-Florent there is another one and also the traces of a Benedictine abbey. But the big tourist draw here are the huge caves carved out of the limestone rocks where hundreds and hundreds of workmen deal with millions and millions of bottles.

Whether it is jealousy or not I do not know, but one hears along the Loire that the Saumur wine community has somewhat rested upon its laurels since the First World War so far as the quality of still table wines goes. In the first place in the mid-nineteenth-century phylloxera crisis the Saumurois were very badly hit because it appears that this little plant louse is harder to eradicate on calcareous soil than on any other. But the real reason probably is that growers and producers alike knew they were on to a good thing when they saw one and put all their energies into the sparkling side of the trade.

Here is a list of some communes of the Coteaux de Saumur district which make white and rosé (the white has by far the better reputation) wines, with a selection of vineyards.

PARNAY

Beniquet	Château de Parnay
Le Gory	Clos de la Folie
Les Cormiers	La Pierre Blanche
Les Roches	Clos des Murs

DAMPIERRE

La Corde	Le Veau
Ferronières	St Vincent

TURQUANT

Clos de la Bâte

BIZAY

Clos de Treilles

BREZE

Bois-Duchesne	Champ-Picard
Clos des Carmes	Château Fouquet

MONTSOREAU

Saut du Loup	Clos des Pères
Les Rôtissants	Les Vignolles

SOUZAY-CHAMPIGNY

Les Bournais	Champ-Chardon
Clos de la Croix	

VARRAINS   SAIX   CHACE

To the south of Saumur is a small region, situated around the town of Montreuil-Bellay (2,500 inhabitants). Here is a region which is the buffer between the Saumur and Anjou districts and wines are to be found at Fontevrault, Méron, Les Ulmes, Bagneux, Courchamps, Distré, Brossay, Cizay-la-Madeleine, Vaudelnay, Antoigné and St-Just-sur-Dive.

★

To end the chapter just let us take a quick look at Cunault, for here is a splendid church, all that is left of a rich Benedictine priory which was suppressed in 1715.

It is the interior here that you want to go for, where among other things are the famous sculptures (over two hundred of them) on the capitals of the pillars. There are also traces of medieval paintings. Rarest of all is the fifteenth-century wooden statue of Ste Catherine.

Most guide-books give you half an hour to 'do' the church in. My advice is to take two hours, and not to forget your binoculars with which to look at the sculptures.

17

ANJOU WINES
AND THE FAMOUS
WINE FAIR

THE EARLIEST REFERENCE TO THE WINES OF ANJOU comes
from that narrow-minded aristocratic literary pedant Sidonius Apol-
linaris, who was born in Lugdunum (Lyons) around A.D. 430. 'Not far
from Brittany', he wrote, 'is a town built on a rock rich in the gifts of
Ceres and Bacchus. It is the city of Angers.'

Some years later, the historian Gregory of Tours confirmed this;
'throughout the Anjou country the vineyards are very extensive. They
constitute one of the riches of the country.'

As to the question which fascinates historians . . . which grapes were
used in the Anjou district first? . . . there is an impressive mass of records
dating from the eleventh and twelfth centuries, showing that the vineyards produced both red and white grapes. Most of the records bear
the signature of the Plantagenets but the Kings of France vied with their
'English cousins' in their admiration for the local wines. Philippe-
Auguste and his successors had much of their table wine brought from
the Saumur region.

And like monarchs in other parts of wine-growing Europe, the
edicts of both these lines of kings show how meticulous they were in
seeing that they had a sufficiency of good wine. Vassals were obliged to
devote a certain part of their land to their cultivation, and the quality
was maintained in part by the strictest enforcement of the *droit du ban*;
this meant that only the King could decide when the vintage should
start.

The Anjou district is particularly rich in works of art in which
husbandry in connection with the vine is portrayed. For example,
there is the charming scene on one of the capitals of the former bishop's
palace in Angers; here is depicted a grape-harvest scene with peasants,
wearing high pointed hats, emptying baskets of grapes into a vat. A

half-naked boy up to his waist in must tramples the fruit and also playfully tries to hit off the hat of one of the harvesters. But the most vinous scene of all in the Middle Ages is in the lovely and famous miniature 'Les Très Riches Heures du Duc de Berri' which I specially chose for the jacket of this book. It shows the marvellous château of Saumur, all resplendently white in its newness and rising amid vineyards under a harmonious, pastel-blue Anjou sky. Among the peasants is one who stands upright to taste a grape. Beside him is a two-wheel wine cart in which are two open wooden containers full to the brim with grapes.

Incidentally, pruning, at the time this picture was painted, may well have been something quite new, for history—or legend?—tells us that at the time of St Martin of Tours the monks of Marmoutier stumbled upon this beneficial treatment and that it was taught them by their asses. One day a number of these beasts escaped from their field and started to nibble off the young vine shoots in a neighbouring plot. The monks thought that they had lost the next crop but to their amazement discovered that the following year their bunches of grapes were the best of the locality.

Another proof of the importance of wine in the region is the number of the local sayings that are connected with it.

Étoiles filantes en septembre,
Tonneaux débordants en novembre.
If you see shooting stars in September,
You will have your casks full in November.

S'il fait beau à la St Vincent,
Il y a du vin dans le sarment.
If on St Vincent's Day (22 January) the weather is fine,
Then the vine shoots will be full of excellent wine.

À la St Martin (11 November)
Bonhomme, bouche ton vin.

This last one is a little more technical; the young wine goes into casks to continue fermenting and in the turbulent process a certain amount is lost. It is essential, of course, that the wine be right up to the bung; otherwise the oxygen would attack the wine and eventually ruin it. *Boucher* means to fill up to the bung, called *l'ouillage*, or, if there is a corresponding English verb, the ullaging.

Quand il tonne en avril,
Vigneron, prépare ton baril.
When it thunders in April,
The vigneron should get ready his casks.

*

The wines of Anjou are divided into five districts but, before enumerating them, let us look at the River Loire and its tributaries in this area, for it is here joined by quite a fripple* of them.

Before we get to Saumur the Loire has running into it, from the south, the Vienne. At Saumur it is joined by the River Thouet, which has been running parallel to it for quite a way. The town of Angers is not on the Loire but just to the north of it. At the town three rivers all flowing down from the north meet: La Mayenne, La Sarthe and Le Loir. After Angers they all become the River Maine, which then flows into the Loire. Then from the south, first the Aubance flows into the river and finally, most important of them all from the wine point of view, the Layon.

Having got the fluvial picture out of the way, we can turn to those wine districts which properly and officially are those of Anjou.

To put you in the picture, I cannot do better than to translate what Pierre Roze, president of the wine-growers' union of Anjou, has to say about the wines of Anjou in his laconic way.

Under the denomination 'wines of Anjou' are grouped different wines. We find white, rosé and red. The white are made from one only variety, called the Pineau de la Loire or the Chenin Blanc.

The rosé wines come from the vinification of red grapes, of appointed species (Groslot, Gamay and Cot). White and rosé wines are light, dry or half dry. They sell principally over the bars in the large industrial towns. They also make excellent carafe wine.

In addition, the wines of Anjou are divided into five Appellations of Origin which are sub-regional and are reserved for wines of fine [haute] quality, and which in the main are made along those rivers which have given to them their denominations.

They are in alphabetical order:

Coteaux de l'Aubance	*Coteaux du Loir*
Coteaux du Layon	*Coteaux de Saumur*
Coteaux de la Loire	

* Not used since the middle of the eighteenth century . . . 'a large number of small rivers meeting a larger one all within a short distance, probably a combination of frequency and ripple.'

The white wines of the Coteaux de l'Aubance are elegant and fruity. Those of the Coteaux de la Loire and of le Loir are firm and yet full of a delicate savour. These are wines both dry and half dry, exactly like those of the Coteaux de Saumur which have a very special [particulier] character, acquired through being grown on a subsoil of chalk.

The white wines of the Coteaux du Layon have a gentler fullness [ampleur]. They are more fleshily fat [charnu], and it is in this region that one seeks, for preference, the great sweet wines.

Furthermore, all over the Anjou wine region, but especially in the Aubance, the Layon and around Saumur, there is produced the Cabernet Rosé which is yearly gaining in reputation, thanks to its elegance and especially characteristic fruitiness.

Lastly, around the town of Saumur, there exists a quite small region making red Cabernet wines, which have a very characteristic flavour which gives them a steady sale among a restricted number of connoisseurs.

Saumur is also known for its production of Vins Mousseux of which the quality is allied [s'apparente] to Champagne, thanks to the similarity of the soil of the two districts.

The range of choice of these Anjou wines is such that there is a wine to please everyone. That is why the reputation of our wines continues to grow.

For a more detailed look at the qualities of these Anjou wines, let us take a look at

A SUMMARY OF THE CONTROLLED APPELLATIONS OF THE ANJOU VINEYARDS

Category	Controlled Appellation	Minimum Degree	Grape Variety
REDS	Anjou		Gamay
	Anjou-Saumur		Cabernet-Franc
	Saumur-Champigny	10° alcohol acquis (see below)	
ROSÉS	Cabernet d'Anjou		Cabernet-Sauvignon
	Cabernet de Saumur		
	Rosé d'Anjou	9° alcohol acquis	
	Anjou	9·5° alcohol acquis	
	Saumur	10° alcohol acquis	Groslot, Cot and Gamay
	Coteaux de l'Aubance	11° of which 10·5° must be acquis	
	Coteaux de Saumur	12° alcohol acquis	
	Anjou Coteaux de la Loire	12° of which 11° must be acquis	

Category	Controlled Appellation	Minimum Degree	Grape Variety
WHITES	Savennières	12·5° of which 12° must be acquis	
	Coteaux du Layon	12° of which 11° must be acquis	
	The communes of Beaulieu Faye d'Anjou Rablay Rochefort St-Aubin de Luigné St-Lambert du Lattay Chaume Quarts de Chaume	13° of which 12° must be acquis	Chenin Blanc
	Bonnezeaux	13·5° of which 12° must be acquis	

In the sense used above, *acquis* cannot be translated in one word. Actually, it means 'acquired' or 'attained' and signifies that, of the 11° of the wines from the Coteaux de l'Aubance for example, only 10·5° of them must have actually fermented out and become alcohol.

When you crush grapes, you get a must which contains a great deal of sugar. The fermentation causes the sugar to break up and become alcohol. If the grapes are very full of sugar all of it cannot be turned into alcohol because there comes a point at which the very strength of the spirit kills off the yeasts which would turn the rest of the sugar into alcohol.

The French call this remaining part of the alcohol *en puissance* and often the 'Minimum Degree' column in the above table is done in a different way. For example, against the Anjou Coteaux de la Loire it would read 'twelve degrees of which one degree putative'.

Needless to say, the less wine permitted to be made per square yard the better will it be, though why Bonnezeaux is half a degree sweeter than Quarts de Chaume, when the latter's production is more restricted, I do not know.

If the information given on Anjou wines is a little voluminous the reader must forgive me, but some years ago I struck up a friendship with a young grower whose way of life I deeply admire and who has greatly increased my knowledge of the Loire.

Jean Baumard came to stay with us in England and later our son George went to work in the vineyards of Rochefort on an exchange basis.

George was there to help with the vintage and to learn what he could about wine. I still have some notes he sent me. What clearly interested a young Englishman used to British licensing laws was the unusual habit of consuming wine at almost any hour of the day.

In Rochefort everyone has his own plot on which grapes are produced for making his own little cru. French law permits anyone to produce wine for his own consumption and to give to his friends. Only when wine is sold does tax become payable. Consequently, wine in a wine-producing area is not a luxury commodity. It would be usual when visiting anyone for a bottle to be opened at any hour of the day and a considerable amount of discussion would result from this. The cafés in Rochefort did a poor trade; I think there were two but I never went inside. The Rochefortais said their water was bad. I discovered soon that this was because the wine was so good.

Wine is drunk at breakfast which consisted of pâté, cheese, cold meats and, on Sundays, hot pâtisseries. I thoroughly approve of the new way of life.

He certainly did.

It was while George was there that I naturally learned something about the Baumard family. Jean's grandfather and his grandfather before him had always been the possessors of a parcel of land on some sun-drenched vineyard slopes near Rochefort called the famous Quarts de Chaume, which makes a luscious sweet white wine of far greater keeping power than the ordinary run of the mill Anjou and which in many a good year rivals some of the great Sauternes.

It was not until several years after George had left that Baumard and I started trading together and I was the first person to whom he sent a cask of wine abroad. These casks are made of chestnut and for identification purposes the name of the buyer is stencilled in great white letters on the ends.

As the years went by my orders for Baumard's white semi-sweet Rochefort grew, and after one longer break than usual I was to experience one of the most pleasant shocks of my life when visiting him, which you will hear about later. Meanwhile we must go to the Angers Annual Wine Fair.

One day around Christmas I received an impressive invitation from the Confrérie des Chevaliers du Sacavin (The Order of the Knights of the Wine Sack).

Twice before the honour of becoming a member of the Anjou Wine Topers (for that is what I take *sacavin* to mean) had been proffered me but this time I felt that to accept was vital. The invitation to their annual banquet is a token of gratitude for the publicity one has given to the wines of Anjou.

Jean Baumard and his wife offered to put me up for a couple of nights but before getting to Angers and Rochefort I got rid of Damp Feet, who had carried his lethargy to such extremes that controlling my temper so far as he was concerned was no longer possible.

Within twenty-four hours I had secured a ticket for the Sacavin banquet for Hanbury, whom I summoned urgently, because I felt a tremendous urge to teach someone a little about the huge range of flavours of Loire wines which would be on show at the annual Anjou Wine Fair, to which I was looking forward with boyish enthusiasm.

The jamboree, now in its fifty-third year, is held in an enormous modern steel and glass hall on the outskirts of Angers. Here no less than 177 stalls managed by as many different growers will offer the visitor an average of six wines each—a thousand different samples all under one roof.

The reader will get more enjoyment and learn more about wine at this fair than at any other in France (and that means the world), with the Alsace Wine Fair at Colmar running a close second.

One of the reasons why these two fairs are so vastly enjoyable is not only that there are such a large number of stalls but that they are manned for the most part of the day by the owner-growers themselves, who never seem to tire of discussing the various flavours of the wines they will offer you.

And the reason why there are so many small individual growers is that neither of the districts has become quite famous enough to be commercially exploitable on a large scale, like Bordeaux, Burgundy and Champagne.

To give some idea of how much more parcelled-up are the vineyards in Anjou than they are, for example, in Bordeaux, be it understood that in this latter department of the Gironde one *viticulteur* farms on an average 2·3 hectares, whereas in the Anjou department of Maine-et-Loire he farms only 0·8 hectares. In Alsace in the Bas-Rhin, north of Strasbourg, he farms less than a third of one hectare, while in the department of the Haut-Rhin whence come the fine wines, he farms less than a fifth part of a hectare; about half an acre.

Bordeaux, Burgundy and the Champagne districts no longer have annual wine fairs because the firms have now grown so large that they have hived off direct selling to the public to agencies both at home and abroad.

The local papers were, naturally, full of the Anjou fair and they had dozens of photos of a cross-section of the owner-growers behind their minute stalls. Jean Baumard's photograph was given slightly more prominence and there was also a special write-up about a vinous experiment he was attempting.

As I have said, Baumard owns one of the most famous plots (he has called a recent acquisition after me) on the most famous part of the Coteaux du Layon: the Quarts de Chaume. The lie of the land here is exceptionally propitious for making great wine in that the hills around the best part of this bowl get the sun all day.

These white wines are traditionally made like Sauternes—sweet—but the trend towards drier wines is inexorable and the wind of change has already been noted by the greatest of them all, Château Yquem. There, in order to meet public demand for a drier wine, or perhaps the falling demand for a sweet one, they have brought out their Ygrec.

Baumard, according to the *Courrier de l'Ouest*, 'was using 1949 as a basis for vinification [i.e. comparing 1964 in quality and style with that year] and was vinifying half his vineyard in the Quarts de Chaume area as dry wine.'

What the paper did not say, Baumard told me later, was: would the Government wine officials grant the dry wine Appellation Contrôlée status?

Once you own vineyards and make wine with the right to this coveted designation you must not only use the permitted species of grapes, prune them in the permitted way and so on, but you must make the wine 'loyal and according to traditional usage'.

*

The enthronement dinner of the Sacavins always takes place at a banquet held on the evening of the first day of the opening of the Wine Fair and Angers thus sees one of its busiest periods of activity. The Fair itself is opened on Saturday afternoon by the Minister of Agriculture and this is very much a time to see and be seen. There are of course the usual opening ceremony speeches, long and of interest only to those in the trade, and made all the more irksome to listen to by reason of having to be standing up, *tastevin* in hand, and rarin' to go.

We made Baumard's stand our focal point and just as we were setting forth on a sipping and savouring spree he thrust a little glass *tastevin* into our hands.

'Are you sure you can spare this, Jean?' I said. 'They have glasses at the stalls.'

'You will need them more than I will', he replied. 'Growers do not like having to rinse their own glasses and so if they supply one they tend to charge. Besides, with a glass in your hand you look more like a real buyer; and then the tasting is free.'

But by far the kindest thing that Baumard did, and which very few other growers of any country would have done, was to introduce me to so many other growers at the fair. This was true open-heartedness, for many *vignerons* have a ruthlessness when it comes to pinching foreign buyers which has to be seen to be believed.

Young Hanbury and I started off in great form, tasting Anjous, Saumurs, Cabernets, Champignys and asking every question under the sun. We also were collecting visiting-cards: Georges Tuffereau of Notre Dame du Marillais; E. Leduc-Frouin of Soussigne; Monsieur Cailleau-Plot of St-Lambert-du-Lattay, who has on his card: 'Si ton sort est amer, bois du St Lambert.'

At first I read this as: 'If your favourite type of wine is something bitter, then you should think of St-Lambert.' Then I realized that it meant: 'If your luck is down, you should drink St-Lambert.'

Then there was J. Cochard, who also specialized in 'Verdelho de Madère'. Again I got hold of the wrong end of the stick; this does not mean that he imports a Verdelho Madeira, but that he grows a Madeira-type Verdelho grape to make a super-sweet dessert wine. There was also Monsieur Alfred Bidet from Rablay-sur-Layon.

As with all these fairs, they have around the outer edges of the hall a section devoted to wine grower's aids: corks, bottling machinery, fertilizers, and particularly salesmen who specialize in *porte-greffes*, or grape varieties upon which can be grafted the European variety (Pinot, Cabernet, etc.) which produces the actual grapes. There are about a dozen of such species along the Loire, the best known being Teleki 5 B.B., Rupestris du Lot and Riparia Gloire, the best being merely numbers, S-04, 101-14, 44-53, 41B, 1202 and so on.

One exhibit that interested me was a vat which was made of wood yet was quite square and also was capable of being dismantled and transported. The makers claim that being square, far less wood is wasted than with traditional casks, and now that quality is again the touchstone people are turning more and more to the one thing which wine needs to be stored and matured in (and that certainly goes for spirits), namely wood.

But I am not quite so sure about this. Wood was the perfect storing-improving agent in the pre-Second World War days, when the *vigneron* made his wines in such a way (leaving the pips and stalks with the juice while the fermentation was on, for example) that maturation was utterly necessary. With lighter wines, especially those which are ready for the bottle within four months of the vintage, I doubt whether wood can be any possible advantage; it is probably a disadvantage, imparting an unwanted woodiness.

After looking at the tractors, listening to a sad tale of woe from a firm specializing in curing vines of their diseases (oidium, mildew, erinose, apoplexy, red spider, etc.), we returned to further tasting and it was then that Hanbury had his bright idea.

'Why don't we fill the van with wine up to the roof and thus avoid transport charges?'

'Like hell we will!' I said.

About two months previously, I had been coming back from the first part of my Loire River study trip and, at Calais waiting for the ferry, had seen the van of a small firm of newly started-up London wine merchants parked at a siding.

This I thought was clever. You go over to France, bring back a lot of wine quickly, cheaply and trouble-free and see your supplier at the same time. I decided when I got back to London to find out a bit more about it. This I did and it was not at all as I pictured it. 'Yes,' said my London wine merchant friend, 'I went to pick up twenty-five cases of Champagne from Rheims. It was a disaster from the beginning.'

He found he had to have an exit permit. This took so long that when he got back to the quayside the boat had gone and he had to spend the night in Calais. Believe it or not there was so much difficulty with the Customs when he arrived at Dover that he had to spend another night there.

That was the last straw. Never again!

So I told Hanbury what I thought about his idea and at about six

The Château of Saumur as
it is today

The Château of
Angers

Quarts de Chaume
vineyards on the
Coteaux du Layon

St.-Philbert-de-Grand-Lieu.
One of the oldest churches
in France

Jean Baumard, testing his
grapes and extracting a
sample of wine for Layton

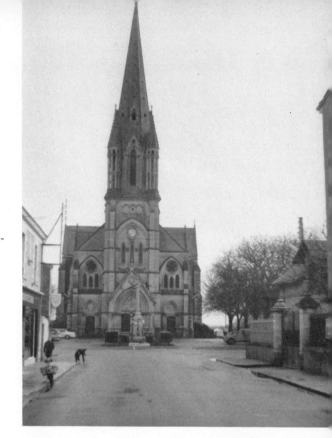

The ugliest church I ever saw—St.-Philbert-de-Grand-Lieu

The Wine Fair at Muscadet

o'clock we called it a day, because we wanted to find him a hotel to stay at, and I wanted to sober up for my big moment.

We found a hotel called the Grand in Rochefort; *Michelin* classified it as fifth category—very plain but adequate. Baumard, who had decided to stay on almost to the end of the first day's fair, got back later, just in time to change and to take us and his pretty wife back into Angers.

The reception was held not in the annexe to an hotel, as I had expected, but somewhere so unusual that I feel it deserves a description. It is in part a medieval salt granary, converted with imagination and charm. The place is immense; so big, indeed, that the Blériot-type biplane which is hanging from the ceiling—a gift of the Aviation Club of Angers—seems almost insignificant.

All was bustle and confusion when we got there, mainly because of a muddle of the place-names of the dozen or so guests of honour, of which I was one. Some of the guests had been placed in far too exalted a position at the top table and others well below—pardon the pun—the salt.

I started by being with the Baumards and Hanbury but shortly after this, and after hanging up our coats in the vestibule, we found we had been split up into three different tables with myself at the top table and Hanbury and the Baumards at opposite sides of the room. A few moments later, Baumard came up to me with a slightly worried look on his face.

'Your friend Hanbury has been separated from us', he said. 'I hope he will be all right.'

'So I see; but he will get along. His French is not too bad.'

'But can he carry his drink well?' he asked.

'No idea', I replied. 'I have not known him that long.'

'There is a fair amount of wine to get through.'

I looked down at the menu.

53me FOIRE AUX VINS DE L'ANJOU
DINER OFFICIEL

Consommé Perles du Japon

★ ★ ★ ★

Cochonnailles

★ ★ ★ ★

Cul de Veau à l'Angevine

★ ★ ★ ★

Savarin

★ ★ ★ ★

Corbeille des Fruits

VINS

Rosé d'Anjou 1964	Saumur-Champigny 1964
Anjou Blanc 1964	Cabernet d'Anjou 1964
Saumur Blanc 1964	Coteau du Layon 1953
Cointreau	

'Yes, it's a pretty hefty toping programme', I said, wondering what *cochonnailles*★ were; 'but he can take things slowly.'

'You see', said Baumard, coming out with it at last, 'he's in between two brothers, who are growers and great friends of mine, and they make a game at these dinners of getting strangers tight.'

'Oh lord!' I replied.

What my drinking commitments were to be for the evening I had still only a hazy idea. Several acquaintances spoke of the honoured enthronee being obliged to drink a huge portion of wine at one fell swoop. My fears, too, were not allayed by reading an account of the ceremony in a local paper.

The suppliant is handed a hanap† *of luscious Anjou. And now before a dignified portrait of Master Rabelais he sees the rest of the members of the order of council placing their hands on the* hanap *which is brimming over with mellifluous Loire wine.*

This the lucky suppliant quaffs in one fell swoop, at the same time saying:
'I swear before our Master Rabelais
That when my glass is full I empty it
And that when it is empty I will fill it up.'

The suppliant is now one of us *and the Grand Master can now invest him with the trappings of the order.*

There was only one thing to do; lay off all serious wine drinking at the banquet. This was a bore because, fearing the amount of wine to be drunk during the feast, I had already declined Jean Baumard's pressing invitation to take something alcoholic with him earlier on.

Teetotal, separated from my friends and having to unearth my veal from a very rich cream and mushroom sauce which I do not like, the

★ They turned out to be considered by Angevin guests to be the most popular dish of the evening and were greatly relished. They consisted of nasty little bits of grilled pork fat and gristle on the bone.

† Medieval goblet of ornate design.

banquet passed with incredible slowness, but at last the preliminaries to the enthronement got under way.

The banqueting hall was a cross between an immense, oblong, clinically sparse hospital ward and a gymnasium, roofed like an amalgam of a barn and a medieval church. At the far end was not only the aforesaid aeroplane, but a screened-off section which housed the kitchen staff and their equipment, the food and vast quantities of wine; not to mention ample stocks of Cointreau in magnum bottles, which was liberally dispensed (the factory is in Angers) after the show.

Less than half of the rest of the room was occupied by trestle dining-tables covered with beautiful linen cloths. At each *couvert* nestled an imposing array of glistening top-quality wine and liqueur glasses. This left the other half of the vast room free for the fun and here was erected what looked for all the world like a great boxing ring, reached on one side by a flight of ancient wooden steps.

Just after we had finished the cheese platter course, which, said the menu, had been 'offert par le Comité Interprofessionnel de Propagande des Produits Laitiers', and while waiting for the fruit basket 'offert par le Groupement des Producteurs de Fruits de Maine-et-Loire' and anticipating the liqueur Cointreau 'offert par la Maison Cointreau',* there was a mighty fanfare of raucous trumpets. We all turned round to perceive that the erstwhile empty boxing ring was now filled with six couples of lusty lasses and lads, dressed in typical Angevin costume and ready to entertain us. This consisted of a traditional dance which to my untutored eye looked like a blend of the Keel Row, an Austrian Schuhplattler dance and ring-a-ring-a-roses. As the dance progressed, the participants became more active, chairs were moved into the centre of the ring and the men and girls were taking flying leaps over them. As the girls were wearing the most frilly of can-can skirts, I was really frightened that an accident would occur. (So were they, you could tell by the apprehension in their faces.) All, however, was well.

Came the great moment. The enthronement!

A mighty trumpet blast, which nearly sundered even this roof, sounded and from the top table there rose the protagonists, who solemnly donned their brilliant, three-cornered hats and made their way to the rostrum or boxing ring.

* I think the Federation's secretary is slipping! He should have had the soup offered by the Japanese Embassy and the meat given by the Society for the Improvement of Veal!

Here a small table had made its appearance. On it, alone in the middle was a huge empty glass goblet, which my practised eye told me would have taken a good litre of wine.

'Of course they may not fill it right up to the top', I thought, hoping that the *toilettes* were not too far off. 'And', I continued thinking, 'thank the god of wine, I have hardly touched a single drop all through the feast.'

Louder blew the trumpets. Slowly ascended those apostles of Bacchus. The fanfares ceased.

A very elderly gentleman stepped forward and started a long speech. It *was* long; it was involved; it was interspersed with dialect I did not understand. But the gist of part of it was that, owing to the dangers of drunken driving, *there would be no drinking from the hanap.*

Quickly, I swivelled round in my chair to fill myself a great bumper from any bottle on the table.

But, to adapt the Walrus and the Carpenter, they had emptied every one!

*

The first person to be Rabelaised was a journalist. Then came a Danish wine wholesaler, a Swedish woman journalist, two more Frenchmen and my good friend Howell of Roger Grayson in London. For each person the routine was the same; they ascended the steps, were asked if they would swear to empty their glass when it was full and replenish it when it was empty, to which they agreed. Thereupon a little china wine cask, suspended by a piece of red and blue ribbon, was placed over the head and a paper scroll was handed out. Then finally the Grand Master came up and gave each person a splendid symbolic kiss on each cheek such as one sees a French Field-Marshal give when he bestows a medal on a brave soldier on the field of battle.

That, I thought to myself, will be an experience to take back to England; I never thought I would receive this honour even in half good-humoured fun.

Several more people went through the ritual and then came an unexpected pause, and some urgent whispering took place up on the rostrum. After a few minutes things were ready to start again and soon there was a tap on my shoulder to say that it was at last my turn. I started towards the rostrum but noticed that two other men were also making their way there. Soon it became clear what the consultation had been about; time was running short and we were now to be 'done' in batches of three.

After we had received our enrolment scrolls there was only a hand-shake—no military kiss!

Suddenly all tension left me and I saw the whole affair for what it was meant to be: a jovial binge and, if there was any publicity to be got for Anjou wines, so much the better.

It was in this mood that I descended the steps, to be confronted by a very inebriated journalist asking what I thought of Anjou wines.

'Perfectly splendid', I said.

'And our girls?' he said.

'Exquisite and desirable', I gallantly replied.

'Have you anything else to say?' he continued.

'Yes,' I replied in mock anger, 'I have come all this way hoping to receive a traditional military kiss and I get fobbed off with a measly handshake. Most galling.'

By the time I got back to my table the rest of the enthronees had been dealt with and the party was beginning to break up. My tardiness in getting back to my seat was due to the fact that I had been trying, successfully, to get myself a tumblerful of Cointreau en route.

Hardly had I settled down, now mellow and relaxed, when one of the officials appeared from nowhere and said: 'I hear you were dis-appointed in not getting a kiss.'

From me came no adequate remark.

'Sir, I have orders from our Grand Master to remedy this. Will you please be upstanding.'

I obeyed, whereupon the six buxom wenches who had been dancing all planted two kisses on my blushing, tomato-red cheeks.

Scarcely had I got over this episode when Jean Baumard and his wife came over with some friends, who started gently teasing me about the barrel now dangling from my chest. More girls came up with more Cointreau and we were about to settle down to a good old heart-to-heart on the prospects of the vintage, when Baumard exclaimed, 'We have forgotten your friend!'

Both of us jumped up from the table and went to the far side of the hall. Here a sorry sight met our eyes. Timothy Hanbury, cold sober, stood up as I approached and thanked me for a good evening. His two companions on either side were well and truly inebriated.

*

The next day, Sunday, was not to be a day of rest, however, for as soon as Hanbury arrived Baumard suggested that we visit Rochefort's famous panoramic view with its *Table d'Orientation*, a plaque showing the direction of various points of interest. People come from miles to see it, for it is certainly one of the most extensive panoramas in France. After this we visited Baumard's cellars.

This was a time of year at which I had seldom visited the wine districts of France, and as we approached the cellars we heard a curious noise which was quite new to me. It was halfway between that of a huge vintage Bentley ticking over and a muffled, deadened machine-gun firing very slowly.

'Whatever is that?' I asked.

Before Baumard had time to reply we were inside the cellar and the source of the noise was revealed. This was a huge ancient heater which was worked by a crude, sludgy oil. I do not think that the oil burned direct but there was some device at the bottom which vaporized it; hence the noise.

'What is it for?' Hanbury and I asked.

'It is to warm the cellars', said Baumard.

'But,' said Hanbury mystified, 'I thought that the thing about cellars was that they should be as cold as possible.'

'Not at this time of year and while the wine is still fermenting', replied Baumard. 'If the temperature falls too low, then the fermentation stops before it has completely finished, and then when the hot weather comes along you get a secondary fermentation which leads either to unsound wines or to expensive and troublesome treatment.'

Jean Baumard's cellars are not the largest on the Loire but I would rather be tasting wines here than anywhere else.

This young man makes each visit memorable, because he brings guileless enthusiasm and great knowledge to each cask he invites you to taste. He is never bored; you are never rushed; and as he goes round with *valincher* in one hand and tasting glass in the other, you realize that here is a man dedicated to going on and on and on improving the end-product of the juice of the vine.

As one goes round tasting, Jean always asks his visitors to comment on the difference in flavour between one cask and the next. Sometimes the difference will be so fractional that even the comparative expert will notice no difference whatever. Jean then patiently explains what to look for; one tastes again and all becomes clear.

As one proceeds, Jean's enthusiasm distinctly waxes as the finer wines follow the less exalted. He himself hardly swallows a drop; though at this stage the guests are throwing less and less wine on to the floor.

Hanbury and I were both enjoying ourselves hugely when my eye, roving around the cellar, caught sight of a cask on which was stencilled in large white letters:

LAYTONS WINE MERCHANTS

I pointed this out to Hanbury with a little pride. Then we noticed another and then more; there must have been nearly a dozen. It was most impressive; I felt as though I was the owner of the cellars.

The explanation of their being there at that time was quite simple. I ship an Anjou in cask for bottling in London. I suppose that by a string of coincidences I had never been there before when the cellar was so full of the new season's wine that every cask had to be pressed into service.

A halt had to be put to such pleasurable instruction for we had two more visits to pay that morning. The first was to the elegant Madame Joly, the wife of a Parisian surgeon who had just become the owner of a vineyard which she had, at the fair, warmly invited us to look over.

'You must come along and see the famous "Cemetery of the English" which is on my land', she had said.

It turned out to be a very interesting piece of history. The English King John Lackland, a Plantagenet and a vassal of the French King Philippe-Auguste, murdered his nephew Arthur of Brittany and was told by Philippe-Auguste to appear before the court in Paris to give some sort of explanation. Jean Sans Terre, as the French called him, failed to turn up, so the French King took away his title of Count of Anjou. John thought this so mean and unfair that he persuaded the German Emperor Otto to join him in a war against the French.

The result was a disaster, for in only a few days in July, 1214 Philippe-Auguste had defeated the Emperor at Bouvines, while his son, the future Louis VIII, thrashed John Lackland at the battle of the Roche aux Moines, which took place on Madame Joly's land.

According to historians, there were between eight and eleven thousand men in the English King's army and if the casualties were as many as is recorded there must have been a great number of dead. It is more than likely that they were buried on this lovely spur, overlooking the Loire, and that a row of cypresses should have been planted to mark the spot. It is rather wonderful, too, that the memory of the event should have lasted in this way for more than seven hundred years.

Madame Joly takes the making of her great wine, the Roche aux Moines, most seriously and has told us in an article exactly how the vinification is carried out.

The grapes are pressed and the juice is run off at once from the press into casks of 225 litres where the must then ferments. The juice of the grape stays at a temperature of at least 16 degrees Centigrade (61 degrees Fahrenheit) for six to seven weeks, so that both the alcoholic and malo-lactic fermentations can be completely finished.

At the end of this lapse of time—the end of December to the beginning of January—the first racking takes place. Then the cellars are allowed to cool down, so that the degree of acidity can be allowed to fall during the cold period of the winter.

The second racking takes place six weeks later, towards the end of February approximately. Then the wine is given a light fining.

After a rest of three to five weeks, when the wine is really bright, a third racking takes place.

Bottling takes place from the beginning of April to the end of June, after the wine has been filtered through asbestos.

Our next visit was to another grower in another château, also in the famous Savennières district—famous for really fine white wines that are so full and luscious. The production is so small that, as early as 1823, the writer J. F. Bochin said: 'It is of such great renown and the production is so restricted that it is hard to come by.'

Apart from his just claim to fame as a good wine maker, Michel Soulez of the Château de Chamboureau is well known in the region as the father of ten fine sons.

Like Madame Joly, Monsieur Soulez has produced a brochure from which there was much to learn; the main thing being that Savennières is the only wine on the Loire that is considered good enough by the authorities to be able to stand on that one word alone.

The Château de Chamboureau wines are, as the owner points out, quite different from the other fine wines of the Anjou regions in that, instead of being sweet, they are dry and pleasantly acid.

Monsieur Soulez' brochure shows that he is not stupidly hidebound, for he rightly recommends that as an apéritif his wine is perfect 'either with a base of cherry brandy, blackcurrant brandy . . . or with a cube of ice.' When did the myth arise that, if you want to make an apéritif as superbly good as the above or a wine cup, a cheap wine is every bit as good as a better one? You might as well say that if you are having Champagne cocktails a cheap raw brandy is as good as a first-rate Cognac—which is nonsense as the flavour will always come through.

We were naturally looking around for evidence of the ten sons; but there was no sign of them and we gently sipped our wine while Michel Soulez started to tell us how he got going.

But this we shall never know for at that moment a trumpet sounded through the french-windows so loudly that no Jericho wall would have remained standing.

Then three very fine-looking young men walked through the door, one dressed as a priest. We were just about to be introduced when, from the other side of the house, an even louder fanfare was pooped off, which made the former one sound like a pipsqueak.

'Ah, that will be the cor anglais', said Soulez.

'Your family must be very musical', said Hanbury.

'Let us go and look at my vines', said the Master of Chamboureau.

*

That afternoon, we again went into Angers for the Fair, and spent some hours sipping, nibbling cheese and discussing vintages. Another good dinner with Jean that night, and because he felt that I had had enough of Anjou wines there was a fine claret with the meat.

The next morning I decided at the last minute to give Jean a small order to take back to London for personal drinking, twenty bottles in all. These were got ready very quickly and then Baumard said, 'I'll just send the boy down to get your permit.'

'What for?' I asked.

'You will need it to show the French customs', he said. 'And in any case it is illegal to carry wine of any sort about in France without a document. Anyway, I should get into trouble.'

Jean went to his desk and got out a formidable-looking form entitled 'ACQUIT-A-CAUTION—VINS DE RAISINS FRAIS BENEFICIANT D'UNE APPELLATION D'ORIGINE CONTROLEE'.

There was a section for an exact description of the wine. Also required were the full address of the seller, the buyer, the time of day with space for the hours, minutes and morning or afternoon that the wine left Rochefort; the number of my van, and how many days the journey would take.

The official at Rochefort had to countersign the document and give the time of day, down to the minute, he had done this.

There was also a tear-off counterfoil which was for me, where all this rigmarole had to be written again.

'These taxes!' said Jean.

'How much was this lot?' I said.

'One and threepence', said Jean.

Three farthings a bottle, I thought. Still if this is going on the length and breadth of France all through the day and for every day of the year, it would be quite a nice sum for the French Exchequer.

'Goodbye, Jean', I said, as we prepared to set off. 'See you again soon.'

He went to undo the huge iron gates of the courtyard and I heard a shout behind me.

'You left this behind in your room', said Jean's wife.

It was the little glass *tastevin* which I had bought at the fair and which had engraved on the bottom:

QUAND IL SERA PLEIN JE LE VIDERAY
QUAND IL SERA VIDE JE LE PLEINDRAY

If, I thought, emptying and filling my glass was any criterion, then the number of times I had done it in the past two days made me a splendid Sacavin.

18

ANGERS

THE CASTLE OF ANGERS DOMINATES THE TOWN and it is a true castle, what the French would call a *château-fort*, and not a *château*. Actually in black and white photographs the fourteen great towers of this vast building look very like those of Avila. In colour photographs or when you have seen the two, however, there is a great difference; for, while Avila's turrets and walls are tawny stone, those of Angers are remarkable for their lovely black and white stripes which come from so much of the material used being slate.

As well as the remarkable, overpowering castle, the town of Angers is built largely of slate. Even in the days of King John this Angevin capital was known as the *'plus sombre et plus maussade'* ('most gloomy and depressing') town in France, and Shakespeare in *King John* speaks of 'Black Angers'. Even now, not only are all the roof-tops made of slate but a great number of houses are entirely constructed of it.

By the way, it seems to me odd that, while our English word comes from the old French *esclate*, the French word *ardoise* comes from the tiny village of Ardes in the Auvergne.

Historically, the castle and town of Angers are remembered for one of the most curious and one of the most likeable men in all France.

Foulques Nerra (the Black) was the former. He was the son of Foulques the Good, who must have been a man of considerable intelligence and courage. For, when Louis IV came to call at Angers, he found Count Foulques taking service in a monk's habit. When it was over, the king started teasing the pious count somewhat sarcastically. 'You know, your Majesty', said the count at last, 'an ignorant king is no more than an ass with a crown upon its head.'

Foulques Nerra got his nickname because of the swarthiness of his face. He came into the title at the age of seventeen and he died at the age of seventy during which span his life was one long battle. Blois, Tours, Le Mans, Nantes; all these towns had been assaulted by him. It is also on record that he once rode from Angers to Saumur, took part in a battle there and returned to his castle without dismounting.

To get what he wanted—and he was as covetous as they come—nothing, crime included, must stand in his way. Then suddenly he was ashamed of himself. The churches which he had built (and he also built twenty dungeons in Anjou and Touraine alone) would have alms showered upon them, and Foulques, pilgrim staff in hand, would go to expiate his crimes on a pilgrimage to Jerusalem.

As he got older he became more and more religious and at length he died while returning from a holy Crusade.

The Foulques family resided at Angers from the tenth to the twelfth centuries.

In the thirteenth century the dukes of Anjou took over and the last of these was called Le Bon Roi René. Surely he would have been the best of good companions.

Good King René was born in 1408, in the sumptuous apartments of the Angers castle which, I have neglected to explain, was rebuilt as one sees it today by St Louis between 1228 and 1238. René's father was Louis II, King of Naples and Duke of Anjou, and his grandfather Louis I, who organized and ordered the tapestries which you, the enlightened sightseer, can see in Angers today. They were done in an epoch when such tapestries were considered to be an essential decorative part of a princely residence and it is considered that those at Angers are the finest examples of medieval and Renaissance work that exist today.

The most famous piece, the oldest tapestry actually made in France, illustrates the stories of the Apocalypse. It was executed by Nicholas Bataille, in his time the most famous of workmen in this field, and was done between 1375 and 1380 in Paris.

But it is only by a piece of good fortune that we can see the tapestries today in their specially constructed building, which is a hundred yards long. Roi René bequeathed them to the cathedral, which took little interest in them. They mouldered away for 450 years, before being sold in 1843 as articles of no value. They were saved by the then Bishop of Angers, who set about their restoration.

Is it surprising that, surrounded as he was with such beauty, Good King René was, to put it mildly, a decidedly artistic person, as was his father Louis II before him?

René, as we shall see, was extraordinarily like Ferdinand; he loved to smell the flowers and fighting was not for him.

It started when his parents married him to a lady whose dowry was to be the province of Lorraine. But his cousin, de Vandremont, thought it belonged to him. They fought—and one is tempted to say *naturally* —René was beaten and taken captive. Many unhappy years were spent in the prison of his adversary; they resulted in posterity inheriting a large number of paintings and some very fine verses.

Liberated, René decided he had had enough of Angers and took himself south to his properties at Aix and Tarascon, 'and in his manor at Gardane and its flowered gardens, the days passed joyfully by'.

He knew, according to the historians, Latin, Greek, Italian, Hebrew and Catalan, and he knew how to play and compose music. He was a poet and a painter and was versed in mathematics, geology and jurisprudence. But he was not and he must have recognized this, a great fighter. He was also, as one writer has said, a *piètre politique*, a wretched politician.

What should he do? He was, in spite of it all, one of the most mentally agile spirits of his time. He did what anyone else with his temperament would have done in his place.

'All right', he may well have said. 'If I cannot fight people I will make them happy; bring some colour into their lives. Have fun, surround them with beautiful things.'

From then on he stayed in his Loire Valley and became just a lovable, generous eccentric.

The first thing he did was to restore his castle at Angers and to re-lay out the gardens, planting therein a whole host of species hitherto unknown to the region. Then by jove! he started what must have been one of the first zoos of the Middle Ages. 'Around the moat of the castle he installed a menagerie of extraordinary animals which from time to time he would have led through the town to the astonishment and glee of the country folk.'

From time to time he would tire of Angers, and then he would move from one rustic country house to another, and wherever he went he partook of the best or entered into whatever pastime was most popular. At La Baumette he found the local wine there so exquisite that he had it transported to Angers in great *tonneaux*, and when he got to Baugé, he found wild boar hunting 'so much in vogue that he needs must join in'. He was all things to all men; at the Ponts-de-Cé he fished with the fishermen, and yet a few days later he was found on the banks of the river enjoying himself in what we now call 'messing about with boats'.

At another place René presided over a 'Baillet des Filles', where afterwards he was served with a platter of cooked bleaks, a small river fish.

Good King René liked to be 'with' people, to mix without pretension with his subjects even to the point of leaving them a little souvenir of his visit; so before leaving he would get out his chalk and leave a portrait of himself on the walls of their abodes.

But the happiest triumph of all, and the one most commented upon by earlier chroniclers, took place at a newly acquired residence, the manor of Launay (which can still be visited), only a couple of miles from Saumur. Here he organized the two most famous tourneys of Christianity, the Pas du Pernon and the Pas du Bergère.

Towards the end of his life he did leave the Loire Valley, dying in Aix-en-Provence in 1480 at the then ripe old age of seventy-two.

*

I said that Baugé was one of the places favoured by René for hunting wild boar but it has something as well much more interesting; a relic with an extraordinary history which can be continuously traced for over seven hundred years; a relic which is connected with de Gaulle and the liberation of France from English shores—the 'real cross' of Baugé.

To get there you may as well make a detour and visit Plessis-Bourré, which many consider is the most beautiful of the not too much publicized châteaux of the Loire. This castle is completely surrounded by one of the largest moats in France, and apart from changing the old drawbridge from wood to stone, the castle has been left just as it was when Louis XI's finance minister, Jean Bourré, built it.

From here it is only half an hour's cross-country run to Baugé, a little town (rather well off in small hotels for its size) which, with lovely old fifteenth-century houses and picturesque streets ornamented with charming wrought-iron balconies, is a place of sheer delight.

First you should visit the Hôtel Dieu, or the St Joseph Hospital, and see one of the most eye-catching, bizarre and delightful old chemist's shops in France. There are very few left intact (there is a fine one at Würzburg) but this, with its fabulous Spanish-Moorish décor and its rich wooden parquet floor, is doubly interesting in that it has come down to us unchanged since 1675.

Come outside; go into the Place Roi René, and leading off it you will see a tourist's sign, 'La Vraie Croix d'Anjou'.

This will lead you to the Hôpital des Incurables and here in the sacristy 'on its throne of silver cloth and bright light', is the true Anjou Cross 'which you, yes even you, on beholding will not be able to withhold a gesture of admiration', says an enthusiastic brochure, in curious English.

It continues:

> For you have never before seen, at such close quarters, a relic of the cross of Christ as big and as sumptuously adorned with gold and precious stones.
>
> Now this cross is not just a miserly fragment of the cross all glued together as are so many others, it is all the same wood in every direction. So it is a true relic and that incidentally is the reason for its historical importance. For there are not in the whole wide great world more than some twelve made with larger pieces of wood (of the cross of Christ) than this one.

One may smile at some small-town priest being perhaps led away by pardonable enthusiasm but the strand of history which caused this piece of wood to be the emblem of the French liberation is enthralling. Every word is authentic, and here is the story.

Quite close to Baugé, and closer still to the pretty little townlet of Le Lude, famous for its national stud, is the beautiful old abbey of La Boissière, founded by the Cistercian monks in the twelfth century.

In the following century, in 1244, the Angevin Jean d'Alluye went on a Crusade and brought back a piece of the cross which he gave to the Cistercians, who chose a clever craftsman to turn it into a double cross, and to embellish it with pearls, rubies and sapphires. On both sides were carved a figure of Christ, surmounted on the one side by a dove and the other by a lamb.

This cross stayed at La Boissière for two centuries, in a chapel specially built for its veneration by the Cistercians, but during the troubles of the Hundred Years' War the monks, fearing that the cross would be pillaged, took themselves, and it, to the protection of the great castle of Angers and Louis I. The relic obviously made a deep impression on the Duke of Anjou, for in 1360 he entrusted it to his goldsmith for further ornamentation, at the same time giving orders for the fabulous tapestries to be put in hand. He also founded an order of chivalry whose emblem was the double cross.

Louis I died before all his projects came to fruition but his son, Louis II, carried on the good work and so did his grandson, Louis III. Thus it was none other than our good friend René who really got it started. He used it everywhere! On the church of St Maurice at Angers for example and also on the coins he struck. But, most significant of all, he used it as a heraldic device and especially 'on the collars of those eagles which served to support his shield'.

René married Isabel of Lorraine and, on becoming the duke of that province as well as of Anjou, his coat of arms became united with those of the Duchess de Bar, and when in 1736 Lorraine became united with France, the double cross was chosen as its heraldic symbol.

After the terrible defeat by the Germans in 1871, the cross became a symbol of the lost town of Metz and the Messins, or people of Metz, placed a broken cross of Lorraine (as it now became called) on the altar of Notre Dame de Sion, with the inscription: 'It is not to be for ever.' In 1920 Maurice Barrès found the two broken fragments and joined them to a palm of gold, on which was written: 'It was not for ever.'

Came June 1940, and through Britain with General de Gaulle passed Vice-Admiral Muselier, who was a native of Lorraine, and as a symbol for the Free French, the double cross of the True Cross, brought back from a Crusade in the thirteenth century, was chosen, six hundred and sixty years after it had been received by the Cistercian monks of La Boissière.

*

But the town of Anjou is not only noted for its castle and its slate roofs; it has an old *quartier* with narrow arcaded pavements and it was here in a second-hand bookshop that I found such a curious old book (disjointed as it is) connected with wine-making that I have translated it as an Appendix (see p. 203).

19

MUSCADET

THIRTY YEARS AGO THERE APPEARED IN MY FIRST BOOK, *Choose Your Wine*, a chapter entitled 'The Four M's'—Madeira, Malmsey, Malaga and Marsala'. Ten years later in the second edition there was a chapter entitled 'The Three M's'; I suppose I felt that to include Malmsey* (or Malvasia—it came originally from Monemvasia, a Greek village) was not quite fair. Another decade passes, a third edition appears and Muscadet makes its belated appearance.

I mention this to emphasize how relatively recently this almost astringently dry white Loire wine has come into favour, though small Parisian restaurants claim to have discovered it some twenty years before I did. I first met Muscadet one hot June evening when the Vallet vineyards were in flower.

Have you ever been in a vineyward of a hot June evening? Did you know that the flowering vine gives off a faint but unmistakable perfume? It is fleeting but it is exquisite and I got it that evening. The faintest breeze will carry it away but, when you get it, you smell a perfume of reseda, also known as mignonette or dyer's weed.

This was the culmination of one of the most intensive days of tasting, cellar visiting, and above all talking I had ever experienced.

The people I had been with had been even more articulate than usual, the conversation more deep, more leisurely, yet more intent than usual. My companions too had been incredibly varied, for not only had peasants and growers been my hosts but a wine poet as well.

Most of the more interesting comments were on tasting and that evening I sat down and knocked them into shape.

---

* Incidentally, how could the Duke of Clarence have been drowned in that butt of Malmsey wine? The cask would have had to have been a very large one and standing upright with its 'head' off. This presupposes a butt with no bung in the staves, for if there had been one the pressure of the wine would have forced it out.

When one tastes, one should never observe the get-up of the bottle in any way or the surroundings. One should shut one's eyes and 'look' with one's tongue, palate and nose.

You cannot taste really well with tobacco-stained teeth, any more than a pair of scales can weigh accurately when they are dusty.

In these twentieth-century days the sense of sight and hearing are most important, but with wine the sense of smell comes into its own.

Machines like tractors have certainly helped one man to do more work, but will a machine ever be made to prune the grapes or get in the harvest?

Sometimes one comes across a young wine tasting as full of bouquet as though it had been in bottle for quite some time; this gives one the same sort of shock as when a child talks like an adult.

Above all a wine taster should possess the quality of impartial disinterestedness; another is that of not drinking the wine one is sounding. After all, a doctor does not succumb to the charms of a patient, nor should one when testing a wine on the palate. In this instant one is an impartial judge. When one is a lawyer that is different; you take sides, drink to your fill and praise as much as you like.

The surgeon's knife cannot open up a man's soul, no more than the perfume of a wine can be analysed by a chemist.

Only those wines which are a little hard at the outset, and which have not got an immediate charm, are the ones with a great future. But contrariwise one gets tired of a wine which is too perfect.

Never serve your finest wines at a large gathering. The compliments paid to the wine will neither be genuine nor true; for one's guests will be frightened of making fools of themselves.

It is possible to love wine without being a good taster, and it is also possible to be a good taster without caring much about wine.

When you are having a serious tasting of wine it is often better to let several people taste one wine at a time and to let them discuss its merits, rather than that they should taste all the range in one go.

Certain wines go from being very young and green to old and decrepit in one fell swoop. They are like cars which as soon as they have been properly run in start falling to pieces, or men of humble origin who pass a lot of brilliant exams when young and then go straight to some dreary monotonous job and badly paid at that.

There is some confusion as to where the word Muscadet comes from and I think one of the best answers is to be found in a little booklet by an unknown author which is given away to guests in an hotel in Nantes.

Take care! Muscadet, the celebrated wine which is produced the length and breadth of the Sèvre-Nantes hillsides, is disconcerting and a deceiver.

It misleads us first by its effervescent name; we all wonder where it comes from.

What is its etymology? Look in the Larousse *dictionary, that splendid refuge for seekers who cannot find what they seek, and you will find: Muscadet, a type of wine which has a slight taste of Muscat!*

Naturally you then look up Muscat and here you find: 'Muscat; a fruit which has a faint taste of musk'. Finally you naturally want to know the exact nature of this musk, the presumed origin of Muscadet, and you discover that 'it comes from an odiferous liquid, which a small European quadruped carries in a pouch under its abdomen'.

And that one supposes is that.

If we are to take this rigmarole seriously we would have expected to have noticed in the bouquet of the wine a slight trace of that extraordinary heavy and clinging scent, so beloved of our great-grandmothers.

Well, well! If that is the origin of the word—and this is not at all certain —it must be stated that whoever baptized our Muscadet in this way was a very mediocre taster.

For between Muscadet and Muscat there is a great abyss; there is not the slightest possible resemblance in either consistency or bouquet.

As for the grape species used, wine historians have not got much to go upon but what there is makes fascinating reading.

In the first place the Muscadet grape is not indigenous to the region but comes from Burgundy.

From documents of the *Département de la Loire–Atlantique* we know that in 1639 several plots of land were grubbed up and replanted with red grapes called 'a good species from Burgundy'.

Then in the terrible winter of 1709, when even the sea froze on the shore, the vineyards were destroyed so completely that it took well nigh thirty years to re-establish them. When this was at last done growers decided to do it with the Muscadet de Bourgogne.

But well over half a century was to elapse before we find the word 'Muscadet' in print on its own.

Actually the grape is none other than that called the Melon in Burgundy and the Jura.

Muscadet has three *Appellation Contrôlée* categories:

1. 'Muscadet', which must contain a minimum of 9·5° of alcohol.

2. 'Muscadet Coteaux de la Loire', a minimum of 10·0° of alcohol.

3. 'Muscadet Sèvre-et-Maine', a minimum of 10·0° of alcohol.

Of the *Muscadet simple* there is nothing further to be said.

Muscadet Coteaux de la Loire. These wines are made around the most attractive old town of Ancenis which has a seventeenth-century castle and old houses, and also around Champtoceaux where, from the Promenade de Champalud, you get a marvellous panoramic view over the Loire.

On the left bank of the river are the following wine-making *communes* or villages:

St-Florent-le-Vieil	Drain
Bouzille	La Varenne
Champtoceaux	La Chapelle St Florent
Liré	Barbechat
St-Julien-de-Concelles	

On the right bank are:

Varades	St-Géréon
Couffé	Le Cellier
Mésanger	Thouaré
Anetz	Mauves
Ligné	Ancenis

Muscadet Sèvre-et-Maine. This region is to the south-west of the above and nearer to Nantes and the sea.

From this area comes seventy-five per cent of the *Appellation Contrôlée* Muscadet, and here is made the best wine.

The following are the most important *communes:*

Vallet	Le Loroux-Bottereau
Mouzillon	Haute-Goulaine
Clisson	Le Pallet
Vertou	La Regrippière
Châteauthébaud	Monnières
Aigrefeuille-sur-Maine	La Chapelle-Basse-Mer
Ste-Lumine-de-Clisson	

Muscadet is of course a heaven-sent partner for oysters, lobsters, crabs and all sea-foods, and great play is made of this in publicity hand-outs as to the proximity of such a suitable wine to the Atlantic Ocean.

The true home, commercial, spiritual and geographical, of Sèvre-et-Maine Muscadet is the most unattractive little town of Vallet and here eighteen years ago in 1949 they started the annual Foire-Exposition du Canton de Vallet, mainly to show the wines of Muscadet and those of the Gros Plant. It takes place in March and each year the organizers have had the bright idea of giving a different theme to the fair; some crudely business minded and some quite amusing.

Probably the most costly—not repeated, I notice—was that of 1950, the year after it opened, when the theme was, 'A Fair of samples, with tastings entirely and obligatory for free' [sic] and the comment written years later states that 'it was a very useful idea certainly, the realization of which did present difficulties'—the understatement of all time.

In 1955 the organizers gave the fair a face-lift and improved the drinking booths and so the theme was, 'Always do Better—both for the exhibitors and the public'.

1957 saw 'The Marriage of Beaujolais–Muscadet'.

Presumably, as I have said, the grape variety originally came from this part of France; then the next year saw 'Muscadet places herself at the service of Gastronomy'.

It was during the course of the fair that a competition was organized among a large number of restaurateurs of Nantes to create a dish using Muscadet, and the Canard au Muscadet was born.

RECIPE

INGREDIENTS

Muscadet	*Grapes*	*Apples*
Butter	*Stock*	*Flour*
Salt	*Pepper*	*One duck (not too fat)*

Cut your duck up raw and sauté in the butter, which should be a golden brown before you put the pieces in. When they have taken on a nice brown colour take them out for a moment and add two tablespoonfuls of flour, half a litre of stock and nearly (à peu près) a bottle of Muscadet, salt and pepper.

Replace the pieces of duck in the stew pan and add two good-size apples cut in wafer-thin slices and a few grapes. Cover with a lid and cook for two hours and a half.

Don't forget to de-pip the grapes.

I owe this information to the *Catalogue Officiel* which is sold at the entrance to the PALAIS OF MUSCADET and which is a veritable mine of information.

Three days are devoted to the fair and the almost hour-by-hour programme of whirlwind events makes hectic and thirsty reading.

At nine on Saturday the whole fair opens with an exposition of the work of the 'Finest Workmen in France', followed by the finals for the SILVER VALINCHER and the SILVER CUP for the best makers of Muscadet and Gros Plant respectively. There is an official lunch and dinner and much time devoted to testing.

Relative quietness reigns on Sunday but at ten o'clock on Monday an important event takes place for all the growers, courtiers etc., march in state into the town of Vallet (the exposition is on the outskirts) to give 'The Banner of Honour' to that café proprietor who has served the best Muscadet during the preceding year.

At one o'clock there is a Grand Déjeuner Gastronomique at which function are served 'dishes which have won prizes in the preceding year and served by the winners'.

Thus ends a fair which I can recommend to all lovers of dry wine.

20

DOWN TO THE SEA

❧

THERE IS NO OFFICAL POINT at which the château country ends but it is generally accepted that it stops at Angers or, stretching a point, past Ancenis to Nantes. This is the largest town in Brittany, with a quarter of a million inhabitants.

I like Nantes better than Angers although it is double the size; it seems neater and more imposing. Maybe I also like it because I have been more successful in selling and publicizing Muscadet than any other wine.

A further reason why I like the town is that a visit to the church calms my ever-jangling nerves. Everything, I so wrongly imagine, has to be done at once. It is worst of all with letters; how I admire people who calmly answer correspondence a full week after receiving a communication and make no apology for the delay. I get in a near panic if four or five letters go unanswered for over seventy-two hours and make elaborate arrangements to have secretarial help for the purpose of sending speedy replies (none are *ever* urgent) seven days of the week.

A *pied à terre* in the shadow of the cathedral of St Peter and St Paul might cure me of this energy-eroding *angst*, for it took 459 years to build, from 1434 to 1893, and what is so exceptionally unusual is that, during this immense stretch of time, no architect has put a step wrong in keeping to the finest of Gothic lines.

The interior is considered to be one of the most beautiful of all the Gothic cathedrals of Northern France; mainly, I think, because instead of using the grey-black granite of most Breton churches a white stone has taken its place which, apart from anything else, has meant that the vaulting could be built up to a height of no less than 120 feet. This is ten feet higher than Notre-Dame in Paris and twenty feet more than Westminster Abbey.

And contemplating the tomb of François II, Duke of Britanny, one of the finest works of the Renaissance and the great decorative master-piece of the cathedral, I get quite a kick out of the fact that those loyal (not a good adjective here) so-and-so's of the French Revolution did occasionally get foiled. In a previous chapter I really let myself go in condemning the way the revolutionaries felt it their duty to tear down and destroy all buildings with royal connections; but in this instance, however, they did not get away with it.

Anne of Brittany, François' daughter, commissioned the tomb from the sculptor Michael Colombe, who finished the work in the first decade of the sixteenth century. It was so beautiful that the revolution-ary tribunal, of course, ordered it to be demolished. With great cour-age, however, the town's architect (Oh! for a statue of him) hid the various bits of masonry in the homes of his friends in such a way that it was possible to fit it all back in the cathedral in 1817.

*

The castle of Nantes, if it did not happen to be in such a large town, would be considered as one of the wonders among the monuments on the River Loire. It is a vast rambling place started in 1466 by Duke François and continued by his dutiful and famous daughter who, incidentally, has given her name to the largest (but not I feel all that good) hotel in the town, The Duchesse Anne.

Nearly every early King of France has stayed for shorter or longer periods at the castle, and almost every well-known personage who has coloured the bright tapestry of French history has been a prisoner there; Gilles (Bluebeard) de Rais, Cardinal de Retz, the Duchesse de Berry, all saw the formidable dungeons, as well as a man I consider to have been one of the most colourful, brilliant, audacious men of all times, Nicholas Fouquet.

This man (not to be confused with the painter Jean Fouquet) was the only person whom Louis XIV, the Sun King, both feared and hated. Several lives of him have been written in French and one which I have by Jules Lair, superbly bound, is, I believe, quite a rarity. I tried to write Fouquet's life some years ago but was not up to it.

Fouquet looked after the kingdom's finances during the early years of Louis' kingship and, I am afraid, though he is my hero, stashed away vast sums for himself. He was a sort of medieval Hatry and, though on paper worth vast sums and though he built fabulous castles and even

bought the large island of Belle-Ile at the mouth of the Loire and fortified it against misfortune, was never solvent.

But there was one great thing in his favour, and of all people Louis
should have been eternally grateful. Fouquet went on and on producing
cash for the King's armies at the last minute when all other supplies
had dried up. Without Fouquet the Sun King might well not have won
several of his battles.

At the height of his power Fouquet, the motto on whose coat of
arms, a squirrel—Fouquet is Breton for a squirrel—read 'How much
higher shall I not climb', became impossibly arrogant.

But the reason Louis hated Fouquet was that the latter had
rather crudely tried to ingratiate himself with Louise de la Vallière,
the King's first mistress and perhaps the person he loved most of
all. Their affair was secret; Fouquet found out and tried to give her
jewellery.

After waiting many years Louis decided to strike. It was D'Artagnan
with his musketeers who was detailed to arrest Fouquet and it was done
discreetly in 1661, when Louis was visiting Nantes.

Poor Fouquet! He was kept in prison for nearly four years before his
trial which, when it did take place eventually, was a farce, but was none
the less one of the longest in all history and I believe is still quoted in
French law. While in prison he wrote his famous, immensely long
book called *Defences*, which is now extremely rare, though there is a
copy in the British Museum.

The final verdict was banishment for life. Louis wanted him to suffer
the death penalty but it was considered too likely to inflame public
opinion.

Then it was decided that, because of the damage such a brilliant man,
with all the state secrets that he held, could inflict abroad, the sentence
should be changed to imprisonment for life. For nearly twenty years
he remained shut up and his incarceration was so long and so severe that
he eventually joined the ranks of the many sufferers thought to have
been 'the Man in the Iron Mask'.

★

You eat well in Nantes and you drink even better, for to the south of
the town is made the last wine of my book and the last wine of the
Loire.

Fifteen miles to the south of Nantes is an immense flat lake called the

Lac de Grand-Lieu. In the vicinity are the villages of St-Philbert-de-Grand-Lieu, St-Colombin, Ste-Lumine-de-Coulais, St-Etienne-de-Corcoué, St-Jean-de-Corcoué, St-Léger-les-Vignes, St-Aignan-de-Grandlieu, Ste-Pazanne, St-Mars-de-Coutais and St-Fiacre-sur-Maine.

'When the Saints come marching in!'

In this region a small, green, acidulous grape is the most important crop, covering hundreds of acres of a flat, vast, almost marsh-like land.

The vineyards are planted here with the same grape species as is planted further south in the Cognac region, the Folle Blanche, also now more popularly called the Gros Plant.

Both names, I assume, refer not to the size of the vine with its berries but to its high yield. As the word *vigne* (vine) is feminine I take it that La Folle Blanche means: 'the prodigious [yielding] white [vine].'

As for the flavour of the end-product, if we can concede that Muscadet is stingingly dry, whatever phrase can we find to describe a white wine that makes even Muscadet taste sweet?

In strength it is one degree lower than Muscadet, which itself is low, and is of course not such a good wine; but it has one quality which Muscadet lacks and which makes it a sound idea to blend the two when marketing it. The Gros Plant wine, which is only of VDQS status, has so much acidity that this will help to preserve the less good Muscadets, which will go flabby if kept too long. Just as there is nothing nicer than a fresh Muscadet, there are few wines more horrible than a flabby one. When this blending is done the French grower does not use this rather dubious word but talks euphemistically about the Gros Plant 'completing' the other.

*

In my travels around France seeking rare and less well-known wines, I have had some pretty odd experiences but the one when I was seeking a few hogsheads of Gros Plant was surely as bizarre as any.

I had been given the names of six growers and had visited five, all with no success (too commercial or too ignorant of the *paperasserie*, i.e. handling of the documents needed to ship wine abroad) and judging by the lack of information vouchsafed by the locals concerning the last grower he was not going to amount to much. People seemed rather embarrassed when I asked anything about him.

The directions from Nantes that I was given took me through the village of St-Philbert-de-Grand-Lieu and then on south to one of the least inhabited and poorest looking parts I have ever seen in France. After a while, I got terribly lost and I was just about to give up when a peasant pointed to a most derelict gate and assured me that a certain Count X really did live at the end of the drive.

It was nothing but a mud track in reality, and the hedges and the fields were in keeping—in a shocking condition.

After a while, I began to wonder cursingly if I had not yet again been misdirected for no house hove into view and I had now motored farther away from the main road than hitherto.

Then a sudden change came.

For once a gate was actually shut; for once it was painted and BEWARE OF THE DOG stared me in the face as I got out to open it.

From now on the road was in splendid condition, the hedges well kept and the fields on one side and the vineyard on the other looked indeed well tended and nourished.

Suddenly a little dream house came into view, well rebuilt, over and around the little mill stream. Here were more gates, one leading to the house itself and another to farm buildings in the distance.

I opened the one leading to the house and as I ascended the steps there appeared at the door a manservant to whom I explained my errand.

The man ushered me into a room and a few seconds later an immaculately dressed, middle-aged man came in to greet me.

'So you would like to look over my cellars and taste some of my wine', he said, clearly pleased to oblige.

This was not what I had told the manservant, for I had stressed that I wanted to make a purchase. Of course, one hopes and expects to be taken around the cellars as one does to be given a tasting. Indeed, the way the latter is conducted influences one's decision to deal with a new grower every bit as much as having samples sent to England and tasting them against one's present supplier's wine. As I walked around with him, I quickly gathered why the villagers had dried up when I had asked them what he was like. He clearly wanted to be and was the *enfant terrible* of the Gros Plant growers.

For I discovered that he believed fervently that the Gros Plant wine should be upgraded and that not one drop of the juice from this vine should ever go to the Muscadet makers, who, he felt, were battening on him and his fellow-growers.

All very well, I thought, if you had as much money as he clearly had, but not so easy if you had a family to feed.

Normally, if one is buying, it is the practice to taste in the cellar but today was to be the exception. The count suddenly lost all interest in the tour and started striding with me back to the house, where a sumptuous array of preprandial croûtons and tit-bits had been arranged. On a silver salver was a set of glasses surrounded by bottles of wine from the estate.

We started tasting and it was clear that the count was considerably impressed by my comments.

Suddenly he said, 'Would you care for a wash before luncheon?'

'But . . .' I stammered.

'Of course, you are staying', he replied.

With the arrival of coffee and liqueurs and a real Havana cigar (very rare in France), I felt that the moment of truth was at hand. If this was the count's way of softening up a prospective customer then he left everyone else I had come across at the starting-post.

Talk about attacking through the soft underbelly!

And as I watched the oily smoke curl lazily up and through the crystal droplets of the chandelier to the gilt ceiling I wondered how hard a sell it was going to be. Was I to be persuaded to take more casks than I wanted, or to pay more francs per litre than was the local ruling price?

'Another Cognac, Mr Layton?'

'Thank you, it's magnificent.'

Now it's coming, I thought.

It did, but not as I expected.

'Tell me frankly,' said the count, 'what do you think of my Gros Plant?'

Damn it! This seems to be carrying non-salesmanship too far.

The situation was delicate but, just because I had been given an exquisite meal, I was darned if I was going to pay over the odds for the wine; I also wanted to give an initial order for the smallest number of casks possible just in case the first shipment was not up to sample.

'Have you got good stocks?' I said, playing for time and praying that his answer would give me something to go on.

'Fair', said the count.

That was what he *said*; but his tone implied, 'What in the name of prying Tom has that got to do with you?'

'How much are you asking a litre?' I said, and it sounded as crude as pouring Worcester sauce over a piece of boiled salmon.

How much can a face express? As I write I can now see on reflection that a glimmer of understanding as to why I had come was passing through the count's mind.

'Mr Layton', he said in a cold voice, 'I don't quite get it. First you ask what my stocks are, which I should have thought would only concern myself; then you ask how much I am selling my wine for.'

'Naturally', I said, still by a miracle holding on to my reason. 'I want to buy a cask of Gros Plant from you.'

The count rose from the table, now making not the slightest effort to conceal his anger.

Now I felt sure I had got the message. Here was a really big wholesaler-grower who thought in ten-cask lots as a minimum.

'Well, two casks', I said.

The count gave a grunt which could have meant anything; I took it as disgust at such a small order.

'Perhaps three then', I said; 'if the price is right.'

The count now indicated quite clearly that the meeting was at an end. He said: 'Mr Layton, I *never* sell my wines to the trade.'

He then touched the bell that he had used to summon his man for the various courses we had had for luncheon and when he came said, 'Put six bottles of Gros Plant in Monsieur's car, please.'

★

On my way back to Nantes I again passed through St-Philbert-de-Grand-Lieu to have a good look at the remarkable Carolingian abbatial church, one of the oldest of its type in Europe.

The land and surrounding district were given to St Filibert (that is his correct name) by Archbishop Ansoald of Poitiers as far back as A.D. 677. At that time it was merely a simple country retreat and used by the monks only in the summer months.

Raids by Barbary pirates from the Atlantic Ocean necessitated something of a more fortified nature being built, however, and so it was to a quite sturdy building that the monks took the remains of St Filibert in 836.

As the years passed the number of pilgrims coming to be cured by touching the saint's bones multiplied so much that a new section of the church was added, the main feature of which was a curious crypt adorned with a *fenêtrelle*, or small window, through which the pilgrims could gaze down at the saint's sarcophagus.

*

We are getting to the very end of the River Loire now and it is at St-Nazaire (the inhabitants call themselves Nazairiens) that we can fairly say it widens out into the sea. This ship-building town, grown up from a village to 60,000 inhabitants in a century because large boats could not get up to Nantes, has only one thing worth visiting, namely the vast concrete, reinforced submarine pens which survived unscathed all the allied bombing in the last war. These giant sheds are above ground and constructed in such a way that submarines could sail right into them underwater. One is at liberty to walk around some of them —a gruesome reminder of the past.

Farther on is La Baule which, on account of a truly glorious, golden-white sandy beach over three miles long, is ousting Dinard as the top seaside resort of the region.

Gastronomically, we are now in the area of one of the nicest of traditional *amuse-gueules* (nibbles) of all France—the savoury and sweet pancake.

The shops and cafés where they are made and where you sit and eat them are called *crêperies* and they are especially predominant in a little fishing town at which I will end this account of my travels. It cannot be said to be on the Loire, possesses no monuments or castles and boasts no vineyards.

Le Croisic has all the charm of a sardine port; the gaily coloured sails bob up and down along the quayside, where each morning the day's catch is sold by auction and where all is noise and bustle. It is a gay and amusing sight. After watching this you have a hot, wafer-thin buckwheat pancake spread with cheese and a glass of local cider, while you sit back and look forward to your lunch of lobster, fresh crab pasties and oceans of Muscadet.

Appendix
A WINE-GROWER'S DIARY

JANUARY

January! Ice like small pieces of broken mirror is to be seen in all the hollows and icicles hang like tiny white candles from the eaves of the buildings. None the less the workman who has to carry the dung up the hillside notices that it is less icy. It is certainly not the time to idle, for in one's bones one feels that the days are beginning to recover a little. True there is not much to sing about—but a pale shaft of weak sunshine occasionally filters through and at least, from beginning to end, a whole hour has been stolen from the night.

By now the new wine has settled down and has cleared and the vent holes of the cellars have been reopened. Now too, on the first day of the week, casks, vats, anything containing wine, are filled up to the brim to prevent any bacteria attacking the wine.★

This is the time to write to the women who snip off the leaves in the spring. The time is now passing by quickly and it will pass more quickly in spite of inevitable weather setbacks; a sky so overcast that it turns almost black. But things will get better. Yet for a moment one worries whether the women will turn up in four months' time. Never mind! The young wine is excellent.

> If on St Vincent's day [17 January] the sky is clear
> Then we shall have good wine that year.
>
> When on St Vincent's day the weather's fine
> Then surely will the vine shoots make good wine.

★ Wines in cask are kept with the bung uppermost during the first turbulent months of their life and it is at this time that the filling up is so important. People often ask what kind of wine is used; this depends on what is most convenient. It may be from a reserve cask of the same year's wine, it may well be from the bottled stock of some much older wine which has got a heavy deposit. The bungs are usually covered with linen for cleanliness sake and are only placed very lightly in the hole. When the wine has quietened down completely, the bungs are then well and truly hammered in and the cask is so placed that the bung is lying sideways (so that it is in contact with the wine) and in this position it is left, for months or years, to mature.

In 1422 12 January was the coldest day in living memory. It was so bad that in three days all the wine, vinegar and musts froze in the cellars and believe it or not the 'coxcombs of all the chickens were frozen right down to the heads'.

A January without rain
Is to the peasant's gain.

When the year comes in on the swim
Then the weather will be grim.

VARIETIES OF VINE AND HOW TO DRESS THEM

For the white grape a short method of pruning called the 'Gobelet' is practised, but for the black Pinot Noir grape a longer one is more efficacious. But in all events it cannot be over-emphasized that the grower must and does sacrifice a part of his production in order greatly to improve his quality.

This improvement of quality has been one of the foremost aims of the Loire wine grower and, not without some sacrifices let it be said, towards this end the better growers have given up growing certain poor-quality species in the course of the last half-century. None the less the grower has good reason for being somewhat conservative in his outlook. He knows for example just what the wine that certain grapes have been producing will taste like, but he does *not* know—until long afterwards—what faults a new grape may give to a wine. Wine growers tend to like the species which their grandfathers liked, and one must admit that had it not been for the terrible ravages of the phylloxera and had not the terrific task of replanting shown that new species could adapt themselves to our soil, no new trials would have been made.

What is the ideal grape to plant in which vineyard? The answer is not readily to hand, but things will not be improved by indulging in the bitter wrangles and disputes which have been taking place in the past years. Fortunately there are so many growers to whom this subject is of such interest that many have turned corners of their vineyards into veritable testing grounds for new types. This is excellent.

FEBRUARY

At last the weather on certain days is such that you believe winter is at an end. But it is always the same and one is deceived. *Vigneron!* Take note of the sun; you will already notice blue flashes on the black of your pruning shears. You should have clipped your young vines first; now it is the turn for the older ones. The old twigs of the vines must now be gathered up just as you gathered up the wine poles in those sad November days. But now winter is a thing of the past. Put your vine faggots in the barn; they will come in useful for the cook later on.

Now also is the time to fill up the gaps in the vineyard and to plant out some grafted vines. These may well have been taken from the strongest of older vines on the property. Thus it is that the continuity of all that is best takes place.

This though is not the only work; with the vineyard now dressed and tidy there is a lot of ditching to do. Manure must be carted and then put in place and covered up. All work is becoming urgent. By the wall there weeds are beginning to show; perhaps they are going to try their luck. Everywhere else the first green shoots to be seen give much pleasure to the eye but those weeds leer in a sinister way. Truly this will be another year when nothing can wait.

> February clear and February bright
> Is worse than a wolf with the sheep at night.

> Snow, water and fog in February
> Are as good as manure.

> If it thunders in February
> All the olive oil you will get will go in a tablespoon.

THE BUYERS

Suddenly the finer days come upon us unaware. This is the time for bottling last year's vintage and wine villages, wine regions, Caves Coopératives, in fact every type of grower-producer now invites that corps élite of buyers (be they hoteliers, café owners, retail wine merchants and so forth) to taste their product. It is an enjoyable minor feast day, but also it is hard work. The buyer is not only the man who pays, he is an ambassador. He may make wisecracks, he may be a bore, but none the less he must be listened to attentively.

MARCH

Now it is clear to all eyes that the sun is no longer rose tinted but takes on a robust yellowish colour. And furthermore around eleven in the morning it is already able to make its presence felt if you decide to bare your back in the vineyards. The bright light skies are now full of bird-song and the women are back in the vineyards raking over the soil after the winter frosts.

The vine starts to give its life blood; the buds swell. Things move too fast; always there is this hurry. This is the time of the 'long wait'; until the grape makes its appearance there will always be grave risks. All April! Half of May!

Eight weeks when one would like to have the steering-wheel of the world between one's own hands. To speed things on; to put on the brake. Hope and then despair; the chance to take risks, the possibility of losing all.

But longer than this short year is the great longevity of the vine. One should remember it quite small in its sawdust.* And it will be some time before it is grown up; one must learn to be patient.

And the patient *vigneron* also alas sees the vine die; many a time he must have to grub up a dead root stalk that a severe winter has killed off. Nature makes everything eternal; the sun is back and so are the weeds.

> Chilly January
> Sleety February
> Dusty March
> Abundant harvest.
>
> A dry and clear March
> Well fills the cask.

APRIL

What a rascally month this is! Though under the sign of the Ram April could as well have been under the sign of the Billy Goat. Both are tenacious butting animals, but above all—like April—they are unpredictable.

Hot and cold, sunshine and downpours; all turn up at the same time.

'Don't cast a clout . . .' says the proverb. Go and tell that to the vine! She will not listen to you. It is the *vigneron* who does the listening *and* the looking. Is it raining? That is all right. Far better than the *bise* (icy north wind) which might at any moment get up and whiten the moon. One of course would try and warm up the vineyards with charcoal heaters but it is a real struggle.

For the return now of frost spells disaster. The sap has risen. The buds have swollen, have opened out and the floss (down) is now showing. It would have been better if this had not happened so soon; one would have preferred to go gently from cold to warmer. But not a bit of it; from a humid heat back it goes to bitter cold and damp. And so crash! If the frost comes it will burn up the little red leaf. And waiting for these possible catastrophes, the grower peels from sunburn; he has manured, dug and hoed. All happens at once.

Oh this April! So glad-making one minute and then a little later as bitter as one's throat after the *bise* has blown.

Up and down, up and down you go, patient *vigneron*; and all you have done you will do again.

* Young vines bought from the nurseryman arrive in sawdust. They are planted out in it too, to guard against slugs.

That moon which starts in April and becomes full at the end of the month or the beginning of May used to be called the *lune rousse*. It was said that the vine shoots and leaves under this light would redden even if the temperature was below zero. This is a case of the moon being blamed for the sun's misdeeds. The fact is that during clear periods the bright sun follows too suddenly the cold night.*

FROST

Listen, you townsfolk! You people who quickly discard one idea when it does not work and try another, do you realize that when disaster strikes, the *viniculteur* who has lost all in his vineyard must none the less continue to tend his vines; that which will give him no grapes must be looked after as well as that which will give an abundant harvest.

Yes, it is a hard life.

MAY

Now is the time for sulphur-spraying and the trimming of the vines.

Sulphuring the vines prevents the pestilential mildew from doing its worst. Canister on back, pump in one hand and spray in the other, the vineyard worker attacks in what seems an endless nightmare. The container empty, he must refill it: this vine finished, he passes to the next. And when all seems done, as in a song, back he goes to the beginning. But this is no happy story, nor something to sing about. It is sheer hard labour, this thankless task of painting blue-green the entire vineyard. One must be more cunning than the disease. One must forestall it as there is no cure. When it attacks, the defences must be in order or it will take hold. It is necessary to be constantly on guard, on guard above all to protect the wine which is to come.

> When the grape is formed in May
> One must prepare for the worst.

> The rain of St John bodes ill for wine,
> Neither will it swell the grain.

THE THINNING OF THE VINES

After the dangers of frost are passed and while the sulphuring proceeds, there comes the happy work of thinning out and trimming. Sun and yet more sun must reach the clusters of grapes.

* This seems to make sense of something I ridiculed when I first heard it: that you get most sunburned during the very early hours of the day.

Pruning and cutting out suckers were done by the family months ago. That was skilled work, knowing what to cut away, what to leave. Now is the time of youth, of pretty young girls singing at their work, their voices fresh but perhaps a little harsh like the north wind.

These girls now work as dressers of the vine. The soil was tended earlier; now it is the turn of the plant itself. Cutting away tendrils, cutting out the newest unwanted growths, they tie in securely the young shoots. They must cast their eye over the whole plant, arranging its 'coiffure' as if doing their own hair.

This is a work of style, and who better to undertake it than a pretty girl.

Merry May, the merry month . . . with its rich green pastures.

Soon the vines will flower. The scent will reveal to the world a small part of this great mystery, without which the world would be a duller place. The appetite is whetted in anticipation of the wine to come, the wine which will have cost so much sweat and toil.

JUNE

At this time of the longest days, if the soil of our land were not so beautiful, how could the *vigneron* endure fifteen hours of daily work? It is a labour of love to spray with sulphur, arsenic, pyrethrum—and not to complain. But the swallow glides through the June sky, its happiness overflowing. It too has no regrets. The vine clamours for attention, the fledgling for food, and everyone is building for the future, working and hoping.

Finally, in the future, will come the day when all troubles are forgotten. The young swallows will sweep the sky while the wrinkled hands of the *vigneron* will happily grasp a glass of the wine which has also fought through and vanquished its enemies.

On that great day, the limitless sunshine of June long past, there will remain only pride, pride in a job well and tirelessly completed. What a wine! What vivid sparkling colour! What a perfume of grapes, all at the command of one man!

THE FLOWERING

The vine, whose flowers resemble those of ivy, has a peculiarity all of its own. The buds open 'the wrong way round'. Held together at their tips, the five petals separate from the calyx and only then does the little cap come away. If a vine flowers normally—like a rose—this is a bad sign and indicates that the plant is sick.

In the lovely first evenings of high summer, the flowering vines give a strange unforgettable scent. This is the time of the croaking frog, the rasping grass-hopper and the trilling cricket. When the vines flower, the *vigneron* applies more sulphur to protect the leaves and, so he believes, to encourage full pollination of the bunches. Disbudding and pinching out the ends of shoots which may have grown too vigorously can also be done at this time. A checking of the sap in this way is likely to encourage the development of the grapes.

JULY

In very hot countries the first grapes are already ripe enough to eat. They are known as Madeleines.

The light has now changed. It has become the hard, white light of high summer. The sky reflects the heat like a greenhouse. The lizard and the vine revel in it. But the *vigneron* feels it wiser to spray with sulphur once again, for perhaps the fifth or sixth time. He is as brown as a berry. Now perhaps a storm threatens; it can be heard on the other side of the hills. There may be no hail, no destruction of the crop, but rain will bring a crop of undesirable weeds which nobody wishes for.

Each day from nine o'clock the shimmering heat begins to grow. The *vigneron* dreams of those lucky people who lie in the shade and clap their hands for refreshment: 'Something really cool which will tickle my palate.' There are even those who can do it all themselves with a bottle of white wine and a soda siphon. Some say that this is sacrilege. But why? The thirsty ones find their discomfort nicely soothed in the insufferable heat, while the soda dilutes but does not detract from the charm of the wine, which remains as fresh as a river breeze. After all, the wine makes a cup that cheers and that is what one wants in days of great heat. Meanwhile, let us drink to High Summer!

AUGUST

The days continue torrid but at night there is something new, a heavy dew which benefits the fruit but encourages, alas! the persistent thistle, growing among the vines. Once again the *vigneron* must hoe the vineyard but the work is much more agreeable, since the grapes smile at him from their shimmering hearts. From now on the grape looks at you, it almost flirts. There is in each berry a spark of light, alive and full of sympathy. An old man will straighten his back and give vent to his feelings in an old country proverb: 'If August does not ripen them all, your wine will lack sweetness and softness.' Thus speaks the old countryman, for the vine must fight hard against hail in August, rain at vintage time and the uncertainties of the market.

> If it rains on the eve of St Peter's Day [1 August]
> The harvest will fall by two-thirds.
>
> Rainy August:
> Full cellar.
>
> Rain in August
> Gives honey and must.
>
> If in August it shall rain
> More oil and wine shall you gain.

KNOW-HOW

One must know which plants to choose and they must be guarded carefully. In the hottest days of August, when the brilliance of the light allows for no errors, the master of the vineyard will be seen walking along the rows marking a vine here and there with paint. He is selecting the growths which in due time will be used for grafting to new stocks. He is protecting his future.

It has gradually come to be believed that there is some association between the uncultivated parts of a district and the vines to which so much care is devoted. Now men of knowledge have their theories, some good, some bad. Certain traditional methods are condemned, only for it to be found, twenty years later, that the old peasants knew what they were doing. Furthermore, by re-examining the mysteries of the vineyard, the clever types have discovered much truth in traditions. Today we are entering a new world.

It is certain that the pollen from roses, eglantine, brambles and raspberries has an influence of some sort. Mysteriously a wine may acquire a scent of roses or of raspberries.

It must also be admitted that some good *vignerons* are not skilled at bringing up their wines. Some step is omitted or a procedure badly understood, so that the resulting wine is flat and old before its time, musty and stale or even in danger of turning to vinegar. The worst offenders overdose their wines with sulphur, a flavour which has nothing to commend it. It is here that science has come to the rescue. The doubtful wine is put on the right road, its faults eradicated and its goodness developed. A fine wine is carefully nursed so as to fulfil its early promise.

For once, then, we may drink a toast to science, to which good wine owes its success. The grapes were sound; know-how has ensured as well a perfect wine.

SEPTEMBER

This rebirth of year, when the rose bush yields its second flowering, also sees fresh shoots growing on the vines. Quickly the *vigneron* removes them, because it is now the time when the sun toils not as a labourer but as an artist. September, they say, gives quality, and the golden sunshine adds the final touch to the wine.

The women are happy. Armed with scissors and baskets, they go forth to choose their own bunches. Formerly the honour of the first picking was offered to an epicure, usually a priest. But now nobody has the patience to wait and is eager to eat those first bunches, ready when the honey-plum is finished. The grapes, still infants and yet mature, must be grasped in the hand and crammed into the mouth. This is the vintage before the vintage.

The grape also has its place at table. The French call it 'a fruit in the hand'. We must agree, therefore, that the grape is the king of all fruits: fresh, rich and full of flavour.

The *vigneron* frowns; he is a man of duty. His wine must take first place and he grumbles at all this gorging of his precious crop. But here again science and experience have shown that, far from lowering the quality, this premature picking of the first ripe bunches gives a chance for the remainder to ripen completely.

And we, happy people, have won our point. Without having to wait some time for the wine itself, we can 'eat the wine' with our mouths full of grapes and more of them firm and ripe in our hands. In the air hangs the scent of the September rose.

You may drink after eating a pear.
After an apple, young man, take care.

Who has not sown by the Feast of the Holy Cross [14 September]
Must plant three seeds in place of one.

In August the ripening, in September the vintage.
The two months lead to a happy ending.

If there's a September comet in the sky,
Sell off your wine and keep your cellar dry.

Shooting stars during September
Forecast a small yield of wine in November.

If September thunders, you will make good wine.

Watch out and believe me on the morrow of Holy Cross Day
If the evening dew is heavy, your crops will be abundant.

THE EVE OF BATTLE

Look at the starlings, *vigneron*. And also the fresh cool evenings, when rain would fill the air with the scent of the woods. We need much water now, but not of that sort. Now each village would like to possess sixty fountains; water, water in plenty, running sweet and cool. This is the hour when all the great vessels for the vintage are brought out, cleaned, washed, scrubbed, hosed fiercely, so that every cranny is penetrated.

Luckily, the days are still hot and the utensils dry out quickly. Otherwise they would acquire a brackish or musty flavour which would ruin the grapes. All this hullabaloo presages a happy battle in the vineyards, where days of hard labour lie ahead. The men ensure that the yokes fit snugly on their shoulders. The *patron* inspects the wine press; mentally calculates the capacity of his empty casks; gets in a muddle; starts all over again; then makes off in search of chaff, sulphur matches, tallow, a thousand and one things. He would like two heads and four pairs of hands. His wife is writing letters, but about entirely different matters! There are always young starlings eager to bid him good-morning in the vineyard each day. But the *patron* has need not so much of these gluttons as of willing hands to do the work, and how grand it is to greet, each year, the same smiling faces. But now that the vintage approaches, there is a twinge of sadness. Yes, another year gone. Happily the heady young wine will banish such thoughts. The vine is for ever young, the wine is always vigorous.

OCTOBER

The year is closing, the sun's flame is flickering. The summer days are already faraway! Thus you dream in the cold hours of a pale morning. Vitality has gone, and if you brush against the foliage as the fine misty rain comes down, you are soon soaked to the skin. Is this the great vintage?

Suddenly by ten o'clock the morning is fair and warm. The wisps of mist are blown away. There is a song on the hillside, a boy blows his horn, a girl laughs clearly. The bunches fall into baskets and buckets, the men hump the heavy hods onto their shoulders. Soon the tubs are so full that the wagons are loaded down to their axles and the horses can hardly pull them away.

Midday strikes and all are assailed by a vicious thirst, as if it were mid-August. It is neither the grapes nor the must which creates this thirst. There is a little madness in the air. When evening comes, there will be a spirit of carnival abroad with dancing in the village street to the strains of an accordion. The smell of fresh must goes to everybody's head. Backs may be aching, but not enough to prevent joining in the fun. The boys and girls will enjoy themselves, but the older men stand seriously in the press-house like mothers round a cradle. One foresees a full-bodied wine, the next a bouquet of great promise. The Jonah of the party suggests with a sarcastic smile that the young wine has been badly made. Instantly comes the retort: No, no . . . it is complete, well-balanced, perfect. Comparisons are made with other great years. The wine is poured into glasses and the talk goes on far into the night.

There is nothing more to say. The year of the vine has reached its conclusion and we must remain confident. Tomorrow in great vessels garlanded with flowers, this new baby will be carried in procession to the nearby town.

If you are still in your vineyards by St Urbain's Day [19 October],
Your crop will have withered away.

Grapes at St Urbain are fit only for wretches.

THE MUST

Up till quite recently this time of year could produce unpleasant surprises. A fine vintage might yield a poor wine, or a must full of promise would go thoroughly astray.

With the aid of the microscope a solution was found. For satisfactory fermentation one requires a good type of yeast. Unfortunately Nature provides far too many undesirable types which are in the soil, in the air, or on the surface of the grapes. Carried by insects or the wind, they bring with them other bacteria which can sour the wine or turn it to vinegar. The bad will overcome the good, and may be present at the picking, the pressing or the fermentation periods, ready to do its evil work.

But today improved methods have enabled us to understand and conquer this danger. Yeasts of the right type are specially cultivated. Furthermore it is possible to hold in check any undesirable yeasts that may be present. The must is sterilized and the selected yeast then added to it.

Thus the good work of the *vigneron* is no longer at the mercy of these tiny particles. Months of sunshine are not brought to nothing by wee beasties, only visible to the naked eye when magnified a thousand times. After having braved the risks of frost, storms and hail, the finest vintage of the soil is not now squandered by what the peasant calls 'microbes'.

Here's to the health of the must, to the health of the wine to follow, to the health of you yourself who look forward in these autumn days to the caress of the drink on your lips. So, when you raise your glass to your mouth and say 'good health', think what that means. It is more than a wish, it is a science. Drink to your health; it is already good health you are drinking.

NOVEMBER

The *vigneron*'s calendar should begin at this season of short days and much work. First there is the tidying up after the vintage: all containers must be cleaned and scrubbed in cold water, rinsed out with hot water or even with alcohol and then well sulphured to counteract mustiness.

Then back to the vineyard where autumn rains have not yet been sufficient to make the soil unworkable. Soil must be carried from the foot of the hillside up to the higher slopes in order to keep the terraces well laid out. Walls may need repair, and this is mason's work. A local proverb tells that mortar applied in winter will endure the fire. This work must be completed before the winter frosts bring everything to a halt.

But the weather is still gentle. Strong winds sweep through the vines, scattering the reddened foliage. Women and children tear up the stakes, tying them in neat bundles of six at the end of each row.

The vines are now ready for the winter, whilst in the cellars (which are if necessary heated) the wine of the year begins to take shape. It is only a beginning, and one hardly dare speak of it and certainly not yet drink it. For comfort one turns to its predecessor, smiling in the glass.

> At St Martin [11 November] drink your wine
> and let water flow through the milk.

> At St Martin, seal your cask and taste your wine.

> At St Martin rack off your wine. The saint has
> started it on its road.

VINIFICATION

For many months the *vigneron* has grown his grapes. Now he must make wine of them and it is not a simple operation. Fine fruit badly handled will make mediocre wine and his ambition is to make the finest. White grapes are pressed, the juice run off at once and fermented separately. For red wines, the treatment is different. Some proprietors first remove all the stalks, while others may wish this wood to remain in the must in order to impart tannin to the wine during fermentation. This practice will vary according to the type of summer which has been experienced. The grapes will in fact start fermenting in the vats before they are completely pressed. Immediately, the small amount of alcohol produced will begin to extract the colour from the skins. The skins remain with the juice until the bulk of fermentation is over. The flesh of the grape is colourless—all the colour is in the skin.

Today fermentation is carefully controlled and assisted by the addition of selected yeasts and the maintenance of a favourable temperature in the vats. But a well-ordered press-house and good fermentation are not enough. Continual watch and care must be exercised; care, to ensure that the vats are covered over or not as required; watch, to see through a glass tube on the front of each vat that all is running smoothly.

A moment is reached when taste and expertise come into play. The fermenting juice must be tasted. Great hopes are raised, pride of achievement foreseen. The proprietor wonders if the young wine shows perhaps the greatest promise; it may become a famous 'year'. He argues within himself: this is *it*! or is it? Each year he would like to make the *vin du siècle*. And if perhaps he is to be disappointed this time, he shrugs his shoulders and assures himself that it will be all right *next* year. And in fact next year has already begun because the vine never stops.

Will you have another glass? This wine is good, isn't it? It will not disappoint us.

> By all Saints your corn should be sown
> And all your harvest gathered in.

> If winter is to follow its normal course
> It should not arrive till St Martin's Day has passed.

DECEMBER

A fire burning unwanted vine wood is most agreeable and is improved by the addition of dead vine stocks. The days are so short that it seems impossible for the cold to be so bitter. It is unpleasant, and everybody does his best to find work under cover. In the barn, there is wood to saw so that the log fire may continue to blaze. When the basket is full, a walk to the four corners of the vineyard will keep one warm. There are larch wood stakes to prepare. Their ends must be pointed and protected against rot. Dry wood is impregnated with tar, green wood with copper sulphate. Should the weather ease up, the hard work in the vineyard itself must be tackled. So long as the ground is free of snow, one must take every opportunity to keep ahead of schedule and to complete the work on the land.

In the village a new smell is in the air. The travelling distillation wagon has come round again. The north wind whistles round the walls but round the machine it is lovely: a little corner of the Tropics saved for the winter. The odour of the *marc* brandy stimulates conversation. It is our turn now to discuss world affairs. We have great plans, noble plans. If only the powers that be would listen to us! But all is gone with the wind, and the small boys, bonneted to the ears, wait eagerly for the snow, for them always too late in coming!

It is also the season of the pig, as ruddy as the pork butcher's arms. This evening, maybe a stew. You eat more than you should and your digestion suffers. What better, to put things right, than a bottle of old good wine? Immediately discussion reopens on the vintage just past. The calm conversation about the old wine heralds the storm about the new. The youth is growing up. It is showing well and is full of promise.

> If there are midges at Christmas
> There will be icicles at Easter.

CHRISTMAS AND WINE

According to custom, Christmas and wine go together. The weather should be appropriate to the season and the holidays bring all the family together. Wine is one of the few things remaining which has a ·close association with individual homes. It also runs like blood in the veins of our country and where else is the link between household and land so close? We should always drink our local wines with love, respect and gratitude. Some of our wines are fit for princes, some for those in good, prosperous surroundings, and some for the most humble folk.

But Christmas is for us all. The French word 'Noël' has a broader meaning. In bygone days people cried 'Noël' on any occasion which merited a demonstration of their joy, admiration or gratitude. In crying 'Noël' to our wines, we are therefore acclaiming all that we produce from the finest to the most humble. At this time of year when Nature stands still, the streams are imprisoned by ice, the earth frozen under a mantle of snow and the trees laid bare . . . the fruit of our vines lives on, living sunshine; the only fruit still able to laugh and to bring a smile to the lips of the older ones, as an echo to the children's happiness.

Noël to our wines! So many of those who have helped to make the older vintages are no longer present when the bottles are uncorked, and this is the last greeting from good, honest men, whose whole lives were devoted to their vines and now who are gone for ever. Noël to our wines, our native earth rekindles the warmth in our hearts. Stony hillsides, sun-baked terraces, vines standing under the blue arc of Heaven, all your promises have been kept and all are now renewed. There is ahead the long tunnel of winter, stretching through January, February, March. But the day will come when the fresh light of spring will recall the light of the wine now gleaming in the glass.

Noël! Noël! to our wines. Let us drink some of this earth which is our home.

INDEX

Acidity, 90
Aix-la-Chapelle, 77
Alacoque, Marguerite Marie, 43–5
Allier, River, 46
Almeria, Spain, 34
Alsace Wine Fair, Colmar, 169
Amalfitano, Georges, 30
Amboise, 101
Amigny (Sancerre), 68
Amuse-gueules (nibbles), 202
Ancenis, 192, 195
Anchoide Corse, 9
Angers, 101, 165, 169, 173, 183–6, 187, 188, 195; Wine Fair, 168, 181–2
Anjou, counts of, 138, 152
Anjou, 163–5, 188; wines of, 165–8; the Sacavins, 168–77
Anjou Cross (La Vraie Croix d'Anjou), 186–8
Anjou-Saumur wine glass, 150
Anne of Beaujeu, 73
Anne of Brittany, 153, 196
Ansoald, Archbishop, of Poitiers, 201
Antoigné, 162
Arbois, 143
Ardèche, 1, 3, 4
Arthur of Brittany, 179
Aubance, River, 165
Aubenas, 3–4
Audouard, Paul, 2
Augustus, St, 44
Avila, Spain, 183
Azay-le-Rideau, 101, 137

Bagneux, 162
Balzac, Honoré de, 45; quoted, 129
Bannay (Sancerre), 67
Barrès, Maurice, 188
Basilicas: Paray-le-Monial, 45; Nevers, 47, 55–7; Carcassonne, 135

Bas-Rhin Department (Alsace), 169
Bataille, Nicholas, 184
Baugé, 185, 186–7
Baule (Orleans), 87, 92
Baule, La. *See* La Baule
Baumard, Jean, 168–71, 173–4, 177–9, 181–2
Baumette, La. *See* La Baumette
Béage, Le. *See* Le Béage
Beaugency, 89, 93
Beaujeu, 37–8
Beaujolais district, 28, 37–41
Beaulieu, 22
Becket, Thomas à, 52
Belle-Ile, 197
Benais, 146, 147
Benedict, St (St-Benoît), 76–7
Bergère, Pas du, 186
Bernard de Clairvaux, 2
Berry, Duchess of, 196
Berry, province of, 63
Berthier, Marshal, Prince of Wagram, 107
Bidet, Alfred, 171
Bilberries, wild, 18
Blois, counts of, 93, 152
Blois, Château de, 101–3, 107, 108
Bochin, J. F., quoted, 180
Bohier, Katherine, 120
Boissière, La. *See* La Boissière
Boniface VIII, Pope, 55
Borgia, Cesare, 154
Bottle-washing machine, 83
Bouchot, Le. *See* Le Bouchot
Bourges, 61–2
Bourgueil, 145–6
Bourré, Jean, 186
Boyer (architect), 107
Breton, Abbot, 142
Brossay, 162

© Cassell & Co. Ltd 1967.

217